D1605396

Acceptance & Commitment Therapy

for the Treatment of Post-Traumatic Stress Disorder & Trauma-Related Problems

A Practitioner's Guide to Using Mindfulness & Acceptance Strategies

ROBYN D. WALSER, PH.D.
DARRAH WESTRUP, PH.D.

New Harbinger Publications, Inc.

Publisher's Note

This publication is designed to provide accurate and authoritative information in regard to the subject matter covered. It is sold with the understanding that the publisher is not engaged in rendering psychological, financial, legal, or other professional services. If expert assistance or counseling is needed, the services of a competent professional should be sought.

Distributed in Canada by Raincoast Books

New Harbinger Publications, Inc.
5674 Shattuck Avenue
Oakland, CA 94609
www.newharbinger.com

Acquired by Catharine Sutker; Cover design by Amy Shoup; Illustrations by Susan Pickett; Edited by Carole Honeychurch; Text design by Tracy Carlson

Library of Congress Cataloging-in-Publication Data

Walser, Robyn D.
 Acceptance and commitment therapy for the treatment of post-traumatic stress disorder and trauma-related problems : a practitioner's guide to using mindfulness and acceptance strategies / Robyn D. Walser and Darrah Westrup.
   p. ; cm.
 ISBN-13: 978-1-57224-472-6 (hardcover)
 ISBN-10: 1-57224-472-0 (hardcover)
 1. Post-traumatic stress disorder--Treatment. 2. Acceptance and commitment therapy. 3. Trauma--Treatment. I. Westrup, Darrah. II. Title.
 [DNLM: 1. Stress Disorders, Post-Traumatic--therapy. 2. Cognitive Therapy--methods. 3. Stress Disorders, Traumatic, Acute--therapy. WM 170 W222a 2007]
RC552.P67W374 2007
616.85'2106--dc22
                    2006102707

09 08 07

10 9 8 7 6 5 4 3 2 1

First printing

Contents

Acknowledgments

We would like to thank all those who have provided support in putting this book together, including friends and family. Most importantly, we each would like to thank our husbands, Mark Castoreno and Andrew Aitken. They have supported and tolerated many hours devoted to writing at the temporary expense of hours devoted to being together. We would like to acknowledge and thank Steven Hayes, whose incredible mind and talent have provided us with this compassionate approach to addressing human suffering. Finally, we would also like to thank our clients, who have struggled through this therapy, changed their lives, and provided hope for others who seek treatment for PTSD.

We would like to offer a special thanks to Susan Pickett (Robyn's wonderful mom) for illustrating this book and for taking the time to put her artistic talents to work. Thanks, Mom!

Foreword

ACT and the Disorderly Process of Trauma

There is a special relationship between Acceptance and Commitment Therapy (ACT) and the field of trauma. There are a number of reasons for it, but I think one of these is deep and philosophical. It has to do with the nature of trauma and a parallel message inside ACT itself.

Behavior therapy has always had a kind of "can do" attitude, linked to an orderly agenda. It was built on the idea that carefully defined and empirically tested interventions, linked to basic behavioral principles, would allow human beings to get their activities more fully in order. When cognitive concepts were brought into the center of behavior therapy in the 1970s, that attitude did not change. Gone was the link to basic behavioral principles, but there was confidence that carefully defined and empirically tested interventions would allow human beings to get their minds more fully in order.

Inside the "can do" attitude of both of these first two generations of behavioral and cognitive therapy was a hidden problem, however. The cognitive and behavioral tradition implicitly adopted cultural beliefs about the importance of getting actions and attitudes "in order." A great deal of effort was put into creating emotional and cognitive lives that were, well, tidy. We would get rid of bad feelings and create good ones. We would get rid of bad thoughts and replace them with healthy ones. Neat.

We are revisiting that issue now in the third generation of behavioral and cognitive therapy. Concepts like acceptance and mindfulness are not focused on the content of thoughts and feelings, but on our relationship to them. This is not a superficial change. It means we are fundamentally changing our view of whether order as we formerly understood it is important.

That very change is a somewhat confusing process. Challenging assumptions always is. Acceptance and mindfulness thus not only question the importance of orderliness in terms of form—they create disequilibrium in the field itself. Challenging order creates disorder. That very effect can be exciting, but it is not easy. In this era of development, everything is back on the table. And at a deep level, what is on the table is the whole issue of purpose. Instead of lives that are orderly, maybe it is better to seek lives that are open, flexible, and connected. Instead of feelings that are positive and controlled, maybe it is better to seek feelings that are deep, known, and accepted. Instead of thoughts that are proper, balanced, and rational, perhaps it is better to seek a relationship with our thoughts that is mindful, defused, and undefended.

The deep philosophical relation of all of this to trauma is based on an interesting parallel process. So far as I can recall, I've never heard anyone question why we use the word "disorder" to speak of psychological difficulties. I suspect it is because of this secret embrace of a culturally established idea that a good life is an orderly process, and that other processes are, well, part of a "disorder."

It does not seem to be true. Human lives generally are not tidy. We are filled moment to moment with feelings, memories, sensations, urges, and thoughts—and they are often messy, painful, and conflicting. Life itself can produce unpredictable challenges.

No one knows that better than trauma survivors. The very nature of trauma raises the issue of order forcefully, unavoidably, and painfully.

You do not have to work in the area of trauma very long before you see how virtually random events can create disorder out of order. The woman in the wrong place at the wrong time is brutally raped. The driver who happens to be in that particular car at that particular instant is terribly burned. The young soldier sees horrors that others can only imagine, for no reason other than a series of the minute choice points and random factors that lead to being exactly there exactly then. And when these things happen, things change. Sometimes, everything changes. Things are mixed up—they don't fit.

This is part of what is hard about trauma, but it is also what is potentially empowering about such painful experiences. Just as learning of a life-threatening illness often causes people to come to grips with their own mortality and focus on what is truly important, so too trauma survivors have an opportunity presented to them by being required to face facts that in normal life many will turn away from and simply refuse to see. If we can find a way forward, carrying these facts, we can reach another level of peace and power that the illusion of control can never produce.

We live inside assumptions of safety, coherence, control, progress, and fairness. We build stories about the way life is supposed to be and who we are. We then live inside these stories, fearfully and uselessly avoiding the massive amount of data that constantly questions them. Unexpected and horrific pain is for someone else, not us. Accidents are somehow the fault of those experiencing them. And after all, good things will happen to those who follow the rules. These illusions suggest that we are in charge of almost everything. Most of all they suggest that the world is orderly. This set of assumptions is safe, comfortable, and deluded.

Trauma experiences show how many of our day-to-day assumptions are based on an insanely thin veneer of "sanity." They show how much of our story is illusion and pretense. Bad things do happen to good people. It does not have to be for a reason. Sometimes children do not grow up. Sometimes careers are cut short. Sometimes innocence is lost. And often these things are beyond our control.

Trauma survivors know how deeply this reaches. We cannot assume that the building will not fall down, or that the car will not swerve, or that the stranger will not attack. Even your own face cannot be relied on to be there tomorrow. Life is not orderly.

This is the sense in which I mean that there is a special relationship between ACT and the field of trauma. ACT asks whether it is possible to let go of conscious, deliberate, purposeful control when that no longer works. Instead it walks through the process needed to come into the present and still to care, even when we have abandoned the security blanket of feel-goodism and the illusion of omnipotence.

This book, by master ACT therapists and trainers, carefully and systematically prepares clinicians to explore this territory. As befits its deep message, the book is not so much a formula as it is a space within which to examine deeper questions. Is it possible and healthy to support trauma survivors to be themselves, to be present, and to care, without trying first to create formal order out of the mix of thoughts and feelings that traumatic experiences leave behind? ACT therapists and researchers think the answer is yes. We are just learning how to do that, and vastly more research and clinical development are needed. But this book provides the first comprehensive starting point for this new journey. We are eager to take it, sensing that along this path lies a way to turn even horror to profound good.

ACT, and the third generation of behavioral and cognitive therapies generally, can be confusing and disorienting because they challenge fundamental assumptions. For researchers and clinicians interested in trauma, perhaps that is as it should be. It puts us into the very shoes of the clients we serve—people whose unbidden experiences have done the same thing. Rather than grab even more tightly at new forms of control, ACT asks clinicians and clients alike to put down the needless defenses, show up, and begin to live in a more open, compassionate, and values-based way, knowing full well that painful events can penetrate human lives at any moment.

—Steven C. Hayes
University of Nevada

Introduction

The single most remarkable fact of human existence is how hard it is for human beings to be happy.

— Steven C. Hayes

Getting Started

This book is a practical clinical guide on the use of acceptance and commitment therapy ("ACT," said as one word) in the treatment of post-traumatic stress disorder (PTSD) and other trauma-related problems. Because mindfulness is a central skill in ACT, we also include mindfulness as an integrated topic. This book is designed to show how ACT and mindfulness apply to these particular difficulties and how they can be used in different settings and modalities (that is, in both group and individual therapy) and with different types of traumatic experiences. It is our hope that the therapists who choose to read and work with this book will find it to be comprehensible and user-friendly, providing both a solid understanding of ACT theory as well as the practical resources needed to apply ACT and mindfulness with this population.

We are writing this book based on the clinical and research experience gained during our long-standing use of ACT and mindfulness with clients suffering from the effects of trauma. We each have more than a decade of experience in treating PTSD and have worked together with ACT for more than six years, using this treatment approach in our private practices, outpatient clinics, and inpatient settings for clients with trauma-related problems and PTSD. We have provided ACT to both men and women in individual and group settings, and we have had experience with many types of trauma, ranging from motor vehicle accidents and natural disasters to sexual trauma and war-zone-related trauma. It is our experiences in using ACT and mindfulness with this population that have inspired this book and the examples provided therein. It should be noted that in the interests of confidentiality we have masked the identities of individual clients or provided examples that are amalgams of various clients and therapy interactions. We would like to add that the text *Acceptance and Commitment Therapy: An Experiential Approach to Behavior Change* (Hayes, Strosahl, & Wilson, 1999), which provides a more detailed theoretical explanation and a full account of this approach, has been an important resource.

In addition to the experience noted above, we have conducted workshops in the use of ACT and have regularly presented ACT concepts and empirical findings at the International Society of Traumatic Stress Studies (Walser, Westrup, Rogers, Gregg, & Loew, 2003; Walser, Westrup, Gregg, Loew, & Rogers, 2004; Walser, Gregg, Westrup, & Loew, 2005) as well as the Association for the Behavioral and Cognitive Therapies (Walser & Hayes, 1998). We also train students to use this approach with individuals who have been diagnosed with PTSD. In fact, one of our more rewarding experiences has been our ongoing supervision group, wherein we not only provide ACT training but also actively work with ourselves and our students to live according to our own values, thus implementing ACT in our own lives.

We are also both scientists and have contributed our own findings regarding the effectiveness of ACT as a treatment for PTSD. We are very interested in empirical work in the area of understanding human suffering and its treatments. Research on both ACT and mindfulness is booming, and there are a number of important studies emerging that support ACT and mindfulness as effective interventions and that suggest that the theory and concepts underlying ACT predict change processes in treatment. The overall goal of this book, however, is not to review the scientific literature, but to provide the nuts and bolts of the intervention. We currently conduct ACT and mindfulness groups on a regular basis and hope to communicate these experiences in a way that proves straightforward to you, the reader, as both therapist and person. We want to not only provide you with a clear sense of how ACT is conducted, but also convey the strength of compassion for human experience found in this therapy. ACT is designed to create both psychological and behavioral flexibility in clients through processes that are applied with warmth and compassion for the client's struggle and for the difficulties that traumatic experience can bring. We are guided by our value of bringing kindness to our therapy and our belief that the client is 100 percent acceptable as they are in this moment. Yet we also hold firm to the notion that clients can always choose to take action that is directly in line with *their* personal values.

We do want to refer readers to a Web site and several publications that provide empirical findings and reviews of the ACT and mindfulness literature. First, please see the Web site of the Association for Contexual Behavioral Science for references to both theoretical and empirical papers plus other ACT-relevant information: www.contextualpsychology.org. We also recommend that you read other key works about ACT, including *Acceptance and Commitment Therapy: An Experiential Approach to Behavior Change* by Steven Hayes, Kirk Strosahl, and Kelly Wilson (1999), *Get Out of Your Mind and Into Your Life* by Steven Hayes and Spencer Smith (2005), *A Practical Guide to Acceptance and Commitment Therapy* by Steven Hayes and Kirk Strosahl (2004), and *Acceptance and Commitment Therapy for Anxiety Disorders: A Practitioner's Treatment Guide to Using Mindfulness, Acceptance, and Values-Based Behavior Change Strategies* by Georg Eifert and John Forsyth (2005). For a literature review of mindfulness, please read Ruth Baer's journal article entitled "Mindfulness Training as a Clinical Intervention: A Conceptual and Empirical Review" (2003). We also suggest that you read *Mindfulness and Acceptance: Expanding the Cognitive-Behavioral Tradition*, edited by Steven Hayes, Victoria Follette, and Marsha Linehan (2004), *Full Catastrophe Living*, by John Kabat-Zinn (1994), and *Acceptance and Mindfulness-Based Approaches to Anxiety*, edited by Susan M. Orsillo and Lizabeth Roemer (2005).

Finally, we have each been profoundly moved by the transformations we have witnessed in doing this powerful intervention. We have worked with many clients who, having previously deemed their lives destroyed by their trauma, are aided by ACT to embrace living in ways that are meaningful and value driven.

How to Use This Book

This book is intended as a practical guide for clinicians who wish to use ACT with clients who are struggling with PTSD and trauma-related issues. The central focus is on the actual course of therapy as applied to this particular population, and, as mentioned, the material draws extensively from the authors' direct experience in using ACT with both men and women with PTSD. As you read the separate chapters, we recommend that you explore how the principles and techniques of ACT might be employed in your own life, as well as considering how you might use the approach with your clients. You may want to complete the homework assignments provided at the end of the chapters specific to the intervention, as they provide a hands-on opportunity to develop your own acceptance and willingness as it applies to your personal internal experiences. As it applies to your clients, each of the therapy chapters (4, 5, 6, 7, 8, and 9) contains two homework assignments. We provide two (in most cases), as most of the therapy topics will need more than one session to be completed. You can use the homework assignments in the way that seems most appropriate for the client and for the amount of time you spend on each topic. If the topic takes more than two sessions, feel free to draw on other homework assignments in the book that went unused or to develop your own—perhaps those that are specific to the client's needs. Finally, as you continue to learn how to implement ACT, you can also try out metaphors or experiential exercises with clients as a way to familiarize yourself with the therapy. We strongly recommend use of ACT and mindfulness in your own life if you wish to be effective at providing this intervention to your clients.

Structure of This Book

The first four chapters of this book serve as an overview and starting point to ACT. Following this introduction, chapter 1 introduces the concept of experiential avoidance and key principles of ACT. This serves as a foundation from which to approach the remaining chapters and is central to understanding the therapy.

Because the concept of mindfulness is a key construct in ACT and one that both clinicians and clients often find challenging, we follow the theory chapter by discussing mindfulness and its importance to the ACT approach in chapter 2. Just as the regular practice to become more mindful must be integrated into daily life, the concept of mindfulness is woven throughout the book as a necessary element that is continually built upon. In chapter 2, we will explore different mindfulness techniques, and we recommend that you practice both personally and with your clients. Additionally, as you read the therapy session chapters (4, 5, 6, 7, 8, and 9), you will see that each session is opened with a mindfulness exercise. Two are provided for each chapter. As noted above, we have included two, as it often takes more than one session to cover any particular core topic of ACT. You can use the second mindfulness exercise in an additional session. Should you find that you spend more than two therapy sessions on any particular topic, feel free to repeat mindfulness exercises, to draw from other mindfulness exercises in the book, or to use your own mindfulness exercises.

We have tried to match the mindfulness exercises with level of experience (mindful breathing at the beginning) or with the core topic that is being presented. We recommend use of the mindfulness exercises that accompany a particular chapter. That said, there is no hard-and-fast rule about which mindfulness exercises are done when. You can feel free to exercise some flexibility around their implementation. Finally, we recommend that you ask your clients to purchase a notebook or journal, as they will be asked to report on their mindfulness experiences, and keeping track in a journal will help them to see their progress. Chapter 3 will explore the process of "preparing to begin." It will address how to describe the therapy to the client, including informed consent and general issues related to beginning the therapeutic process from this approach.

In chapters 4 through 9, we present the major ACT components in chronological order. That is, ACT is a "building block" therapy, wherein the client is taken on a journey that (a) systematically undermines problematic control and avoidance strategies; (b) establishes a framework wherein clients can directly experience their thoughts, feelings, and sensations without employing harmful change strategies; and (c) helps clients arrive at a place where they can choose to take committed action in accordance with their values—ACT's main focus of change. It is recommended that first-time readers read the text front to back in order to best appreciate this step-by-step process. Once you become facile with the material, then it is easier to loosen the step-by-step structure and more readily pull in pieces of the therapy from the different core areas wherever they are needed.

Chapters 4 through 9 will explore and describe the core components of ACT, which are introduced in the same order as they would be conducted in the therapy: "Creative Hopelessness" (chapter 4), "Control as the Problem" (chapter 5), "Willingness" (chapter 6), "Self-as-Context" (chapter 7), "Valued Living" (chapter 8), and "Committed Action" (chapter 9). Each chapter details how to introduce and work with each concept as it pertains to the client with PTSD, and case examples are used to highlight particular challenges associated with each topic. The sections also include exercises and homework that will assist the clinician to move the client through each core component.

ACT is a very hands-on therapy, and the therapist's own stance with regard to experiential avoidance and acceptance can serve to both significantly enhance and seriously impede the work. Chapter 10, "Therapist and Treatment Considerations," addresses issues of therapist compassion, authenticity, and self-care as viewed from an ACT perspective and addresses training considerations. Chapter 11 further examines specific treatment considerations such as the application of ACT in various PTSD populations and comorbid conditions that are often present when working with traumatized individuals. This chapter also discusses assessment as it applies to ACT—specifically, ways in which therapeutic movement in such areas as mindfulness, trauma, and acceptance can be evaluated and monitored. Finally, in the conclusion we briefly present data and offer our final thoughts about working with individuals recovering from trauma.

CHAPTER I

Acceptance, Mindfulness, and Trauma: The Problem of Experiential Avoidance and the Verbal Nature of Trauma

When we finally look at horror and joy, birth and death, gain and loss, things, with an equal heart and open mind, there arises a most beautiful and profound equanimity.

—Jack Kornfield

The experience of a traumatic event can have a profound effect on an individual's life. Multiple aspects of functioning can be negatively affected, including social, occupational, physical, and financial areas. Perhaps more fundamentally, as a result of these consequences and the trauma itself, psychological functioning can be enormously impacted and can result in serious long-term consequences. That is not to say that all trauma survivors experience long-term problems. In fact, most recover and are able to go on and live normal lives. For those who do suffer long-term effects, their lives can come to be ruled by the experience of the trauma, costing them vitality and engagement in personal values. The goal of acceptance and commitment therapy, or ACT (Hayes et al., 1999), is to bring vitality and valued living back to the traumatized individual who has been unable to recover.

One of our goals in this chapter is to explore the problem of *experiential avoidance* (efforts made to change, eliminate, and/or avoid negative internal experience such as thoughts, emotions, memories, and sensations) as it particularly relates to posttraumatic stress disorder (PTSD), and to define the verbal nature of trauma and how it is related to ACT. We will first look at general epidemiological information, the American Psychiatric Association's definition of PTSD, and comorbidities of PTSD as an introduction to the relevant issues of experiential avoidance and verbal behavior as related to trauma and its negative outcomes. We also include sections on mindfulness and ACT in comparison to other therapies.

Chapter Objectives

■ Provide an overview of PTSD

■ Discuss experiential avoidance in PTSD

■ Explore experiential avoidance, PTSD, and comorbidity

■ Discuss the roles of experiential avoidance and control in PTSD

■ Explore the verbal nature of trauma

■ Examine mindfulness in relation to ACT

■ Compare and contrast ACT with other CBT interventions

Overview of PTSD

Epidemiological research conducted by Kessler, Sonnega, Bromet, Hughes, and Nelson (1995) found that 50 percent of U.S. women and 60 percent of U.S. men are exposed to a traumatic event during their lifetime. Similarly, the Detroit Area Survey (Breslau et al., 1998) found that 75 percent of individuals are exposed, at some point in their lives, to a stressor that meets criteria for a diagnosis of PTSD. Rates of PTSD, though, are much lower than the trauma exposure rates. The National Comorbidity Study (Kessler et al., 1995) found lifetime prevalence rates for PTSD to be 7.8 percent, and the Detroit Area Survey (Breslau et al., 1998) indicated lifetime prevalence rates were between 9.2 percent and 9.8 percent.

In order to receive a diagnosis of PTSD, an individual must meet *DSM-IV-TR* (American Psychiatric Association [APA], 2000) criteria defining the disorder. PTSD is viewed as a psychological disorder caused by exposure to a traumatic event. The traumatic event must involve actual or threatened death or serious injury to self or others, and it must include a response of intense fear, helplessness, or horror. Some examples of these types of traumas include sexual assault, child physical or sexual abuse, natural disasters, sudden loss of a loved one, firefights during war, being a prisoner of war or experiencing captivity and torture, viewing mutilated bodies or dead bodies and atrocities, motor vehicle accidents, and acts of terrorism.

In addition to the traumatic event criterion, there are three major symptom clusters in PTSD (APA, 2000). For a diagnosis of PTSD, at least one *reexperiencing* symptom is required, as well as at least three avoidance symptoms and two hyperarousal symptoms. *Avoidance* symptoms include efforts to avoid thoughts, feelings, or conversations associated with trauma, efforts to avoid activities and places that are reminders of the trauma, inability to recall important aspects of the trauma, a diminished interest in significant activities, feeling detached or estranged from others, restricted range of affect, and a sense of foreshortened future. Reexperiencing symptoms include recurrent and intrusive distressing recollections of the event, recurrent distressing dreams of the event, acting or feeling as if the event were recurring (reliving the event in the moment), intense psychological distress when exposed to internal or external cues or reminders, and physiological reactivity when exposed to reminders. *Hyperarousal* symptoms include difficulty falling or staying asleep, irritability or outbursts of anger, difficulty concentrating, hypervigilance, and exaggerated startle response. These symptoms cause significant distress or impairment in social, occupational, and other important areas of functioning. For example, they can interfere with relationships (Carroll, Rueger, Foy, & Donahoe, 1985), they can affect physical health (Schnurr, Spiro, Vielhauer, Findler, & Hamblen, 2002) and they can cause reduced quality of life (Allen & Bloom, 1994).

Two central challenges confront the individual experiencing a trauma. The first, of course, is to survive the event. The second is to somehow come to terms with what has happened so that one's life or personhood does not become defined by it. The first, while difficult enough, draws upon automatic survival strategies—the hardwired fight/flight/freeze responses. The second task calls for abilities that many of us have never been taught, and much of what we *have* been taught may actually stand in the way of recovery. That is, attempts to "not have" the trauma and the thoughts and feelings associated with it may account for much of the distress seen in PTSD. As we review the consequences of trauma, you can begin to see how the disorder may be defined as one that is largely due to experiential avoidance that is associated with the trauma. In addition, if we review the common comorbidities of a PTSD diagnosis, the role of experiential avoidance becomes even clearer.

Experiential Avoidance and PTSD

As conceptualized in ACT, experiential avoidance is a process wherein an individual is unwilling to contact certain private experiences and actively works to escape such experiences. It is related to PTSD in two ways. First, individuals with PTSD are unwilling to contact, in the present moment, private experiences such as negatively evaluated emotional states, traumatic memories, negative thoughts, or unpleasant physiological sensations such as rapid heart rate or sweating, and second, these individuals attempt to change the form or frequency of those events, even when there is negative cost to doing so (Walser & Hayes, 2006). For example, a sexually traumatized client may avoid intimacy and will lose important relationships as a result, a fearful motor vehicle accident survivor may refuse to drive although it is her only means to get to work, or a soldier may drink heavily so as not to experience arousal related to traumatic events experienced in the war zone. One of the aspects of experiential avoidance that can make treatment difficult is that often these initial attempts to avoid can in fact help the person feel better momentarily—the anger pushes someone away, the fear lessens, and the anxiety decreases. This temporary solution gives the false impression that the strategy is actually working and that the client just needs to find better ways to implement the avoidance strategies as a means to feel better and thus "be better" (recovered from the trauma). Rarely, however, do avoidance strategies make things better in the long run. For the most part, they impact the person quite negatively and soon the individual needs help not only with recovery from trauma, but also with recovery from the problems that their long-standing avoidance behaviors have created.

If we review the avoidance symptoms of PTSD, you can easily see how the avoidance strategies and attempts to escape private experience point directly to the role that experiential avoidance (the avoidance of internal or private experiences, such as emotions, thoughts, bodily sensations, and memories that remind the person of the trauma) plays as a key mechanism in the development and maintenance of PTSD. However, PTSD is not only about avoidance of internal experiences, it is also about the avoidance of places or things that may remind a person of the trauma and that may cue the internal experiences. The cost of experiential avoidance becomes evident as the individual's life becomes smaller due to the avoidance tactics. The other symptoms of PTSD may also be related to experiential avoidance. For instance, with reexperiencing symptoms such as intrusive memories, many clients will report the desire to avoid these distressing memories, and they will ask the therapist to help these memories go away. Furthermore, clients will report efforts to not sleep or efforts to take medications to induce sleep as a way of avoiding nightmares or unpleasant dreams about the trauma, or they will use drugs as a way of simply avoiding everyday experiences of anxiety.

Avoidance is also evident in symptoms of hyperarousal. When clients report difficulty with concentration, they will often report feeling spaced out or out of touch.

Both of these experiences can be conceptualized as avoidance of self or of the world or as a desire to not be present (escaping from the current moment). All of these avoidance maneuvers are conceptualized as experiential avoidance. In ACT, then, this concept offers an explanation of how avoidance functions in the development of trauma-related problems, e.g. disconnection, lack of concentration, isolation, and so on while also lending coherence to the understanding of the long-term negative consequences seen in PTSD (Walser & Hayes, 2006).

Experiential Avoidance, PTSD, and Comorbidity

Between 62 and 80 percent of individuals diagnosed with PTSD also meet criteria for at least one other disorder (Davidson & Fairbank, 1993). For instance, the strong comorbidity of PTSD and depression has been well documented (Keane & Wolfe, 1990; Kessler et al., 1995). Research also suggests a shared vulnerability in persons with PTSD and persons with depression (Breslau, Davis, Peterson, & Schultz, 2000). That is, major depression increases the risk for PTSD subsequent to trauma (Breslau, Davis, Peterson, & Schultz, 1997; Kessler et al., 1995) and PTSD increases the risk of developing first-incidence major depression (Breslau et al., 1997). These researchers conclude that individuals who develop PTSD and major depression may represent a vulnerable subgroup whose preexisting vulnerabilities are exposed by and potentially exacerbated by the trauma. We suggest this shared vulnerability is expressed as experiential avoidance, an argument that is supported by research showing that avoidance is a significant risk factor for not only PTSD but for depression as well (Shipherd & Beck, 1999; Tull, Gratz, Salters, & Roemer, 2004). Both syndromes are characterized by a fundamental nonacceptance of one's private experience, be it a traumatic memory or feelings of sadness; both disorders are marked by dysfunctional, avoidant behaviors that powerfully and negatively affect one's quality of life.

Co-occurring PTSD and substance abuse is also a common problem (Najavits, 2001; Ouimette & Brown, 2003; Ruzek, Polusny, & Abueg, 1998). Use of substances is consistent with the model of experiential avoidance (Walser & Hayes, 2006). For example, substance use is often the manner in which individuals escape, dilute, or change their internal experience of emotion, and it may operate as a reinforcer by helping trauma survivors to escape feared emotions (Ruzek et al., 1998). Researchers have found that trauma survivors report substance use as a means of numbing traumatic memories (Root, 1989), and other research has shown that individuals who abuse alcohol are often drinking as a means to regulate negative emotional states (Marlatt & Gordon, 1985). Furthermore, those who have been diagnosed with PTSD may experience a heightened sensitivity to anxiety, which has been defined as a fear of the consequences of anxiety symptoms (Taylor, Koch, & McNally, 1992). Higher levels of alcohol consumption have been linked to anxiety sensitivity (Stewart, Peterson, &

Pihl, 1995). In our own work with trauma survivors, we often hear that alcohol and drugs are used as a means to manage unwanted thoughts and feelings.

While a grief reaction after the loss of a loved one is considered normal, there is consensus that some individuals develop a pathological and debilitating syndrome referred to as "complicated bereavement." Some experts in the area prefer the term "traumatic grief," as it points to the syndrome being a stress response and because many of the symptoms (such as numbness, disbelief, anger, and the loss of trust and sense of security) resemble PTSD (Shear & Smith-Karoff, 2002). The trauma in this case is the forced separation from the loved one or separation distress (Prigerson et al., 1996) Several studies indicate that separation distress is a core factor in traumatic grief, manifested by excessive loneliness following the loss, difficulty acknowledging the death, and intrusive, distressing preoccupation (yearning, longing, or searching) with the deceased person (Prigerson et al., 1997; Shear & Smith-Karoff, 2002).

The "complication" in complicated bereavement can be best understood when we consider what would be a more adaptive reaction. This would mean that instead of disbelief and anger, the individual could acknowledge the loss, could remain connected with others, and could believe that life can still hold meaning and purpose. In other words, acceptance in lieu of emotional avoidance is the key to effectively coming to terms with such a painful event (Walser & Hayes, 2006). The importance of this is not constrained to being able to reconcile with loss. Several studies have shown that individuals suffering from complicated bereavement have greater quality of life impairments and more mental and physical health problems (Prigerson et al., 1997; Silverman et al., 2000). In sum, the examples of the comorbid diagnoses used here lend further support to the model of experiential avoidance.

Experiential Avoidance and Control

It is not unusual that traumatized individuals would want to avoid negative internal experience. Not only is it uncomfortable, but in fact, much of experiential avoidance is learned, and clients are taught that the thing to do is rid themselves of negative emotion and negative thought content. They are taught that they should be in control of their personal emotional and mind states. Control has both good and bad aspects. Being able to control one's environment is a good thing when one is feeling cold, for instance. Control can be powerful when one is trying to repair something that has been broken. We are taught how to solve problems by fixing them. If we don't like something, we figure out how to fix it and then fix it: if you don't have enough education, get more education; if you would like a better time, go to the movies; if you would like a different hairstyle, go to the beauty shop. This same kind of control can be applied in difficult areas also: if you don't like your living circumstances, make it better, whether by divorcing, moving across the country, or changing friends.

Control can work in positive ways to improve our lives. However, these same kinds of control strategies—attempting to be more, better, different—can also work in ways that cause pain and suffering when misapplied (Walser & Hayes, 2006). Trying to create more self-worth, or a better feeling, or a different "you" can become an exceedingly painful process. If you are working from this position—that you need to control internal experience and think, feel, and be something other than what you are—then you are automatically placed in a position of "non-wholeness," a lesser place wherein who you are is fundamentally broken. This is a "first you lose then you play the game of life" position. It would be a very different thing to experience oneself as fundamentally whole with all negative and positive private experiences in tow, including the trauma and its associated feelings and thoughts. Furthermore, the struggle to heal from this lack of wholeness, this brokenness, following a trauma, can become a vicious cycle and further proof of being broken when the strategy of avoidance inevitably fails to create a permanent solution (which would involve no more fear, no more anxiety, no more trauma). The fruitlessness of this agenda is even more apparent when we consider that history only works in one direction—it is additive across time. We cannot go back in time and undo the traumatic event. Moreover, if clients spend ongoing time trying to control their experiences of a past trauma, then the trauma and its associations will grow, in some cases even to the point where an individual's full identity and life experience is, in some way, about the trauma. Whole pieces of the individual can become lost to the experience.

The Verbal Nature of Trauma

Misapplied control as the solution to healing from trauma may, in fact, be part of the problem. Moreover and paradoxically, efforts to control these internal events by avoidance can actually amplify the experience of the event (Walser & Hayes, 2006). For example, deliberate attempts to try not to think about the trauma may actually bring the trauma to mind. It's not surprising that humans would try this strategy—we are not to blame for the efforts we make at control of internal events. Control as a strategy for solving human suffering is built into human language (Hayes, Wilson, Gifford, Follette, & Strosahl, 1996). If we examine the impact of the verbal behavior (to speak, form thoughts, use our minds) of humans as a whole, we will see how it can come to affect a trauma survivor's life more globally. Our human ability to be verbal can play a critical role in moderating the damage caused directly by a traumatic event. For instance, given the nature of human language, the description and evaluation of the trauma itself can become aversive (Hayes et al., 1999; Walser & Hayes, 2006). Simply telling the story of a trauma can evoke negative emotions and experiences; the actual trauma does not have to be present. In addition, verbal behavior takes place in all contexts, so that self-talk about traumatic events can appear for an unlimited period of time and in multiple situations, again growing the potential problems and pain associated with the trauma (Walser & Hayes, 2006).

Melting with Language

Verbal knowledge, or our ability to create and grow our language, is our miracle and our misfortune. Knowledge helps us to build cities, improve our lives, be creative, plan, and have fun. Knowledge also brings with it self-awareness or awareness that we have a mind. Our minds, however, even with their vast knowledge, do not always know what's good for us. With our minds we judge, categorize, catalog, sort, label, and group. Again, these are useful human language tools—most of the time. A problem arises when we hold the content of our mind to be literally true; literally as *who we are*. From the ACT perspective, we refer to this problem as "fusion" (Hayes et al., 1999). If we review the definition of fusion, it provides a good metaphor for what we mean by this concept. The definition of "fuse" is "to blend, to be united as if melted together." As meant here, when we hold thoughts and interpretations to be literally true, when we buy them without recognizing them for what they are, then we are melted together or fused with our thoughts and interpretations. From this position, responding to the content of the mind can lead to problematic behavior that diminishes vitality. If a sexually traumatized individual makes the judgment that she is ruined or worthless due to her history, and she holds those judgments to be literally true, then it seems she must work diligently to undo the ruined part herself or get rid of the feelings and thoughts of worthlessness so that she can be whole and engage the world again (Walser & Hayes, 2006). If the sense of worthlessness is traced back to the trauma, then the trauma has to be undone or eliminated, too.

There are a number of more obvious ways in which fusion with mind can lead to problematic behavior, such as when we hold our stories or our reasons as the causes for our actions. This might be exemplified by hitting someone *because* you have a *feeling* of anger, staying inside *because* you have a *thought* that you are unattractive, or being unwilling to engage in intimate sexual behavior *because anxiety* related to a trauma has surfaced. These verbal explanations (stories) for causes of behavior can both amplify avoidance and increase rigidity in responding. When we believe our stories cause our actions, we take them to be true and accept them as legitimate causes of dysfunctional behavior. The conclusion is that the reasons need to change so that the behavior can change. However, it is unlikely that feelings of anger, thoughts of unattractiveness, or anxiety will be permanently removed, and they are not the causes of the behavior anyway.

Other problematic ways of responding to mind include strategies trauma survivors employ in reaction to excessive worry and rumination, intrusive thoughts, and trauma-related memories. For instance, we have worked with trauma survivors who manage cognitive intrusions and worry by isolating in the garage, by nagging their partner, or by taking drugs. Many of the methods used to manage these experiences involve straightforward avoidance of persons and places; but they also include other types of avoidance wherein feelings, thoughts, and memories are escaped, including being overly competent and motivated to achieve at the cost of personal well-being. The potential reactions to internal content, then, can set behavior in motion that is damaging and increases suffering. Furthermore, when you ask clients how well these strategies work to solve their dilemma, they will often report some small amount of temporary relief. However, if you ask them to tell you how much time they spend worrying, the answer is closer to "all the time," and they acknowledge they are still painfully struggling.

There are more subtle ways in which fusion with our verbal content (or mind) can cause us problems in terms of remaining psychologically and behaviorally stuck following a trauma. For instance, knowledge and verbal capacity gives us the ability to construct possible futures (Hayes et al., 1999). One the one hand, we can imagine winning the lottery or being married and what the consequences of such events would be. This same ability, on the other hand, allows us to imagine what it might be like if we had not had particular traumatic events happen in the past. Clients will say to themselves or in therapy, "If only I hadn't been molested as a child, then my life would be better." The message is that a historical event, one that can never be changed, is now *the* reason as to why the person's life is in shambles (and is also the reason for current suffering). As noted, history cannot be undone; yet many a struggle has been waged for years in a vain attempt to undo the past. We have seen trauma survivors make the most futile and painful attempts to have some other history than their own. These attempts range from pretending to be someone else, to marrying repeatedly as a way to redefine oneself, to hiding out for years on end, to suicide.

Another subtle way in which our relationship to our verbal content can be problematic pertains to "imagined ideals" (Hayes et al., 1999). Trauma survivors, like anyone, can compare their current lives to an imagined ideal. This ideal sense of self can have many forms, and it sometimes shows up in the clinical setting when clients make statements like "If I only had what you have, then my life would not be a problem," or when the client strives toward a perceived ideal that takes the form of being a good-looking, well-liked, prosperous, and popular person. Both ideals are usually viewed as being trouble free and certainly as being without the experience of anxiety, depression, sadness, memories or other negative thoughts and emotions related to having had a traumatic experience. In order to reach the imagined ideal goal, it becomes even more important to rid oneself of negative internal experience as a means to achieving this state. A personal battle of self-hatred and failure then promises to increase suffering and postpone healthier ways of living.

Additionally, when we fuse with our mind's evaluation, judgment, and the like, it seems as if the evaluations actually reside within the object being evaluated (Hayes et al., 1999). If we say that something is good or bad, it suggests that "good" or "bad" exists in the thing itself. We lose contact with the fact that evaluations do not exist within the object being evaluated but rather are comments that we are making about an object. This is problematic when trauma survivors evaluate themselves as damaged. If one is fused with "damaged," it can be difficult to move in life-enhancing directions. It appears as if you must believe some other evaluation first, like "fixed," before you can live well. Again, the overall problem with all of these forms of fusion is that they can lead to avoidance of self, the current moment, and the world. This avoidance is often manifested in attempts to control private experience, which, in turn, limits the range of behaviors that can occur and narrows exposure to emotion. In the end, behavioral and psychological flexibility are compromised.

In sum, trauma survivors, through processes of holding the content of their minds to be literally true (fusing with verbally constructed futures, imagined ideals, reasons as causes of behavior, and evaluation), get entangled with their minds and become overidentified with the content of their mental lives in ways that keep them stuck in psychological turmoil and traumatic pasts. It is important to remind the reader at this time that this is not about blaming the trauma survivor. Control of private experience is what these individuals have been taught to do, as have humans more generally. We are all in this human language deal together, and the overarching goal is to decrease suffering. We are simply suggesting that the tool used to decrease suffering, rigidly applied control, is the very strategy that ultimately causes pain to linger and grow. We verbally construct with our minds the world, our future, and our past; and we can act on these constructions. It is for these reasons that we struggle and hold on when we should let go. We live in a derived, verbally regulated reality rather than experiencing the world as it unfolds in the here and now.

Is there an alternative to misapplied control? With ACT, we believe there is. In the place of literal meanings there are multiple meanings to your experience (for instance, your thinking, what is present, context, history, and feelings); in the place of the fusion, there is defusion from mental content, seeing it for what it is—content of the mind; in the place of reason—acknowledging your reasons and choosing to behave in ways that promote personal values, committing to a course of action; and in the place of emotional and experiential control, moving into emotional and experiential acceptance (Hayes et al., 1999).

A Word About Mindfulness and ACT

Mindfulness has been defined as "bringing one's complete attention to the present experience on a moment-to-moment basis" (Marlatt & Kristeller, 1999, p. 68). It is the practice of compassionate, moment-to-moment presence. It entails openness to experience and the practice of observing thoughts, feelings, and sensations as an ongoing flow of events that don't necessarily need to be acted upon. ACT uses mindfulness practice and various techniques to help the client establish this sense of openness. There are generally four processes in ACT that support the development of mindfulness as it is defined above. These are acceptance of experience, defusion from the literal meaning of thought, continuous contact with the present moment, and a transcendent sense of self (Hayes, Follette, et al., 2004; Hayes & Wilson, 2003). These processes provide the opportunity for the client to experience both positively evaluated and negatively evaluated internal events without necessarily treating these events as real or the truth. In fact, from this observer perspective they can be seen for exactly what they are—thoughts, feelings, and sensations. This can help clients disentangle themselves or defuse from private internal content without any effort to make the content change. It is observation *without* effort to make something more, better, or different. ACT, however, does not rely on the practice of mindfulness alone as the intervention but also addresses personal values and the ability to make and keep commitments related to those values. There is an intricate interplay between being present in the moment and heading in a personally valued direction. These ideas will be further explored in chapter 2.

ACT and Other CBT Interventions for PTSD

It is ironic that ACT is considered an innovative, recently developed therapy given that it is based on relational frame theory (RFT), one of the most empirically substantiated theories of human behavior, language, and cognition. RFT has undergone decades of empirical research on derived stimulus relations. A full account is beyond the scope of this chapter (we direct the interested reader to *Relational Frame Theory: A Post-Skinnerian Account of Human Language and Cognition* by S. C. Hayes, D. Barnes-Holmes, & B. Roche, 2001), but the point is that the theory upon which ACT rests is hardly new. Yet with its emphasis on acceptance of internal phenomena and on valued living, ACT is markedly different from traditional approaches. In this section we will briefly discuss some of the more common treatments for PTSD and how these treatments compare and contrast with ACT.

One way to view differences between the various treatments for PTSD is to consider the intended point and purpose of intervention. That is, in cognitive therapy the idea is to first target and modify problematic thoughts in order to subsequently affect emotion (to feel better) and behavior (to behave better). Some approaches, such as exposure therapy, focus on preventing avoidance behavior so that clients' reactivity to trauma-related stimuli can be unlearned, or deconditioned. Others (such as systematic desensitization, stress inoculation therapy, and assertiveness training) add behavior acquisition as a way to control or counter problematic responses. Another example is the psychodynamic approach, which focuses on making previously unconscious material conscious in order to increase one's ability to cope with the material.

As you can see, despite the varying targets, these treatments share the idea that some aspect of the client's internal experience is not as it should be and needs modification. As discussed, ACT explicitly does not try to modify the client's thoughts, feelings, or physiological reactivities. Rather, ACT alters the *functions* of those thoughts, feelings, and physiological reactions. The client is helped to see that such reactions are just that—internal phenomena that are distinct from the self and that one's ability to make life-affirming choices is not dependent on modifying or otherwise controlling such phenomena. At a fundamental level, rather than changing a person's internal experience, ACT loosens the grip such phenomena can have over the person's life, freeing them to live intentionally rather than reactively.

It is interesting to also consider commonalities between ACT and alternate treatments for PTSD. One aspect is particularly worth noting as it may represent a powerful mechanism of therapeutic change. That is, regardless of the stated purpose of the therapy, these approaches all ultimately offer the opportunity for individuals with trauma to develop a different, more helpful relationship with uncomfortable thoughts, physical sensations, and emotions. For example, exposure therapy and ACT both assist individuals to stay in contact with their internal and physiological reactions to trauma stimuli, thereby experientially learning to view them differently (for example, one learns that these reactions don't in fact signal impending danger; one learns not to buy into such reactions and that they can be experienced safely). Whether implicitly or explicitly stated, the individual develops a different perspective of the relationship between their self and their thoughts, feelings, and physiological reactions. As another example, in cognitive processing therapy (CPT; Resick & Schnicke, 1993), individuals learn to challenge their thoughts, to balance distorted interpretations with more accurate and insightful conclusions. This entails a different relationship with one's thoughts, a reexamination of cognitions that often have been held for years without question. This process of identifying and challenging one's thoughts requires distancing from those thoughts (in other words, defusing). In addition, though not explicitly addressed in CPT, clients come in contact with a self that is distinct from (larger than) their cognitions. That is, the self is the entity that is doing the examining and challenging of certain thoughts. As the literature on ACT and other PTSD treatments evolves, it will be interesting to see whether additional light is shed on the issue of relationship to private events as a mechanism of change in therapy.

CHAPTER 2

Mindfulness and Acceptance

There is no baser folly than the infatuation that looks upon the transient as if it were everlasting.

—Tiru Valluvar, *Tirukkural* 34:331

"Acceptance" means "to willingly take in what is offered, to hold without protest or reaction." In ACT, we are actively working to help clients accept internal or private events such as thoughts, feelings, memories, and sensations. We are working to help them willingly take what is offered, inside the skin, and to hold it lightly, as if holding a butterfly in the palm of their hand. While this may seem simple, to practice doing this can be quite hard and requires an ongoing commitment. The mind readily pulls us into its space, dragging us around like a fish being pulled on a hook. We get caught and away we go with what the mind has to say, rarely recognizing or being aware of this process.

The mind is exceedingly tenacious, rarely giving us a break from its ongoing commentary on our lives, situations, and how we're being in the world. On the one hand, the constant flow of thought so captures us, it's difficult to see that thinking is what is happening every day and every moment. Given this ongoing river of thought, we come to overidentify with our minds in ways that can lead to inflexibility—holding ourselves to be the things that our minds tell us we are. The problem here, of course, lies in the knowledge that the mind holds. If you know one side, you know the other. If you know "good," then you know "bad." The evaluating and judging processes of the mind, when held as something to be believed, can create painful and difficult struggles that impact quality and meaning in life. Being mindful of this process, on the other hand, can allow us to surf this wave, seeing it for what it is—an experience called thinking.

Chapter Objectives

- Discuss the ins and outs of mindfulness

- Understand some of what is known about mindfulness

- Introduce clients to mindfulness

- Explain how to use the mindfulness exercises in this book

What Is Mindfulness?

Mindfulness is an ancient Buddhist practice that can have a powerful impact on our lives today. This does not mean that you need to become a Buddhist or even practice Buddhism to engage in the practice of mindfulness. Mindfulness is a simple concept. John Kabat-Zinn provides us with a useful and ACT-consistent definition: "Mindfulness means paying attention in a particular way: on purpose, in the present moment, and non-judgmentally" (1994, p. 4). He notes that this kind of attention brings greater awareness to the present moment, and that it creates clarity and acceptance. All of these goals are in the ACT approach.

The Present Moment

One of the key problems in getting stuck in the literal meanings of the mind is that it can keep us out of the present moment. This is true for all of us, but can be particularly painful for clients who have been diagnosed with PTSD. If we take a moment to observe the places where our mind spends its time, we generally find that it is focused on the past or worried about the future. We rarely show up to what is there to be experienced in the moment as it unfolds. In practicing mindfulness with our clients, we will speak to the moment not only in mindfulness exercises, but also by just pausing and asking the client to observe what is happening right now. We may ask them to just listen or see. We may ask them to just feel or sense. On nearly every occasion of doing so, our clients learn that it is a relatively good moment (comparatively speaking), and there is much to be aware of that has little to do with the trauma of the past or the worries of the future. We have had many clients report after doing a mindful walk that they got back in touch with something that they had lost—a sense of wonder and beauty about the world.

The Past

We can spend hours in our minds thinking about what happened yesterday or years ago, engaging in a process of evaluation about how things should have been different, especially if we don't like the places that we are visiting in our memories. We may also spend time thinking about the fallout of a particular event, such as a divorce or death of a loved one. As we review these memories, we build narratives or stories that explain what happened, what should have happened, and how to avoid having a similar negatively judged event happen again. The stories that get built around this can be extensive and can come to function in interesting ways. For instance, the story around divorce may be that the person can never again get married because it was all too painful and devastating. Rather than risk that kind of pain again, the person limits contact with potential partners and then constructs a story about that, giving yet more reasons for avoiding intimate contact. Here, you can easily see how stories around trauma can lead to negative functioning. Stories get built about the trauma (for instance, one story might be "I am ruined because of my trauma and am unloveable as a result") and lives get smaller based on these stories ("Therefore, if I am unloveable, I cannot be in relationships"). Loneliness is born in these places and lives remain cut off and out of balance.

It's natural to experience pain in the face of trauma. In fact, it would seem odd if someone did not experience difficult emotions in response to a traumatic event. The issue becomes what we do once the pain arises. We often begin to evaluate it and react to it in ways that are problematic and increase suffering. The circle of suffering in the illustration shows how the original painful reaction to the trauma occurs, and the person is then beset by judgments, arguments, evaluations, struggle, proclamations, wishes, shame, and desires to control or have some other experience. It is in this place that suffering occurs and grows. Pain is the original natural response to a harm like a trauma. Suffering is all that we do to judge and eliminate the pain—we evaluate it as bad, then battle with it to make the natural experience go away. Suffering can grow around the original pain,

Pain is a naturally elicited emotion. Suffering is all the stuff we add to it with our minds.

potentially leading to years of problematic behavior. Take the following example of an interaction with a client:

Therapist: Tell me what has been keeping you stuck.

Client: Well, … the government has screwed me and the war ruined me.

Therapist: Can you say more?

Client: *(with emphasis)* My whole life has been impacted by this. The government has destroyed me and being in Vietnam has ruined my life. The government never recognized me for what I did … No one appreciated that I was risking my life in Vietnam.

Therapist: If I recall correctly, you told that same story a few weeks ago and then again a few weeks before that.

Client: Well, it's true.

Therapist: Okay. But let's just take a moment and notice that you've told this story multiple times since I've come to know you. How many times have you told this story in your life?

Client:	*(pausing)* Thousands of times.
Therapist:	How many years have you been telling it?
Client:	*(pausing)* About thirty-five years.
Therapist:	*(quite seriously)* Has anything changed after telling the story? Are things different for you now? *(Therapist pauses; client is looking a little confused.)* What do you think will be different if you tell that story one more time?
Client:	*(long pause, then whispers)* Nothing. *(pause)* But you don't get it, the government screwed me and Vietnam destroyed my life.
Therapist:	*(solemn and compassionate)* Yes, I hear that story ... And it is clear to me that something went wrong in your past around this. And ... now you've told the story again. What do you think will be different now?
Client:	Nothing, but you don't seem to see... *(Client trails off, confused.)*
Therapist:	I do see something. I see years of pain and the story you've built around it, but I also see how telling the story hasn't seemed to be the answer. It hasn't fixed the problem. You have told it thousands of times across many years, and here you are sitting in front of me ... telling it again. What are you hoping telling the story again will get you?
Client:	Out of this problem, out of this pain.
Therapist:	*(thoughtfully and without judgment)* So something is really amiss here. If you've told this story thousands of times, you would think you would be out of the pain by now, that it would have worked. Would it be fair to say that telling the story isn't working? That isn't to say that these things didn't happen to you—it's clear to me that they did. Bad things happened to you at the hands of the government when you came back from Vietnam, and you saw horrible tragedies and events while you were in Vietnam. But something funny happened when you got back— repeating this story got linked to a means to get rid of the pain. But the pain is still here, correct?
Client:	*(quietly)* Correct.
Therapist:	Telling and retelling this story as a way out of the pain must not be the answer. It doesn't work. If it did work, it would have by now. And in some strange way, it seems that your whole life has become about this story. Your life has been about the past.
Client:	Right.

Therapist: *(gentle and earnest)* The real tragedy will be if I see you again in a year or two and you're still telling me the same story.

Client: *(very quietly)* True.

The interaction with this client poignantly brings to the fore the problem of hanging out in the past. These kinds of stories can be small, interfering with our lives and values in ways that are not particularly problematic, but they can also be large and extremely limiting, telling you that you cannot have the love or life you deserve or berating you with self-doubt and encouraging you to give up because you will fail anyway. And what are these limitations based on? They are based on a story about one's past that the mind has created and the story is usually linked to the desire to have had a different past—a different history. However, there is no other history to be had. Part of what we are doing with ACT is pointing to the fact that history cannot be undone, while also working on decreasing suffering by targeting the relationship that we have with pain, which is a naturally occurring experience related to a traumatic event, rather than what the story tells you it is—that you are damaged and unlovable. Being aware, in the moment, of this experience of pain is very different than trying as hard as one can to not have the experience. Suffering is found in the latter.

Other things that you might say in response to these kinds of stories include giving the client the position of absolute rightness. For instance, you might say, "You are correct; you are 100 percent right about this story. Now what?" Or you can prepare the client for more of the same, saying something like "I think we should go over this story every time you come into session, but be ready for the same outcome that you've always had. Sound okay?" Both of these interventions, if done with sensitivity to the difficulty of the situation, will not only point to the unworkability of the situation but will also point to the problem of spending so many moments in the past. These kinds of interventions are useful throughout ACT and play a particular role in one of the core interventions—creative hopelessness—and in undermining literality in the area of reason giving. Each is presented in greater detail in later chapters.

The Future

As with the past, we can spend hours in our minds worrying about the future. This, too, keeps us out of the present moment. The desire to dwell in the future can often be driven by wanting to control internal experiences arising out fear of what *could* happen. Trauma survivors are often burdened with notions about the amount of time that will be filled in the future with their current problems (feeling anxious, afraid, etc.). In fact, we have heard many clients ask, "Am I going to feel this way forever?" or say, "No matter what I do, it will always be this way." In some sense they are right. We are thinking, feeling, sensing creatures, and there is always something to be thought or felt. It is also most likely true that clients will experience the thoughts and feelings that they don't want to experience many more times in their lives. Anxiety will come and then it will go; fear will come and then it will go; the thoughts will rise and fall in the same manner. We lose sight of this ongoing process in worrying about things never being different in the future or by trying to control the future with worrying rather than experiencing what is happening in the now. Additionally, if you are anxious about what the future holds, and given that the future is unknown and uncontrollable, then that is also something to be anxious about. You can even get to a place where you are having anxiety about your anxiety. This is not a process that tends to promote feeling "better" in the future. Again, suffering is increased under these conditions. Practicing being present in the moment and being aware that thinking and feeling are ongoing experiences that change with each new moment may be the antidote to this kind of suffering.

Interestingly, if your goal is to keep the past from becoming your future ("I don't want to ever have trauma again or any of the feelings and thoughts associated with it"), and you work hard to make sure this comes true by avoiding all things related to your trauma, then the trauma is always present. It is a paradox—you don't want the trauma, and that is exactly what you get. Your past becomes your future. Mindfulness allows us to sit on the bank and observe the flow rather than getting hooked by this process.

Creating Clarity

An important aspect of mindfulness is its value in creating clarity. There are at least two characteristics of this clarity that can encourage vitality. First, when we are mindful of our experience, we can see it for what it is; we can see it clearly and disengage from holding the experience to be literally true. For instance, when being mindful of an emotion, you observe the emotion, noticing its nuances and sensations. From this position, there is no need to fight with it, to make it come or go. The emotion is a collection of sensations felt in a particular way. When we are willing to experience it in this manner, the emotion itself is untainted. It can be viewed as its simple form—an emotion (or memory or thought). There is vitality in this approach as it makes room for all manner of thought, feeling, and sensation, bringing to bear the large variety of human experience that is available.

Second, when experience is seen clearly, one gains the opportunity to respond differently to it. When you can see a thought or feeling as just that, a thought or feeling, rather than something that you literally *are*, then a freedom arises in how you respond to the thought or feeling—you no longer have to try to control it or make it something different. This clarity about experiencing, then, sets the stage for choice. If you are no longer the actual things that you think and feel, but rather you are a context in which these events occur, then they no longer have the control over your life that they seemed to have. You are freed to make choices that are consistent with your values. There is much more vitality in living a valued life than in living a life trying to control your internal experiences.

Acceptance

Mindfulness creates a place from which acceptance is possible. If we are beings who are the context for the ongoing flow of experience, then the efforts to eliminate experience become unnecessary (and in fact nearly impossible). Experience will change momentarily—just watch and wait. Additionally, if these experiences are only the content of our lives and are unchangeable once they have occurred, then holding them lightly, contacting them at a given moment, is the essence of acceptance. In this moment we take the experience as it is offered, without protest or reaction.

Some of What We Know About Mindfulness

The practice of mindfulness has been around for centuries and has been used for both secular and nonsecular reasons (Hirst, 2003). It is generally used as a means to transcend suffering. For instance, Ruth Baer provides a definition of mindfulness practice that includes "bringing one's attention to the internal and external experiences occurring in the present moment" (2003, p. 128). Dimidjian and Linehan (2003) specify three principles found in the behaviors of mindfulness—observation, description, and aware participation—and include how one should participate in these behaviors —nonjudgmentally, in the present moment, and effectively. Additionally, Hayes and Wilson (2003) specify acceptance, cognitive defusion, and exposure as the core of mindfulness practice.

Recent research on mindfulness indicates that mindfulness has a positive impact on many difficult life experiences. For instance, studies have shown that mindfulness is an effective treatment for psychological burnout in health care practitioners of differing disciplines (Cohen-Katz et al., 2005; Beddoe & Murphy, 2004). Mindfulness practice has also been shown to have a positive relationship to marital satisfaction (Burpee & Langer, 2005) and has been found to improve chronic pain and stress in the elderly (McBee, 2003).

Mindfulness has also proved useful in treatment of mental health patients. For instance, Ma and Teasdale (2004) found that a mindfulness-based form of cognitive therapy was effective in preventing recurrence of depression in recovered patients who had previously experienced at least three previous episodes. Other recent research suggests that mindfulness meditation is effective in preventing relapse among substance abusers (Breslin, Zack, & McMain, 2002).

Mindfulness has proven effective in reducing stress and anxiety symptoms in patients with medical conditions. For instance, Sagula and Rice (2004) studied the impact of mindfulness on patients suffering from chronic pain. They found that those who practiced mindfulness, as compared to controls who did not, had significant reductions in depression and anxiety and moved more quickly through the stages of grief often associated with chronic pain conditions. Tacon, McComb, Caldera, and Randolph (2003), found that the mindfulness-based stress reduction (MBSR; Kabat-Zinn, 1994) program was effective in reducing anxiety in women with heart disease, and Weissbecker and colleagues (2002) found that patients with fibromyalgia who participated in a mindfulness-based cognitive behavioral therapy intervention reported improvements in general well-being and both functional and psychological status. Finally, there has been sizable research into the use of mindfulness in helping patients who have cancer. Speca, Carlson, Goodey, and Angen (2000) found that a mindfulness meditation program effectively decreased mood disturbance, stress symptoms, and cardiopulmonary and gastrointestinal problems in both male and female cancer patients, and Carlson, Speca, Patel, and Goodey (2004) found that participation in mindfulness practice improved quality of life and decreased stress symptoms in breast and prostate cancer patients. These studies are promising and are increasing our knowledge about the potential benefits of mindfulness practice.

Introducing Clients to Mindfulness

To introduce clients to mindfulness, we spend time talking about why mindfulness is helpful and then open each of our sessions with a guided meditation that focuses on the breath, the body, or some situation we ask them to imagine in their mind. We generally engage in the mindfulness exercises for about ten minutes, taking a few minutes afterwards to talk with the clients about their experiences during the exercise. We also ask clients to practice mindfulness on their own.

Why Mindfulness

When we first talk to clients about why we would like them to engage in mindfulness exercises, we explore its utility at a number of different levels. First, we talk about how mindfulness is a way to practice observing different aspects of the self, including the body, mind, and sensing. We couch this in terms of awareness and the benefits that awareness can bring. Being aware of oneself in the moment can help individuals to better know their experiences, allowing them to understand what it is that they are feeling and thinking at any one time. Many clients who have been diagnosed with PTSD have lost touch with their current experience, finding it difficult to describe their emotional states. They feel disconnected from their own sense of self. We work on awareness to help them get reconnected.

Second, we explore the state and experience of what is occurring in their minds much of the time. That is, we talk about how PTSD can lead one to spend large amounts of time either dwelling on the past or worrying about the future. On the one hand, time is spent either reflecting on the trauma or how the trauma has impacted them and their lives. Time is spent evaluating, arguing with, wishing for, and describing things in "if only" scenarios, and in wanting to undo the past. On the other hand, time is also spent thinking about what will happen if their situation or PTSD doesn't improve, thinking about what might happen next, trying to control future outcomes, or evaluating how they will not be able to face the upcoming challenges. In addressing these scenarios, we might say something similar to the following:

Therapist: Can you see how your time is taken up by thinking about what has happened in the past or by thinking about what will happen in the future? Very little time is spent with what is happening right now, right in this moment. In fact, if you stop and notice this moment, it's pretty good, as moments go. All I'd like you to do is notice what you see, … what you hear, … and what sensations you feel in your body, … If we evaluate this moment and just notice what's happening right now, it's not too bad. And, in fact, it may be that this moment is filled with rich and varied experience.

We then continue by pointing to the power of being in the moment:

Therapist: Did you also notice that while you were being aware of this moment, you weren't in your past or future? You were here. You caught a break. What if mindfulness was like that—you could show up to the richness of each moment and observe?

Many clients agree that this would be helpful, although they also point out how difficult it is to do. We emphasize practice, explaining that mindfulness is like building a weakened muscled—you must exercise it in order for it to grow in strength.

Third, we actively link mindfulness to the ACT processes of defusion and self-as-context. Each of these will be explained in further detail in later chapters. Briefly, defusion is the process by which we help clients to loosen the literal connection between what the mind says and what the mind is referring to. For instance, the word "cup" is not literally contained in the object we call a cup. In the same way, the word "broken" is not contained in the person. Additionally, the verbal relationships to a particular word and their associated functions are often present. You can *imagine* washing a cup in your hands and you can notice what the "feel" of the soap, water, and hardness of the ceramic container might be like. You may even be able to "smell" the soap as you think about this scenario. It doesn't mean that you are literally washing a cup, but it can seem that way as all of the functions of cup washing are present as you imagine it. In this same way, again, you may be able to imagine that you are broken and the associated experiences of brokenness (sadness, thoughts about trauma, etc.) may be present. However, it doesn't mean that you are literally broken—"broken" doesn't literally exist in you (or the trauma survivor).

There are many defusion techniques and exercises in ACT that help clients to see this process of what we call deliteralization. The idea is to help clients get defused from their minds. Practicing mindfulness helps with this process.

In addition, with ACT we are actively helping clients to see themselves as a context in which their content—their experiences of emotion, thought, memory, and sensation—occurs. We work to help clients see themselves as ongoing, continually changing experiences that they can actively observe, rather than holding themselves as the content of their experience and a final outcome of their experience ("I am broken"). Here, too, mindfulness is useful in developing this perspective.

Since both defusion and self-as-context processes occur later in the progression of the therapy, we only make brief reference to these concepts in the first session. For instance, we may say something like the following:

Therapist: Mindfulness is also going to help us further down the road when we begin to explore issues related to how our minds seem to make things out to be true that may actually not be so. This is not to say that you don't know about your trauma or that it didn't happen; but it is interesting to see what our minds do following the trauma, how they begin to evaluate and judge and perhaps cause problems for us. Make sense? (*Clients generally agree and know what we are referring to here.*) Also, we're going to be working on finding a new relationship with our history, emotions, and thinking. Mindfulness is going to help there too.

Following the mindfulness exercises, clients will generally make a number of comments about the experience. Initially, the comments will often be about how they were unable to follow the instruction (such as focusing on the breath or scanning the body). We remind the clients that this experience is typical, and that in mindful practice, if you notice yourself drifting away from focused attention, you just gently notice that this has happened and where you've been pulled, then gently bring yourself back to the task at hand.

Dispelling Misconceptions

There are a number of misconceptions about mindfulness that can interfere with its practice. First, many people will have the misconception that practicing mindfulness is a form of religion. This is generally based on misunderstood notions about

Eastern philosophy and Buddhist religions. Practitioners of mindful meditation may have certain ideals and goals (such as enlightenment), but these are not necessarily linked to religion. It may simply be a philosophical practice or a desire to improve one's life. When talking with clients about mindfulness, we remind them that it can serve many purposes; some may be religious in nature, but others are simply about creating health and well-being, being more connected to the moment, or improving attention.

A second misconception is related to the view that mindfulness is a form of hypnosis (Gunaratana, 2002). We have had clients ask us if our plans are to place them in a trance and then "force them to bock like chickens." We generally get a good laugh out these ideas and then spend time informing clients about what is practiced in mindfulness, letting them know that the goal is not to create a trancelike state where one can be manipulated but rather to be present in the moment—to experience and be aware.

A third misconception involves the notion that mindfulness is a form of relaxation or is designed to be a relaxation exercise. Although some may find mindfulness relaxing, others find it to be anxiety producing. Observing thoughts and memories can bring with it feelings of anxiety. These, of course, are to be observed too, but they may not be very relaxing. We remind clients that they may or may not feel relaxed after participating in a mindfulness exercise or when practicing on their own. If they do feel relaxed, we talk about it as a by-product of the experience rather than a goal. Generally speaking, most of the clients we have worked with report feeling more relaxed after a mindfulness practice than before. However, we occasionally get a client who reports increased anxiety following such an exercise. We have learned that in these cases, the client has generally been hooked by a thought or memory and then has traveled with it, buying it, evaluating it, and holding it as reality. They get lost in the thought and forget to return to observing the thought for what it is—a thought. We gently remind the client of the process of returning to the position of observer, asking them to notice the thought or memory while also being aware that they are the context in which the experience is occurring. We find that, initially, clients may struggle some with this notion, but after the sessions on self-as-context we can easily point to exercises and metaphors (the continuous you exercise and the chessboard metaphor—see chapter 7, on self-as-context), and clients are more readily able to link with the observer perspective.

Related to the notion that mindfulness is a form of relaxation is the idea that mindfulness is a form of avoidance or a way to escape reality. Mindfulness can be used in this fashion, but if it's done correctly it won't generally function this way. Additionally, if one practices mindfulness with the goal of achieving a "special" feeling that is not negative, then the practitioner can get caught in increased tension about not being able to create the emotion or in disappointment that a good feeling, once attained, is subsequently lost (as are all feelings).

A fourth misconception involves mystical notions about mindfulness. Some may see mindfulness as a mystery that cannot be solved or as a "magical" practice where individuals are placed into some kind of alternate realm. Here again, we merely remind clients that there is nothing magical about mindfulness. It is a way to be present and experience—nothing more, nothing less.

A fifth misconception that is more often held by therapists than by clients is that mindfulness can be dangerous. This usually involves ideas about encountering "bad" memories or unpleasant emotions during mindfulness and the impact that the encounter may have. This is similar to concerns that therapists have about exposure therapy. Of note, it is well documented (Riggs, Cahill, & Foa, 2006; Shipherd, Street, & Resick, 2006) that exposure is a useful technique for treating PTSD (exposure therapy and ACT are further explored in chapter 10). Exposure techniques, on the one hand, are done with trained therapists in clinical settings (although exposure homework may be done by the client at home, it is still monitored). Mindfulness, on the other hand, can be practiced anywhere and does not need to be occurring under controlled circumstances.

Therapists can explore and address these issues in multiple ways. It is important to remember the purpose of mindfulness: to be aware in the moment, to be present to ongoing experience. This in itself is not dangerous. In fact, it is designed to be helpful. This said, you will want to spend time talking with your clients about the many ways that mindfulness can be practiced. It can be practiced in very small doses or for longer periods of time. Mindfulness can include guided imagery or activity (mindful walking or working). It can include focusing on the breath or body scans. The key is to be engaged in the moment with awareness. Focusing on workability—how to use mindfulness when feeling stuck—can also be beneficial. Mindfulness is not intended, from this perspective, to confront negative internal content purposefully; rather, the purpose is to simply notice negative content as it shows up, just as one would notice other internal content. Practicing with clients during session is also helpful. We recommend that therapists who are asking clients to practice mindfulness also practice themselves. That way, you can more directly answer questions about the experience and understand the process in ways that are helpful to the client.

Finally, some clients mistakenly think that if they practice mindfulness for a short period of time, then their struggle will be "fixed" and they will no longer have difficult emotions and thoughts (Gunaratana, 2002). Mindfulness, as with accepting and committing, is a process, not an outcome. There will always be another negative feeling to be felt or difficult memory to be had. Life presents these events and will always provide opportunities to practice mindfulness.

The Mindfulness Exercises in This Book

We start each of the core components of the ACT therapy presented in this book with two examples of mindfulness exercises. With each example, we talk through the exercise as if we were presenting it directly to the client. Given that we often cover a component in ACT across several sessions, we provide two mindfulness exercises per intervention chapter (4, 5, 6, 7, 8, and 9), so multiple exercises are available to you. However, we do start with focusing on the breath and a body scan as a beginner's foray. These are mindfulness exercises that can be practiced immediately and are basic examples of mindful practice. In addition, these initial examples of mindful practice are very focused on in-the-moment experiencing. Later examples of mindfulness focus more on imagery. Feel free to mix these exercises around or use them whereever they seem appropriate or fit.

There are a couple of things to keep in mind when teaching mindfulness to clients who have been diagnosed with PTSD. First, we talk about practicing mindfulness with eyes open versus eyes closed. Generally speaking, most mindfulness practice is done with the eyes open. Others suggest closing the eyes. For clients with PTSD, we let them know that they can keep their eyes open and focused on a spot in front of them or they can close their eyes if they wish. Allowing the client the choice is important. Many people diagnosed with PTSD feel that they can participate only if they can keep their eyes open. For some, closing their eyes is so uncomfortable and disconcerting that they are unable to even try the practice in the first place. The main point is to get the client practicing—eyes open or closed.

Additionally, asking clients to practice between sessions is helpful. However, if for any reason, a client begins to dissociate or if they find themselves drifting into trauma memories and getting stuck there, rather than dispassionately observing the memories as they pass, then ask the client to reorient with an eyes-open meditation where they are focused on the sights, sensations, and sounds of the moment. By the way, these practices can be short in duration. Starting with even five minutes worth of practice a day can be valuable. Eventually, with practice, even trauma memories can be dispassionately observed for what they are—memories.

Lastly, in ACT we are working to help clients get reconnected to their sense of experiential knowing while simultaneously loosening the grip of verbal knowing. Many of the imagery exercises help to make this reconnection. Describing this to clients can help them come to make the distinction between these two ways of knowing the world.

CHAPTER 3

Preparing to Begin

The tragedy of life is not that it ends so soon, but that we wait so long to begin it.

—W. M. Lewis

In this chapter we focus on how to introduce ACT to clients and review the overall structure of the therapy. It is designed to orient and provide general guidance to the therapist.

Chapter Objectives

- Orient the therapist

- Discover the structure of treatment

- Explain informed consent

- Understand the general session structure

Therapist Orientation

Acceptance and commitment therapy is based upon relational frame theory, one of the more studied areas of basic behavioral analysis (see Hayes et al., 2001; Hayes 2001, for a nice review). It is a distinct therapy with an explicit philosophy—functional contextualism—that therapists need to both understand and embrace in order to conduct the therapy properly. In short, ACT therapists need to understand that the various thoughts, feelings, memories, and so on that clients experience are not the problem so much as the function they serve. That is, the urge to drink is problematic only if clients then choose to drink in order to alleviate that urge. The thought "I'm ruined" is problematic if the client believes it to be literally true and allows that thought to function as a barrier to living fully. The central focus of ACT is to support clients in having what they already have (uncomfortable thoughts, feelings, sensations, etc.), to make a distinction between having these experiences and holding them to be literally true (for example, "I'm having that thought again about never having a life" versus "I'll never have a life"), and to help them move forward in valued directions.

As it applies to PTSD, the ACT therapist recognizes that clients' number one wish, to be fixed, is not doable in the way they are wanting and is not a goal of the therapy. The clients we have worked with who have PTSD come to therapy with a burning desire to be different. Even clients who state that they want to "get [their] life back" or that they want to "move beyond the trauma" reveal, when more closely questioned, that what they really want is to have the trauma erased—to be as they were before. As nothing can erase past events, nor the thoughts and feelings associated with them, this is clearly a setup for failure and frustration. More than that, the strategies clients have used in an attempt to control or escape such thoughts, feelings, and memories have made their lives untenable. ACT is a bold therapy, challenging this unworkable agenda at the very outset of the therapy.

Interestingly, we have noted that while many of the trauma survivors we work with are initially disturbed at the idea that they can't be rid of their traumas or fixed in the way they'd like, some also express relief at hearing what they have suspected all along. They confess that even in that moment, as they sit with a new therapist commencing a new treatment, part of them knows this too will not work ("work" as in get rid of the trauma and associated effects).

At the same time that ACT boldly challenges cherished but unworkable avoidance strategies, it is a deeply compassionate therapy. The ACT therapist believes clients are 100 percent acceptable as they are. In ACT, clients will never hear they should get over it or that something is wrong with them for suffering the way they do. In ACT, the end goal for clients with PTSD is to recognize that they can carry the burden of their traumatic experiences without being overwhelmed or defined by it, and that they can live the lives they want to live despite their trauma histories.

Treatment Structure

This book describes an ACT protocol for PTSD that occurs over eight to sixteen, sixty-minute sessions. (Note: When conducting ACT in group settings, we utilize a ninety-minute session to accommodate multiple participants.) The wide-ranging number of sessions speaks to the flexibility of ACT. Sessions are organized around key content areas that complement each other, and all are needed to fully complete the therapy. That said, there is flexibility in the order and timing of how ACT components are presented to clients. Therapists can remain on one key area for several sessions if that seems appropriate, or topics covered previously can be revisited if the need arises. We recommend that therapists new to ACT follow the suggested order of the sessions for clients with PTSD. However, it's likely that as you become more familiar with the various components of ACT, you will begin to pull in key ideas as optimal moments arise in the course of therapy. Of note, we have written six chapters (4, 5, 6, 7, 8, and 9) around the core interventions for ACT. You will find that each core may take several sessions, and we provide an estimated range of number of sessions that may be needed to cover the core topics.

While many ACT protocols commence with the values component, we often wait to introduce this component until later in the protocol when working with PTSD. This is because so many of the trauma survivors we have worked with are hard-pressed to identify values. It is difficult to know what one wants if one doesn't have a sense of self or a sense of being able to live values in the face of current difficulties. In these instances we have found it more effective to lightly point to the idea of values at the outset of therapy by asking clients what is not working in their lives and what might be keeping them from the lives they would like to be living. Later, when clients have a stronger sense of themselves as context versus content and a better awareness of their ability to make valued choices, we introduce and work on the values component more explicitly.

Our clients with PTSD often complain of memory and attention problems; for instance, they don't remember their last ACT session, or everything seems a blur. Clients we have worked with in residential treatment almost always report feeling overloaded with new information. For this reason we have found it helpful to spend a bit of time at the outset of each session in review, reminding clients where they started and where they have come in terms of the ACT journey. We have found this works nicely to solidify previous insights and to pave the way for new learning. New material is then introduced with ample time provided for discussion and participation in the experiential exercises. Therapists may determine that material needs to be repeated—this is fine. Additionally, we have provided several metaphors and exercises for each key ACT component so that therapists have more than one option to draw from as they proceed through each core area.

Informed Consent

As when initiating any therapy procedure, therapists should review limits of confidentiality with their clients, as well as the terms of their treatment contract more generally. Providing clients with enough information to allow them to make an informed decision about ACT can be surprisingly tricky. ACT is an experiential therapy; that is, much of the learning occurs in the doing, and explanations of the therapy cannot sufficiently depict this experience. Further, explaining the process or point of ACT can teeter dangerously close to sounding as if ACT will be (as clients are expecting) "the answer," when in fact, much of ACT is about helping clients see there is no answer, at least not in the way they are anticipating. ACT therapists are therefore faced with the dilemma of how to provide enough information for clients to ensure informed consent but not so much that it undermines the very therapy they are commencing. Because the therapy is largely experiential, clients need to know that it's likely they will be intensely feeling, not just thinking, during the therapy. We have also learned through experience that individuals with PTSD are already in a fearful place before any explanation occurs about the therapy. Whereas some clients really do need to be made to understand that therapy won't be easy, clients with PTSD are already predisposed to imagine the worst when hearing that this therapy can be a bit of a roller-coaster ride. This means that a second dilemma faced by the ACT therapist is how to provide a realistic sense of the therapy—one that offers fair warning but isn't unduly alarming for the client with PTSD. Here is an example of a brief explanation of the therapy:

Therapist: This treatment, acceptance and commitment therapy, is essentially that—what happens in the therapy is contained in its name. We will be working on accepting what can't be changed and committing to things in your life that matter to you. Given this, it will probably be different than what you expect, what you may think the therapy is, or even what you may have heard. It is a therapy where what happens is difficult to describe with words. It is in the actual doing of the therapy that the therapy becomes clear. Part of what is required here is a bit of trust about where we're going. I know that may be difficult, especially as many people who suffer from PTSD struggle with trust. So, part of what I am going to ask you to do is to hang out long enough to see if this is working for you. I think by that time you'll have a sense about how the therapy can work for what you're struggling with. If, after five or six sessions, it doesn't seem to be working, we'll do something different or I will make the appropriate referral. We'll work together to see what is best, and you can let me know what your choice is. Are you willing to give that a try?

The above informed consent approach works for individual or private-setting groups. For residential or inpatient settings where ACT is part of the curriculum, consent to participate in the therapy can be included in the overall treatment contract.

Session Structure

Each session takes the following structure: 1) open with mindfulness exercise; 2) prior session and homework review; 3) main topic and exercises; and 4) hand out homework for next session. Each session begins with a mindfulness exercise so that (a) both client and therapist can become centered and focused for the session, and (b) both client and therapist can continue to develop their mindfulness practice. This typically takes about ten to fifteen minutes to complete. A note about the mindfulness exercises: As with all aspects of this therapy, experiential acceptance is key. That is, rather than hurry though the mindfulness exercise in order to be done with it so that the "real" session can begin (as one of your authors is prone to do), the exercise should take as long as it takes. Time is also provided after the exercise for clients to express any thoughts or feelings they want to share about their experience.

Next, clients are provided a brief review of the topics previously covered and a review of homework. Following the review, new material is presented. All of the above is done with mindful awareness of what is happening in the room with the client, and this always takes precedence over following the protocol (one of the reasons therapists should not take the actual ACT protocol with them into session). For instance, if a client appears to be having an emotional reaction, the therapist would make room for this rather than soldiering on with what they had planned to say and do in the session. "Making room," however, does not mean delving into content or the whys of the client's experience but rather simply supporting the client in whatever experience they are having without engaging in control or avoidance strategies. The following two dialogues demonstrate the difference between doggedly continuing with the plan for the session and using the therapy more flexibly. We will begin with the former. This dialogue takes place after the mindfulness practice, and at the beginning of the session on control as the problem.

Therapist: So, last week we left the session in a place where you were noticing being stuck, that digging your way out of holes doesn't work.

Client: I think I remember that.

Therapist: What have you noticed about what you felt with respect to being stuck?

Client: Not too much. I can't remember exactly what we talked about.

Therapist:	We talked about all those things that haven't worked in your life in terms of trying to fix the problem of negative emotions and thoughts, the problem of struggling with PTSD.
Client:	Oh.
Therapist:	So what if it's the case that the struggle is the issue, that your very efforts to fix the problem are the problem.
Client:	Sorry, I'm a little confused. I'm still not really remembering what we did last session.
Therapist:	Perhaps what we talk about today will solve that for you. Are you willing to move on?
Client:	I guess. Yeah.
Therapist:	Suppose that control works in 95 percent of the world…

Above, the therapist has truly lost the flexibility of the protocol and has entered head-on into rule following. This tendency can be a beginner's problem in trying to get the therapy "right," but it can also be a problem for more seasoned therapists if they are missing the nuances and purpose of ACT. Next is an example of flexible use of the protocol. This dialogue takes place at the same point in therapy as the previous example.

Therapist:	So, last week we left the session in a place where you were noticing being stuck, that digging your way out of holes doesn't work.
Client:	I think I remember that.
Therapist:	What have you noticed about what you felt with respect to being stuck?
Client:	Not too much. I can't remember exactly what we talked about.
Therapist:	We talked about all those things that haven't worked in your life in terms of trying to fix the problem of negative emotions and thoughts, the problem of struggling with PTSD.
Client:	Oh.
Therapist:	So let's back up a little. Let's revisit last week and tie it into what might be happening for you right now. Sound okay?
Client:	Sure.
Therapist:	We built a list of the things that you struggle with … memories, anxiety, disconnection, … and then we explored all the avenues you have tried to make the memories stop, to get rid of the anxiety and reconnect. Remember that?

Client:	I'm having a bit of difficulty.
Therapist:	That's okay, we are right where we need to be. On that list you said you had tried such things as alcohol, drugs, medication, therapy, running away, and a bunch of other things.
Client:	I think I remember that.
Therapist:	*(gently)* And here, in the therapy right now, is a potential addition to that list … forgetting.
Client:	What do you mean?
Therapist:	How often do you forget?
Client:	All the time. My girlfriend is always telling me I forget, but I don't think there's anything wrong with my memory. I mean I can remember lists and dates and numbers, the whole works. I just seem to forget certain things.
Therapist:	Is it possible that forgetting is also a strategy to try to make difficult experience go away? Last week we were talking about some pretty tough stuff. We were talking about how all the strategies you have tried have failed and about how you find yourself here, in therapy. Could it be that forgetting helped to get you out of that stuck place?
Client:	I hadn't really thought of it that way, but as I think about it … I suppose it's possible.
Therapist:	So forgetting might be another way to dig.
Client:	I guess. I think so.
Therapist:	So we might need to slow things up a bit and check in more about forgetting. Is that okay with you?
Client:	Yes. But what if I forget? *(chuckling)*
Therapist:	That's okay. We will start where you are and work on how to let go of forgetting as a strategy, on how to drop the shovel with this one. It might mean showing up to some difficult emotions. Are you willing to do that?
Client:	If you think it will help.

In this second example, you can see how the therapist quickly abandoned the agenda and moved back to meet the client where he actually was. In this session, the therapist and client continued with unworkable strategies and the cost of forgetting. It was several more sessions before they were able to move on.

The Big Picture

One way to state the overall goal of ACT is that it enhances clients' psychological flexibility and behavioral choices. To accomplish this, both client and therapist need to have (a) an awareness of what sort of life the client would ideally be living, (b) recognition of what has stood in the way, (c) awareness that most of the perceived barriers are not actual barriers, and (d) awareness that one has the ability to make choices in the direction of that desired life. Each of these core ideas will be presented and discussed at length in this book, particularly in terms of how to best work with these topics when providing ACT to clients with PTSD. When conducted well, ACT offers the PTSD client both relief and freedom.

In the next six chapters of the book, we will take you from the beginning of the therapy—opening the client up to something different through creative hopelessness, to the end—making and keeping commitments that are in accordance with personal values.

CHAPTER 4

Creative Hopelessness: Finding the Place Where Something New Can Happen

Deep inside I know that trying to figure things out leads to blindness, that the desire to understand has a built-in brutality that erases what you seek to comprehend. Only experience is sensitive. But maybe I am both weak and brutal. I have never been able to resist trying.

—Peter Høeg

In the first stage of ACT the therapist works to establish creative hopelessness. The term "creative hopelessness" is meant to represent the position in which clients find themselves after letting go of fruitless attempts to change their experience (hence the hopelessness), which actually makes room for the creation of something more workable. It is imperative that clients experientially connect with their failed efforts to make their internal lives different. Most PTSD clients are actively working to have feelings that are different than the ones they currently experience. They often report that they would like these experiences to change and go away. For instance, if a client is struggling with feelings of anxiety or sadness associated with PTSD, there are often great efforts made by the client to get rid of the anxiety or sadness (or other negatively evaluated emotion). Additionally, they may be trying to do the same with thoughts or memories about the trauma. There is a strong belief that if they can eliminate these negatively evaluated experiences from their lives, they will be healed and able to go on and live well. The problem with these efforts, however, is that the very attempts to eliminate the experience often enhance and prolong it. We have had clients report that the harder they try not to think about the trauma, the more they find themselves thinking about it. This only makes sense. If you're spending time trying not to think about something, you have to bring that thing to mind in order to know that you don't want to think about it. A paradox is set in motion, and a vicious cycle of thinking about the trauma and trying not to think about the trauma is established. This dynamic comes into play with emotions also, where clients will report anxiety about their anxiety, or fear of fear, or sadness about their depression. Clients can get into lengthy battles with themselves around efforts to eliminate this kind of internal material. For instance, we have worked with Vietnam veterans who have been trying to rid themselves of their traumatic experiences for more than thirty-five years.

Essentially, what clients are trying to do when they are struggling is to find ways to feel and think that are more, better, and different than the way they feel and think at the moment. Unfortunately, this effort sets them up to be in a place where who they are right at this moment is not acceptable. They must have some other history, or a different feeling, or a better thought in order to be cured. The pursuit of this agenda is largely due to social training, and looks like something along the lines of "Whole and happy people do not feel, think, or remember the things I remember." We human beings are told that we should be able to control our thoughts and feelings. This can be a double-whammy for trauma survivors, as not only were they not able to prevent the trauma from happening, but they are also failures because they cannot control their reaction to the trauma. The focus of this session is to point out the problem of trying to avoid what cannot be avoided.

Session Format (1-2 Sessions)

- Open with mindfulness

- Review prior session (if more than one session)

- Jump into the therapy

- Review the usual suspects

- Create creative hopelessness

- Solve problems and discover when solutions aren't solutions

- Explore hopelessness about the right thing

- Recognize the cost of negative change efforts

- Stay with feeling stuck

- Give hope to hopelessness

- Explore sticking points for clients

- Explore sticking points for therapists

- Assign homework: creative hopelessness

- Moving forward

Opening with Mindfulness

Opening the session by completing a mindfulness exercise serves two purposes. The first, of course, is getting practice at being mindful or being present in the current moment. The second is to help the client get centered and focused on the session. You will also want to pay attention to how you deliver the mindfulness exercise. Using a soft voice and paying attention to timing is important—you will want to pace the exercise, allowing time between statements. As it may be the first time clients have engaged in a mindfulness exercise, it is important to start with the basics, such as focusing on breathing and being aware of sensations or the environment. Below we provide a couple of examples of mindfulness exercises that may be used.

> ### MINDFULNESS EXERCISE 1:
> ### ATTENDING TO BREATHING
> #### (Approximately 5-10 minutes)

Therapist: I would like everyone to start this exercise by placing your feet squarely on the ground and sitting up in your chair so that your back is straight but not rigid. Make sure that your head feels square to your shoulders and place your arms in a comfortable position at your side. (*Demonstrate for the client by modeling the posture.*) This posture helps us to stay alert and focused. There is nothing particularly difficult about doing a mindfulness exercise—it just requires your attention. So let's begin by first noticing or paying attention to the fact that your body is actively sensing the environment. Notice that you can feel yourself sitting in the chair and you can feel your feet on the ground. Also notice that you can feel the clothes on your skin and perhaps your jewelry. Notice, too, that you might feel the bend of your knees or elbows. Now, gently close your eyes or locate a place in front of you, like the floor or wall, where you can fix your gaze. Notice as you close your eyes that your ears open. Take a few moments to pay attention to all of the sounds that you hear. (*Take a short bit of time and list the different sounds that are present in the room, the blow of the heater, for instance, or the sound of your voice.*) Just take this time to follow sound. (*Allow a few more moments for focusing on sound.*)

Now gently release your attention from sound. I would like you to place your attention at the tip of your nose and begin to notice the sensation of air moving in and out of your nostrils … paying attention to your breathing. You may notice that the air coming in through your nostrils is slightly cooler than the air moving out of your nostrils … Allow yourself to just gently follow your breathing, paying attention to the gentle easy air as it passes in and out … You may also notice the rise and fall of your chest. Be aware of the expansion and contraction, be your breathing … If you become distracted by your thoughts, just take a moment to notice where your thoughts took you, notice where your mind went, and then, without judgment, let go and return your attention to your breathing. If you get distracted a hundred times, bring yourself back to your breath a hundred times. Now let's just take the next few minutes to focus completely on breathing. (*Allow several minutes for focused breathing.*)

Now I would like you to gently release your attention from your breathing and bring your attention back to hearing. Take a moment or two to be aware of the sounds that you notice in the room. (*Allow a few moments for listening.*) Now, releasing your attention from sound, gently focus on your body and how it feels to sit in the chair. Notice the placement of your feet … and arms … and head. Picture what the room will look like, me sitting here, the chairs and colors, and when you are ready, rejoin the room by opening your eyes.

MINDFULNESS EXERCISE 2: BODY SCAN
(Approximately 5-10 minutes)

Therapist: I would like everyone to start this exercise by placing your feet squarely on the ground and sitting up in your chair so that your back is straight but not rigid. Make sure that your head feels square to your shoulders and place your arms in a comfortable position to your sides. (*Demonstrate for the client by modeling the posture.*) This posture helps us to stay alert and focused. There is nothing particularly difficult about doing a mindfulness exercise; it just requires your attention. I would like you to begin by closing your eyes or by finding a place on the floor in front of you on which to fix your gaze.

Now I would like you to turn your attention to your toes. Wiggle them for just a moment to help you get your focus there. (*Time the next instructions so that clients have about five to ten seconds to become aware of each of the areas you are focusing on. We have included ellipses to denote pauses.*) Now slowly begin to scan from your toes to the bottom of your feet, feeling the ball … and the arch … and the heel. Now circle your attention around to the top of your feet, taking a moment to notice that you can sense that area of your body … Begin to scan further up to your ankles, taking a moment to notice the sensation that is present in your ankles … Now scan up to your calves, becoming aware of your calves, and then wrap around to the front of your lower legs, taking a moment to notice your shins … Scanning up further, place your attention on your knees, feeling the bend there … and then move up to your thighs, feeling the sensation of your thighs … Now gently circle around to the back of your legs, feeling the area of the hamstrings … and then gently scan up to your hips, feeling the bend there … Then scan up to your lower back, feeling the sensation in that area of your body …

Now scan around to the front of your body, becoming aware of your abdomen … scanning up, notice your stomach … and scanning higher, become aware of your chest … Circle around to the middle of your back … and then scanning upward notice the area of your upper back and shoulder blades … Now scan out across your shoulders … and gently move your attention to your upper arms, noticing the biceps … then, wrapping around, also notice the triceps, or the back of your upper arms … Scan down to your elbows, noticing the bend in your elbows … and then scan to your lower arms, noticing the tops of your lower arms … and then circle around to the bottom … Scan further to your wrists … then to your palms … and knuckles … and scan right out to the tips of your fingers …

Now, releasing your attention from the tips of your fingers, place your attention at the base of your neck … Begin to scan upward, noticing your neck and then the base and back of your head … Scan around to the front of your head, becoming aware of your chin… Begin to scan upward, noticing your lips … nose … cheeks … eyes … forehead … and then scan upward, right to the top of your scalp, becoming aware of the sensation at the very top of your head …

Now, gently releasing your attention from the sensation at the top of your head, I would like you to take a minute to notice your whole body sitting in the chair … Be aware of the sensations of pressure,

Creative Hopelessness   **45**

noticing where your body touches the chair and the floor and where it does not … And releasing your attention from your body, gently place your attention on the image of this room and this group of people … Now, when you're ready, open your eyes.

Upon ending the mindfulness exercise, take a few moments with clients to process the experience by asking if they had any reactions to the exercise. For some, it will be the first time that they have paid attention that closely to their breathing or body in some years, maybe ever, and they may have both positive and negative reactions. Survivors of sexual trauma occasionally note that they did not enjoy the exercise, as it reminds them of the trauma. Many survivors of sexual trauma will actively avoid or neglect their bodies as part of their overall avoidance following the traumatic event. When this is the case, we generally ask clients to just notice their reactions, to pay attention to the thinking that has led them to believe that focusing on the body is not okay. We don't want clients to do anything with these reactions necessarily, rather, they should just note where avoidance has led them—to believing that parts of themselves (in this case their bodies) are not acceptable. We return to this notion later when self-as-context is established.

Other clients will report that they feel relaxed following the exercise. To this, we would respond by stating that relaxation following these exercises is a by-product, not a goal. The goal is not to become relaxed; rather, it is to become aware. Feeling relaxed following the meditation deserves further comment. Some trauma clients believe that doing these kinds of exercises is fully about relaxation. They often fear this outcome, as they can interpret relaxation as a loss of control. Again, we emphasize that relaxation is not the point of these exercises; rather, awareness is the goal. Finally, some trauma survivors will dissociate when they close their eyes, which is why we typically give them the option to do such exercises with their eyes open and focused on the floor or wall.

Prior Session Review

Begin to review homework at the appropriate session. You should begin to give homework assignments at the end of your first creative hopelessness session. Two homework assignments are provided at the end of this chapter that you can use as needed in conjunction with multiple sessions on creative hopelessness. Take a brief period of time during the second session to reflect back on the prior session and to check in with clients about their experience. Spend about five to ten minutes reviewing the homework, if any, from the previous session and exploring responses to working on it.

Jump

Open this next part of the session by asking a number of questions designed to get clients thinking about how difficult their personal struggle has been and how long it has lasted. This is the first leap into creative hopelessness and gets clients thinking about the length of time of their struggle. You also want them to look at the types of emotions and thoughts that accompany their sense of struggle. Ask the following questions:

- Tell me about your PTSD, including how many years you have been struggling with the symptoms.

- How have these symptoms and the struggle interfered with moving forward in your life? What are the barriers to improvement?

- Other than the trauma, what are the biggest problems you struggle with?

- What barriers can you identify to being able to deal with those problems?

- What would you like your life to look like five years from now?

With these questions you can more clearly see how the trauma has affected the individual, and how the barriers associated with the trauma have prevented the life the client wants. Get full descriptions and look for any form of experiential avoidance that may be present in these explanations.

The Usual Suspects

Clients, across trauma types, age, and gender, often have similar answers to the above questions. They can fairly easily describe their symptoms and generally report on how these difficulties have made their lives unlivable. Often the symptoms are the barriers to moving forward. Clients will report that once the trauma memories, their anxiety, or their feelings of wanting to isolate are gone, *then* they will be able to start living. In fact, much of the report about barriers generally has to do with the thought that once they are gone, the client will be able to feel or think better, be able to have more of something like confidence or less of something like anxiety, or be able to have a different history, particularly one without a traumatic experience. Despite the recurrence of these themes, it is always important for the therapist to remain open and compassionate about the difficulty of the struggle, to remember how painful it can be to be working so hard to be other than who you are.

Clients also tend to identify other problems aside from the PTSD that are manifestations of emotional avoidance. For instance, other problems may include drug and alcohol use, dissociation, eating disorders, relationship problems, suicidal behavior, depression, social anxiety, obsessive-compulsive disorder, and weight problems, to name a few.

Finally, when clients talk about what they would like their life to look like in five years, they may report wanting to live in a particular location or wanting to have a better job. But usually the responses have to do with being free from PTSD and its associated struggle, such as living without anxiety or fear or creating intimacy without loss or sadness. In essence, these desires tend to center on a long-imagined ideal—a life free of pain and trauma.

Creating Creative Hopelessness

Once you have a good idea about the client's overall struggle and how it has interfered with the client's life, then you and the client can develop a list of all the ways the client has tried to get rid of difficult emotions, thoughts, or physical sensations. First, ask the client, "Please tell me everything that you have tried to change or fix these things that you have been struggling with." It is possible to keep a mental list; however, we have found it helpful to write these responses down on a notepad or whiteboard so the client can clearly view the different emotions and thoughts being generated. In our group sessions we keep a large whiteboard available and write the answers to this first question on the top quarter of the board, leaving the bottom three-quarters for the second question. Once the list of things clients desire to change has been generated, ask clients to list all of the different strategies they have used to make the things listed on the upper quarter of the whiteboard (their difficult feelings and thoughts) go away. This list can entail everything from small efforts (for instance, "distract myself by watching TV") to very large efforts ("I moved across the country") and can include strategies that are both negative and positive in nature. See the following example of a whiteboard list created after asking the above questions in a group situation.

Things you have struggled with (stuff you have tried to make go away):

PTSD, pain, anxiety, isolation, nervousness, sadness, fear, thinking "I'm not worthy," low self-esteem, powerlessness, anger, disappointment, lack of confidence, feelings of emptiness, loneliness, memories, thinking "I'm damaged goods," feeling unliked, feeling confused, not being forgiven, not enough willpower, feeling crazy, thinking "Why me?"

Positive efforts to make the above go away:	**Negative efforts to make the above go away:**
■ Self-help books	■ Use of alcohol and drugs (misuse of prescribed drugs)
■ Positive self-talk	■ Isolation
■ Self-affirmations	■ Moving from relationship to relationship
■ Therapy (group and individual)	■ Changing jobs frequently
■ Medications (multiple dosages and types)	■ Moving frequently
■ Alcoholics Anonymous (or NA or ALANON)	■ Running from relationships
■ Religion and spirituality	■ Avoiding people, places, and things
■ Planning for the future	■ Sexual encounters or other sex acts
■ Talking with family and friends	■ Driving fast
■ Exercise and diet	■ Being angry
■ Getting out of bad relationships	■ Overeating or not eating enough
■ Getting a better job	■ Throwing up
■ Learning more about PTSD	■ Cutting or other self-injury
■ Understanding my self better	■ Attempting to commit suicide
■ Mindfulness	■ Never going anywhere
■ Acceptance of the trauma	■ Always saying no or always saying yes
■ Alternative health approaches	■ Pushing away people I care about
■ Vitamins	■ Staying quiet, never telling anyone about my insides
■ Acupuncture	■ Workaholism
■ Taking legal action	
■ Inpatient programs	

The example is a tidy copy that summarizes much of what we hear in group; however, our clients are often throwing things out so quickly that the board is usually quite chaotic looking in the end. In fact, we intentionally scribble down the various strategies so that there is essentially a mess on the board—a graphic depiction of the problem with making one's life about being more, better, or different (one of our clients suggested we add "and faster" to this phrase). Of course, there are actually many more positive and negative efforts that can be generated besides those listed here. Additionally, this is a place where therapists can level the playing field by joining the client in developing the list. For instance, we will often give an emotion or thought that we personally struggle with and add it to the board, and then later also provide our own strategies for trying not to feel bad or think negatively. Some therapists might shy away from doing this as they may not want their clients to see them as weak or incompetent. But being open in this way not only points to the humanity of the therapist but also demonstrates to clients a willingness to work and be vulnerable together.

As an example, in one group therapy session, Robyn wrote on the whiteboard that she was struggling with feelings of incompetence and that working harder was her strategy to make the feelings go away. One client was quite curious about this, worried that if Robyn felt this way, Robyn might not be able to help her. Robyn asked the client if she had had the same concern in the past—that others would not be able to help her. The client noted that she felt that way all of the time. Robyn then added "No one can help me" to the client's list of struggles. Robyn then followed this line of inquiry out a little further and asked the client if people in her life had worked hard in efforts to help her and she said yes, that some people had tried very hard. Robyn then asked if "working very hard" had changed her thought that "No one can help me." The answer was no. Robyn also noted to the client that working harder didn't change Robyn's personal thought either, and that in fact it made the thought even stronger. It seemed that Robyn couldn't work hard enough to make the thought go away. Both the client and Robyn wondered out loud how hard a person would have to work to make that thought go away, and they decided mutually that there was no amount of work that could be done to quell the thought. In this way Robyn was able to join with the client and both were able to laugh at the difficulty of the situation. The client was also able to see that Robyn's thoughts of incompetence may not have anything to do with her ability to provide assistance. These kinds of interactions not only demonstrate empathy, but also provide room for the human experience that comes with knowledge—once you know something, it's very difficult to not know it anymore.

Once a fairly exhaustive list is created, we ask clients to review it and give any reactions they might have to the list. It is important to give them adequate time to survey the list. Although there is typically a fair amount of energy in the room, even laughter, during this exercise, having clients sit back and look at the struggle depicted on the board almost always results in a somber, palpable sense of despair. Most often our clients report a sense of frustration and sadness about all of the efforts they have made to solve their problems without any resulting change or movement, or they note that the change was temporary. That is, although they may have found that some of these strategies, usually the positive ones, were helpful in the past, they also find themselves still struggling and still seeking therapy to be fixed. Long-term workability becomes the issue. Sometimes clients confuse these positive strategies with the ability to eliminate negatively evaluated histories or with the ability to prevent negative events from happening in the future. However, life doesn't really seem to work that way. We cannot eliminate our pasts, and simply trying to have a positive response to a painful memory doesn't change the memory. Additionally, life offers up many opportunities to experience pain, whether it comes from loss or unexpected happenings or just everyday stress. We will all experience a variety of emotions, including negative ones. So part of the deal in going through life isn't that you respond positively or well to every event, rather that you acknowledge the event as it is and focus on workability that is in accordance with your values.

Here's an example of how the therapist can point out that nothing seems to work:

Therapist: As we look at this list, it appears that none of these strategies have worked in any long-standing way, and that you have tried a lot of different and good things as well as those that weren't so healthy. I also want to note that this isn't anything that we are deciding about you—this is something that you know by your own experience. Check to see if it isn't so ... None of these have worked. Furthermore, the reason they didn't work wasn't because of lack of effort or trying. Obviously you have tried very hard and for a long time to make your PTSD, your life, different. So let's just take that as a given—you have put in a lot of effort and you have tried hard, ... and yet, the problem still remains. The struggle is still there.

At this point clients will frequently offer more solutions to the problem by stating that they just need to understand PTSD better, or by noting that they know they need to try harder. Again, we place these strategies on the list of things previously attempted (for instance, "understand more" or "try even harder"). In fact, anything the client offers is probably another strategy, whether it's a question they ask in order to get clarification or a comment on how they think they know where you are going with all this. All of the client's attempts to fix the problem similarly turn into more strategies for getting rid of negative internal experience. Verbal understanding is so firmly entrenched in the human experience that it can hardly be anything else at this point in therapy. It's good to be suspicious of anything the client offers. Attempts at understanding or figuring it out are part of the problematic verbal system, and you can be confident it is most likely something that has been tried before:

Client: So what I need to do is understand this whole thing better. Once I figure this out, I'll be able to fix my problems.

Therapist: Check and see whether, in your experience, you have tried understanding already. You have been trying to figure this out for quite some time, in fact. It must be that understanding and figuring it out is not the answer, otherwise you would have this licked by now.

Client: But perhaps I wasn't trying hard enough.

Therapist: Look there too. Isn't it the case that you *have* tried hard? All we have to do is look at this long list to know how very hard you've tried. So trying harder can't be the solution either, or that would have worked by now too.

Client: Well, what will work then?

Therapist: I could give you a quick answer to this question, but it feels to me like that might be ripping you off in some way. Almost anything I could say is something that you have probably tried before, and it would feel like one more therapist telling you the same old thing, and to just try to do it harder. Maybe even asking more questions is part of trying to figure it out. So even that—asking questions—can go on the list of things you have tried to make this different.

Client: I'm confused.

Therapist: *(gently)* Good. That's a good place to be.

At this point in therapy the only goal is to identify the client's struggles and all efforts to eliminate the stuff struggled with (thoughts and feelings).

When Solutions Aren't Solutions

Another area that can be tricky has to do with when the client offers mindfulness and acceptance strategies as the solution to the problem. This can feel like the right answer to both the client and you. However, if you follow it out just a little bit, many times you will find that these are offered as strategies ultimately designed to be rid of negatively evaluated thoughts and feelings. Here's an example:

Client: Well, I think I finally understand where you 're going with this. I just need to be more mindful and accept my feelings.

Therapist: *(curiously)* So that you can what?

Client: So that I can stop fighting everything.

Therapist: Why do you want to do that?

Client: So that I can feel better.

Therapist: But here is the trap. You noted that you've tried this before; you put it on the list … And we have already established that trying harder isn't it. So it seems that if you just accept this, it will go away. How many times have you tried to just accept it?

Client: Many times.

Therapist: So that can't be it. If acceptance, as you know it, had worked, you wouldn't be sitting here right now.

Client: I guess so. Then what's left? There is nothing left. Why should I even be here?

Therapist: That is a good question. But let's just start with this—you have tried a lot of different things and found that none of them has solved your problem—the problem of making all this PTSD stuff and the related fallout go away. Don't simply believe what I am saying right now, check your own experience and see if this isn't so.

Client: That's right, it hasn't gone away.

Therapist: So you are stuck.

Client: I'm stuck.

Therapist: Let's start there then, right where you're at … stuck.

Clients will respond to this kind of approach in a variety of ways. It is extremely important at this point for you to remain compassionate but grounded in the work of creative hopelessness. We have had clients ask, "What are you trying to do to us?" or "Are you toying with me?" in this section of the therapy. They are generally referring to our efforts and persistence at undermining the change strategy, and these comments often stem from not having questions answered in a way that makes them feel better. In fact, if you respond to these kinds of questions with long explanations of the therapy or with answers that are about relieving anxiety or confusion, then in some way you are playing into the very problem that the client has been failing to resolve all along. You can respond to these kinds of questions by stating something along the lines of this example, which includes a helpful metaphor:

Therapist: I'm not trying to do anything to you or to toy with you. I am trying to create a place where something different can happen for you. I don't want to become a part of this same system that brought you here in the first place … and I definitely don't want to be just another example in that list of strategies that haven't worked for you. (*pause*) It's like we're standing in a forest and all of the trees are burned and dead. What I want to do is help you grow a new lush and green forest, but we can't do that until we clear out all of the old burned and dead trees. Once we get them cleared, then we make space for something new to grow. This first part of this therapy is like that—we are clearing the forest so that something new can grow.

Clients may also say something like "You don't understand how hard this is! Why don't you just give me the answer?" It is effective to follow this question with "So you can get rid of what?" The response will inevitably be about getting rid of the feeling that accompanies "not knowing." You can, however, agree with the client on how very hard it is.

Hopelessness About the Right Thing

As mentioned, when clients look at all of their efforts to make their struggle go away, they frequently feel a sense of hopelessness and will report that they are discouraged, disappointed, and in some cases angry. You can help clarify this issue by noting to the client that *the situation* is hopeless. We regularly say to clients, "We are not saying that *you* are hopeless, we are saying that the *situation* is hopeless. The misapplied change agenda is a hopeless agenda." It is important to remember that the fruitlessness of the change agenda is not something you have to try to prove to clients; all they need to do is check their personal experiences to see if efforts to make negative content go away have worked. Rather than solve the negative content, we support the feeling of discomfort and "not knowing" as a positive thing, as an opportunity for something new. If clients are feeling confused or unsure, then they are more likely to be open to new possibilities. Here, the focus is on inviting discomfort, for it too will be something to be felt and accepted rather than avoided.

Recognizing the Cost of Negative Change Efforts

When focusing on the efforts to make internal experience go away, it is particularly important to point out the costs of engaging in these strategies. You can ask the client what costs have arisen out of doing all of the different things they have tried in order to not feel or think what they feel and think. Clients usually report costs ranging from loss of important and valued relationships, to loss of jobs and money, to loss of a sense of self and quality of life. These costs are often extensive and related to what clients currently are "missing" as compared to their idealized self in the magic-wand scenario. Also, these costs have often compounded the struggle—the pain of the trauma is followed by efforts to not have the trauma, which are followed by costs due to the effort and followed by more pain. Sometimes we see clients for whom the costs of the struggle outweigh the costs of the actual trauma. The fallout can be very painful and ultimately add to the desire to be free from the trauma so that the ensuing problems will somehow be undone.

Staying with Feeling Stuck

As the session begins to wind down, a final metaphor is offered to describe and capture the main ideas introduced in this section of the protocol. This metaphor points to the useless strategies designed to promote experiential avoidance. The person-in-a-hole metaphor (Hayes et al., 1999) may be presented as follows:

Therapist: It's as if you have been living your life in a large field. But before you were placed there, you were blindfolded and given a bag of tools. Once in the field, you were told to go live your life and you did. Unknown to you, spaced throughout this field are some fairly large holes, and soon enough, as you're walking along, you fall into one—a trauma happens. In this dilemma, you do the sensible thing and open your bag of tools to see which tool you might be able to use to get yourself out of the hole. When you open the bag, however, you find only one tool—a shovel. So you start to do what one should do with a shovel … you dig. What you find, though, is that the hole isn't getting smaller and that you are not getting out. So you dig harder, and still you're in the hole. You dig faster, and still you're in the hole. You try all styles of digging—short quick scoops, deep earthen-filled scoops. You try digging sideways, and you try digging slowly and methodically.

You may pause from time to time to try to retrace your steps and figure out how you got in the hole, but it only leads you back to the idea that you must use what you have been given to get out, and you once again begin to dig. As time passes, what you learn is that the hole isn't getting smaller and that you're not getting out. In fact, you find that the more you dig, the bigger the hole gets. You know that this must be the way out; this is what you were told to do. So you dig even more dutifully, and you persist. Yet, you find yourself in an even larger hole. You are so used to digging by now that sometimes you don't even recognize that you're digging—it just happens naturally … What I would like you to do is to take just a moment and notice that you're holding a shovel and that you are trying to dig your way out of a hole … The problem is that digging doesn't get people out of holes—it only makes holes bigger. So let's take a moment to stop digging and just see that you are in hole. You're stuck.

Clients identify with this metaphor to a large degree. They do feel stuck, and it does seem that they are in a large hole. It is not uncommon for them to add to the metaphor, saying something like "And you should see the hole I've dug! I've got a suite in there." As you end the session, you can ask the client to do nothing but notice that they are stuck. You don't want them to solve anything at this time. You give the client the homework to be done before the next session, at which point you will pick up at the place of being stuck.

Giving Hope to Hopelessness

A few cautions should be addressed. One is that regardless of how carefully the therapist avoids sending the message that clients themselves are hopeless, some will nonetheless hear that as the overriding message. It is important to repeat, more than once, that although the situation is hopeless, *they* are not, and that "there is a direction we are going with this therapy." Clients will also hear that it is their fault that they are not getting out of the hole, because they are the ones doing the digging. It is central to remind clients that they were blindfolded when they fell in the hole. They didn't see it. They are not responsible for being in the hole. They are not to blame for what has happened. It is especially important for trauma survivors to hear this piece. They are often stuck in blaming themselves or are angry about feeling blamed. Reminding the client about the blindfold can serve to loosen this thought and its grip on the client. At this point you can tell the client, "You are not responsible for falling in the hole—you were blindfolded, remember? The trauma was not your fault. However, you *are* responsible for getting out of the hole. You are response-able; you are able to respond … to do something different … But let's just start with the awareness of being in the hole."

Sticking Points for Clients

Clients may struggle with creative hopelessness in different ways. We have noted a variety of responses to this session. First, many of the clients feel validated in an unusual way. Often they have felt bad about themselves for not being able to make these strategies work, for not feeling in control of their emotions and their lives. Pointing to this dilemma validates the client's experience of something about this system not working. Clients hear over and over how they need to try harder or how something is wrong with them since they're not getting over the trauma. A sense of relief often comes with this recognition that although clients have tried hard, it still hasn't worked, and there's a reason that it hasn't worked, one that isn't about them.

Second, although some clients will feel validated, they will also feel confused and unsure of things. You should view these sorts of responses as more opportunities to work on acceptance, and encourage clients to notice their feelings without any effort to make them come or go. Let clients know that you are working on something with them and that part of it might involve feeling confused. It is not necessarily a "bad" place to be; rather, it is a place where opportunity is possible—a place where not knowing the answer may lead to something different and new.

Finally, some clients argue that control *does* work and subsequently view the points raised in the session as pointless. It is helpful, however, to get clear with clients about what they mean by control "working." There are some clients who react strongly to this session and who may try to argue with you about the benefits of controlling private experience—how, in fact, they have experienced benefits and want to further understand how they can control even better. This situation requires a judgment call by the therapist. It is important to tease out whether this argument is about emotional avoidance or if such clients are truly coming from a place where the workability of control has led them to the kind of life they would like to lead. (We very rarely have clients who fit this criterion, but occasionally one will come along.) This may require some questioning of how control has worked, but from a curious rather than an argumentative stance. If you find yourself arguing or trying to convince the client, then that is a signal that you are caught in content and not flushing out the workability.

Here is an example of a conversation with a young client in group therapy who had found that, in her experience, control had worked. She had come to therapy to learn how to control her internal experience better. The other women in the group had found that, in their experience, none of the strategies had worked in any long-term and fulfilling way. It had been agreed that if any of these control strategies had worked, the clients would not be in therapy at this time—they would be using the strategies that worked to live well. The younger client, however, did not agree with the group and had positioned herself to argue the veracity of her point.

Client: Some of these strategies work very well for me. I don't know what you're talking about when you say they haven't worked.

Therapist: Well, let's look to see what's true for you—not true because I say so, but true because your experience says so. Have these strategies worked in any long-standing way? Be sure to check your own experiences.

Client: Yes, they have worked very well, and my experience tells me that they have worked, and I don't understand why you're doing this. (*Here the client was getting more argumentative and upset and seemed to be baiting us to argue with her.*)

Therapist: Let's look again, as I want to be sure before we move on … In your experience, these strategies have worked?

Client: (*proudly*) Yes.

Therapist: (*gently*) Then what brings you to therapy? Why not use those strategies that have worked and be done with therapy?

Client: (*pausing*) I just need to learn how to use them better. They have helped me.

Therapist: (*gently*) I believe that they have been helpful in certain situations and for short periods of time, and they may have even pulled you through some difficult times, … but I'm suspicious. Why not just do more of what has worked, apply the control strategy, and be done with the bad feelings and thoughts, be done with therapy?

Client: Because I need to learn how to control better, and that's what I came here to do. If you ask whether in my experience I have found that control works and I say yes, then I don't understand why you would tell me that it doesn't work. I don't like this, and it's not what I came here for.

At this point, other group members had begun to make small comments such as "Can't you see that you wouldn't be here if it worked?" or "Trust us; you just need a few more years of getting burned by this stuff, and you will see that it doesn't work." Also, it seemed that in this case we needed to join with the client rather than continue to point at the system that had somehow led her back into therapy, and we therefore changed direction.

Therapist: Well, so here is this kind of difficult spot we find ourselves in, and what I want to do is focus on workability—finding what works for you so that you can lead the life you have wanted to lead. The other women in the group have found that these strategies don't work for them, so I want to spend just a little time following this line of thinking out so that we can press forward. Would it be okay, as you sit in on this group, to look for those things that you find helpful, that you think you can use? Are you willing to stay and do that?

Client: *(pausing)* I guess I can do that.

The client continued in the therapy and, as time passed, found the therapy to be useful to her. It worked to gently point at the system but not to make the client feel she was wrong. This can be a helpful strategy when bumping into these kinds of difficulties with creative hopelessness. In our experience, these kinds of situations do not occur very often, but it is helpful to be prepared for them when they do.

Sticking Points for Therapists

A key to conducting ACT well is to remain aware of the various ways you can make a clinical error. The following are some of the more common challenges therapists encounter when working with their clients on creative hopelessness and other components of ACT.

Getting Caught in Content

One of the places that therapists get stuck when implementing this therapy, especially when they are first learning how to do it, is when they get *caught in the content* of what the client is saying. This happens when the therapist loses contact with thinking as an ongoing process (in other words, gets caught up in the content of what clients are saying rather than the function it is serving in the moment). In this case, the therapist gets caught up in believing what clients have to say about the struggle or other aspects of their experience. It is good to issue a word of caution here, which is not to say that you shouldn't be empathetic to the client's situation. Rather, the focus is on how the efforts to get rid of internal private experience don't work. Keep the spotlight on the client's personal experience of how workable their efforts have been.

The "story," although important, may be part of what is keeping the client stuck. For instance, Darrah was once working with a PTSD client who reported every week that the government screwed him, and that Vietnam ruined his life. The facts of the case—being screwed by the government and the difficulties stemming from his experience in Vietnam—were not up for debate. Darrah said to the client, "I believe that awful things happened to you in Vietnam and that the government didn't do the things you needed when you returned." Rather, the more important piece was to examine how telling the story repeatedly was serving him now. Was there something to be gained in telling the story over and over again—thirty-five years after the war? By this time, the story of the government and Vietnam was functioning to keep him stuck rather than to help him move on.

There are a couple of ways that you can respond to these events when they show up. First, as with the example just given, you may want to ask questions like "Let's assume you are 100 percent correct—now what would you like to do?" or "If you tell the story again, what do you think will be different?" or "How is this story serving you?" Finding the function of the story will be far more useful than buying into the story as something that is true in the moment. Second, you can point to the process when you find yourself getting caught up in the content with the client. Here you can simply note that you are getting caught up in the story. You can ask how easily this happens and how often. After pointing to the process, you can then move back to creative hopelessness and what hasn't worked.

Trying to Convince the Client

This stumbling block occurs when the therapist is trying to convince clients that their efforts haven't worked. If you find yourself arguing with a client or explaining too much and intellectualizing about creative hopelessness, then you have probably moved into a place where you are trying to convince the client that what you have to say is true. This would be like getting caught in your own content. The best thing to do under these circumstances is, first, stop arguing, explaining, or intellectualizing, and second, check with the clients' experience. They will know best about how these solutions have worked. If they are sitting in front of you, it's probably the case that their efforts haven't worked, but they need to arrive at that realization themselves.

Lastly, convincing may be occurring if the therapist is failing to move to the next component of the protocol when doing so would be a good judgment call. It is important for therapists to remember that beginning with control as the problem, rather than creative hopelessness, may be the place to start for a few clients. Making this distinction is a clinical judgment call and is usually indicated when the client determinedly resists creative hopelessness (as in the example given earlier) or when the client hasn't been burnt enough by the failure of the "more, better, different" strategies.

Not Letting Clients Feel What They Feel

In this situation the therapist feels the need to change the way the client is feeling. Many therapists have been trained to think that if the client leaves the session not feeling better, they have failed in some way. From the ACT perspective, working to make the client feel better is part of the same problem—nonacceptance of self and private experience. This is a good place for you to check your own emotional state and see if you're having anxiety about clients feeling confused or sad during the session or when they leave. It may be that you are not making space for your own feelings. Therapists have said to us, "I don't like it when the client is sad or upset when they leave the session. I feel bad and am worried they won't come back to therapy." This is a time for self-acceptance, a time to stay with your own anxiety while also letting clients stay with theirs. Make room in the session for whatever shows up in the realm of private content. This is radical acceptance, not just acceptance of things we like.

Homework

Homework assignments should be copied and handed out to the client at the end of each session. Hand out one homework assignment per session. Two are provided here in case creative hopelessness is covered in two sessions rather than one (creative hopelessness rarely goes beyond two sessions). If you complete creative hopelessness in one session and you feel the client can complete both homework assignments, feel free to assign both. Be familiar with the assignments so that you can answer any questions that the client might have. Ask the client to bring the completed homework to the next session for review.

HOMEWORK ASSIGNMENT 1: CREATIVE HOPELESSNESS

Instructions: Between now and the next session, I would like you to spend time noticing that you are stuck. Think back to our session and the space that we got to just before you left the session. Notice how long the struggle has been there for you and reflect on the feeling of being in this struggle. Write a paragraph on your experience of being stuck in the struggle.

Reflect on the costs that you have experienced as a result of being stuck in the struggle. Describe some of those costs and how you have felt as a result. Throughout the week, take time to monitor your negative experiences such as bad moods or negative thoughts, especially as they relate to your PTSD or trauma. When these experiences are present, notice what it is that you try to do to deal with these experiences.

Take notes regarding these efforts. However, don't try to change anything at this time. If nothing happens on a particular day of the week, leave the boxes blank.

Day of the week	Situation	Experience (negative thoughts or emotions)	What you did to try to deal with the experience and what was the cost, if any?
Example	*I got in an argument with my partner.*	*I felt angry and thought that I was wrong/bad for yelling and fighting.*	*I drank alcohol in order to decrease my anger and mellow out.*
Sunday			
Monday			
Tuesday			
Wednesday			
Thursday			

Friday			
Saturday			

Please write out some of the costs that you experienced as a result of trying to "fix" negative emotions.

HOMEWORK ASSIGNMENT 2: PRACTICE MINDFULNESS MEDITATION

Instructions: Take time during the week to practice mindfulness. Do this exercise three times on three different days between now and our next session. Find a quiet place to sit and make sure that you will not be distracted (turn off the TV and the radio, unplug the phone, etc.). Sit and place your feet squarely on the ground and sit up in your chair so that your back is straight but not rigid. Make sure that your head feels square to your shoulders and place your arms in a comfortable position at your sides with your hands in your lap. This posture will help you to stay alert and focused. There is nothing particularly difficult about doing a mindfulness exercise—it just requires your attention.

Begin by first noticing or paying attention to the fact that your body is actively sensing the environment. Notice that you can feel yourself sitting in the chair and you can feel your feet on the ground. Also notice that you can feel the clothes on your skin and perhaps your jewelry. Notice, too, that you might feel the bend of your knees or elbows. Then, gently close your eyes or locate a place in front of you where you can fix your gaze. Notice as you close your eyes that your ears open. Take a few moments to pay attention to all of the sounds that you hear. Take a short bit of time and listen to the different sounds that are present in the room.

Then gently release your attention from sound, place your attention at the tip of your nose, and begin to notice the sensation of air moving in and out of your nostrils, paying attention to your breathing. You may notice that the air coming in through your nostrils is slightly cooler than the air moving out of your nostrils. Allow yourself to just gently follow your breathing, paying attention to the gentle, easy air as it passes in and out. You may also notice the rise and fall of your chest. Be aware of the expansion and contraction—*be* your breathing. If you become distracted by your thoughts, just take a moment to notice where they took you, notice where your mind went, and then, without judgment, let go and return your attention to your breathing. If you get distracted a hundred times, bring yourself back to your breath a hundred times. Take five minutes to focus completely on breathing.

Then gently release your attention from your breathing and bring your attention back to hearing. Take a moment or two to be aware of the sounds that you notice in the room. Then, releasing your attention from sound, gently focus on your body and how it feels to sit in the chair. Notice the placement of your feet, arms, and head. Picture what the room will look like when you're done. Then, when you are ready, rejoin the room by opening your eyes.

Moving Forward

Creative hopelessness helps clients to see all that they have tried in order to make their histories, memories, painful emotions, and thoughts something more, better, or different—something other than what they are. This struggle can be distilled down to one word: control. Get in control of your thoughts, memories, and emotions and you will be better. Problem is, it doesn't work. Misapplied or rigidly applied control turns out to be the problem rather than the solution.

CHAPTER 5

Control as the Problem: Experiential Avoidance and Unworkable Solutions

Sometimes surrender means giving up trying to understand and becoming comfortable with not knowing.

—Eckhart Tolle

In the second stage of ACT the therapist is working to help the client discover how misapplied control may actually be part of the problem. If you review synonyms of "control," you will find such words and phrases as "be in charge of," "have power over," "direct," "be in command of," or to "rule" or "restrain." If you listen to the request of the trauma survivor in therapy, it is often a request to do the same with mind and emotion. It is not unusual to hear clients say things like "I would like to have power over my feelings" or "I want to be in command of my thoughts." The solution is perceived as being to rule or restrain unwanted private content, to rid oneself of negative emotion, thoughts about the trauma, thoughts related to the trauma, or memories of the trauma. Much effort can be spent trying to solve the problem by controlling negatively evaluated internal experience. From the ACT perspective, however, this very attempt to rule and restrain can actually increase or prolong the problem. If it's very important for a person not to think or feel a particular way, paradoxically, it will most likely be the case that the person will think and feel that very way.

Session Format (1-2 Sessions)

- Open with mindfulness

- Review prior session

- Explore the paradox of trying not to think about something

- Explore the nature of paradox

- Understand the costs of misapplied control

- Examine how we learned to control

- Explore sticking points for clients

- Explore sticking points for therapists

- Assign homework: control as the problem

- Moving forward

Opening with Mindfulness

Open the session by completing a mindfulness exercise. This provides the client with an opportunity to practice observing experience rather than trying to control it. When considering how to deliver the mindfulness exercise, prepare to use a soft voice and time the exercise so that it allows the client time to experience its intended purpose. Below we continue with examples of mindfulness exercises that may be used.

> ## MINDFULNESS EXERCISE 1:
> ## EXPANDED ATTENDING TO BREATHING
> ## WITH LIGHT IMAGERY
> ### (Approximately 5-10 minutes)

Therapist: I would like you to start this exercise by placing your feet squarely on the ground and sitting up in your chair so that your back is straight but not rigid. Make sure that your head feels square to your shoulders and place your arms in a comfortable position at your sides. This posture helps us to stay alert and focused. So let's begin by first noticing or paying attention to the fact that your body is actively sensing the environment. Notice that you can feel yourself sitting in the chair, and you can feel your feet on the ground. Now, gently close your eyes or find a place on the floor to fix your gaze should you choose to keep your eyes open ...

I would like you to place your attention at the tip of your nose and begin to notice the sensation of air moving in and out of your nostrils ... Pay attention to your breathing. You may notice that the air coming in through your nostrils is slightly cooler than the air moving out of your nostrils ... Allow yourself to just gently follow your breathing, paying attention to the gentle, easy air as it passes in and out ... You may also notice the rise and fall of your chest. Be aware of the expansion and contraction—be completely aware of your breathing ... If you become distracted by your thoughts, just take a moment to notice where your thoughts took you, notice where your mind went, and then, without judgment, let go and return your attention to your breathing. If you get distracted a hundred times, bring yourself back to your breath a hundred times. Now let's just take the next few minutes to focus completely on breathing. (*Allow several minutes for focused breathing.*)

Turn your full attention to the rise and fall of your chest. Notice how your chest rises and falls, expands and contracts ... Notice that you are bringing life-giving energy, oxygen, to your lungs, which then transfers to your body ... Imagine that you are breathing in this energy in the form of light ... Choose a soft color like light blue or soft pink, and imagine that with each breath you are bringing in this colored oxygen to fill your lungs ... Picture your lungs expanding and contracting and being filled with this soft light, and just as oxygen spreads, imagine this light spreading to your heart ... bringing energy to your heart ... And now imagine the light growing and spreading further throughout your body, just like oxygen would ... Picture the light traveling to your abdomen ... and growing ... so that it spreads to your legs and arms ... Imagine this light filling your body and flowing up into your head ... Picture the light spreading out to your fingertips and to the tips of your toes ... And now imagine that the light can pass outside of your skin. Imagine it spreading until it completely circles you ... as if you were enclosed in a ball of light energy ... Allow yourself to just rest in this energy ... breathing in and out ... feeding your body with the breath. (*Take a few minutes to allow the client to be present to this image*).

Now, releasing your attention from the light image, gently focus on just the rise and fall of your breathing ... and then on your body and how it feels to sit in the chair. Notice the placement of your feet, your arms, and your head. Picture what the room will look like when you open your eyes and, when you are ready, rejoin the room by opening your eyes.

Therapist: I would like everyone to start this exercise by placing your feet squarely on the ground and sitting up in your chair so that your back is straight but not rigid. This posture helps us to stay alert and focused. I would like you to begin by closing your eyes or by finding a place on the floor or in front of you to fix your gaze. Now I would like you to turn your attention to your hearing. Notice what you hear as you sit in this room. Perhaps you hear the sound of the heater ... or the sound of your breath. Perhaps you hear sound coming from outside and the sound of my voice. (*List several sounds that are present in the room.*) Turn all of your attention to hearing ... If you find that your mind gets caught on a thought and pulled away from hearing, just gently notice where your mind went and then gently bring your mind back to sound ... focusing on just listening ... become fully aware of hearing ... Focus on each sound at it moves into your awareness, letting it pass, and then focus on the next sound that moves into your awareness ... Be present to hearing. (*Allow several minutes for focused hearing.*) Now, releasing your attention from your hearing, I would like you to gently place your attention on the image of this room and this group of people ... and when you're ready, open your eyes.

Upon ending the mindfulness exercise, take a few moments with clients to process by asking if they had any reactions to the experience. Clients should be starting to increase their ability to participate in such exercises. Some clients may still feel very uncomfortable and may continue to express that they cannot participate in such exercises. Spend time processing both positive and negative reactions to these exercises. Remind clients that the goal is to work on accepting experience even if they continue to report negative reactions. These exercises are not about being comfortable and relaxed—they are about observing and contacting experience. A client may also report feeling relaxed following an exercise. In response, just briefly state that although relaxation can happen as a by-product, it is not a goal. If clients continue to practice mindfulness, of course, it will come more naturally to them.

Prior Session Review

Take a brief period of time during this session to reflect back on the prior session and to check in with clients about their experience. Spend about five to ten minutes reviewing the homework and exploring responses to it. Themes of the homework:

- Write about your personal reflections on being in the struggle.

- Write about the costs of being in the struggle.

- Record and monitor any negative experiences and report about your reactions to them.

Don't Think About Vanilla Ice Cream

Open this part of the session by helping the client to come into contact with how their solution—experiential control—may actually be part of the problem, if not *the* problem. The goal of the session is to experience the scope of the problem but not to necessarily do anything about it. You may suggest here that not only has control not worked, as demonstrated by the extensive list generated in the creative hopelessness stage, but that it actually can't work, especially as it relates to getting rid of traumatic experience. Here, you can focus more directly on issues of rigid control and how much of a role it plays in the client's life. You may hear things like "It is very important for me to control everything; it's how I keep from being retraumatized." There is an important point to highlight with clients at this time, and it needs to be done with some finesse, as it can be misinterpreted as blame (which is addressed later in this chapter). The point is that in the very effort to prevent themselves from being retraumatized, much of their lives have become about the trauma—avoiding people, places, or reminders, working not to remember the trauma, building a life that would prevent reminders of the trauma from being present, and so on. Here we might say to the client, "In all of this, it seems that the trauma has remained ever present, and by virtue of the fact that you are here to see me, it has not only been present but it has become bothersome. So help me to understand this plan to control and how it has worked for you. Here is this strange deal—you are trying to control your trauma as a means to keep from being retraumatized, and your life has become about your trauma. You are your trauma. (*Said kindly and compassionately.*) Can you see the problem?"

We often ask if the client has ever had the experience of trying very hard to not have a certain outcome (Hayes et al., 1999), for instance, trying very hard to not feel embarrassed or be rejected, and then finding that they felt embarrassed and rejected. The more important it is to not experience a certain thing, the more likely it will be that you will experience it. So, in fact, the human story is more along the lines of "If you aren't willing to have a particular experience, you've got it" (Hayes et al., 1999). It can be helpful to return to the person-in-the-hole metaphor from the last session to help demonstrate this problem:

Therapist: It has the quality of being in the hole and digging faster to get out, only the hole gets bigger.

Client: I have had the experience where I got exactly what I didn't want.

Therapist: Exactly! We can find out about this in even very small ways ... I would like you to *not* think about the next thing I am going to say. I will even let you prepare. You can do anything but close your ears. Are you ready? Try not to think about this next thing. Are you ready? Don't think about vanilla ice cream, vanilla ice cream with warm chocolate fudge on top, and with bananas around the edges and a little cherry right on the top. (*Often at this point you get laughter and clients saying things like "You forgot the nuts!"*)

Client: It's impossible not to think about it.

Therapist: Right, you can see the problem ... Dig, dig, dig. Now try not to think about the problems stemming from your trauma or the trauma itself. (*pause*) See the problem?

Occasionally, we will get clients who report that they were able to not think about vanilla ice cream. They will suggest that they were able to block it out of their mind:

Therapist: (*with curiosity*) Block what out of your mind? What is the "it" you're talking about?

Client: The thing you told us not to think about.

Therapist: What was that?

Client: Well, I just blocked it out by thinking about something else, by thinking about cookies.

Therapist: Something other than what? How did you know to think about cookies?

Client: Because it wasn't vanilla ice cream.

Therapist: (*playfully*) Aha! You did have vanilla ice cream. Even if you did shift to cookies, you had to contact vanilla ice cream in order to know to shift to cookies. See how this works? You have to have it in order to know you don't want it. Once you contact it, whatever the "it" is, and if it is especially important not to have, then you could spend a lot of time on making sure that you don't have it by contacting it over and over again.

It can be useful here to give a couple of examples. We point to things like dieters being unable to stop thinking about food or worriers being unable to stop worrying. There is also an example in the racing car industry: Drivers had difficulty not hitting the walls on a track when they were going around turns. The teams of advisors instructed them, "When you're driving fast around the corner, whatever you do, don't hit the wall." Paradoxically, the drivers kept hitting the walls despite their very best efforts to follow the instructions. Frustrated, the advisors finally told them to look away from the wall and toward the direction they wanted to go when going around the turns. You know what happened next: The drivers stopped hitting the walls.

If you are familiar with the suppression literature and the effects of suppression, you can also spend time talking about these during the session. Essentially, research has shown that if you suppress a thought or emotion, there is a rebound of that same thought or emotion following the suppression period (Wegner, 1994; Wegner, Erber & Zanakos, 1993).

Paradox in Action

At this point it is very helpful to explore the polygraph metaphor (Hayes et al., 1999):

Therapist: Imagine that I could hook you up to the perfect anxiety detection machine. (*Other emotions could be substituted here; for example, fear is often a powerful one for trauma survivors, but embarrassment, anger, and others can all work for the purposes of this exercise.*) Imagine that you have wires and leads connected to various places on your body, and they feed into a computer that I have sitting in front of me. Note that this is a very sensitive machine; it can detect even the smallest amounts of anxiety. Now, imagine that I give you a job while you're hooked up to this machine, just one job. Your only job is to not get anxious. (*Here you will often have trauma survivors report that they would have failed the job already—as therapists we usually nod our heads and agree with the difficulty of asking such a thing.*) But ... I want to motivate you to not get anxious because it is very important that you avoid anxiety right now. So, in order to motivate you, I am going to hold a large stick, and if I see you get anxious, I'm going to give you a whack! (*Clients will often display a bit of surprise at this last statement but will immediately see that this would cause them to become even more anxious.*) What will happen? (*Clients will report that they will get whacked.*) Right, it will be almost instantaneous! I say, "Don't get anxious or I will whack you," and the next thing you know, you're getting whacked. (*If the therapist has been playful up to this point, which is often the case, the following statements*

made by the therapist need to convey a serious and important message.)
Well, think about it: You *are* hooked up to the perfect anxiety detection machine. It's your own central nervous system, and you have become so good at being aware of your anxiety that you are quickly attuned to it. And there's something else that's really important here. Something that *is* motivating you and that is tied to your own self-worth, who you are as a human being. It looks like this: "If I get anxious, who I am as a human being is not okay." Now don't just believe me, check your own experience and look to see if this isn't the case—if you don't want it, you have it, and if you have it, it means something bad about who you are as a human being. Look to see.

In our experience, clients connect to this statement very readily and the whack with the stick suddenly makes sense: If I have negative feelings, I am worthless, I am broken. At this time it is good to repeat, "If you aren't willing to have it, you've got it."

It can also be useful to spend a little time talking about how things can show up in odd or unintended ways. Robyn will occasionally share a personal story as an example of this to help clients find similar experiences in their own histories. She relates a story about a time that she was on a panel with a famous psychologist where each was delivering a presentation. It was standing room only, with over three hundred people in the room. For some reason, Robyn began to fear that the famous psychologist might see her flush or turn red while delivering her own presentation, and the idea of this became unacceptable. Robyn believed that it would be embarrassing and horrible if this famous psychologist saw her turn red. So, she started the process of working very hard to not turn red. She kept repeating in her mind, "Don't turn red. Don't turn red." Her entire focus became about not being red. After completing her talk, she returned to her table and noticed that she was somewhat relieved as she did not feel the red hotness in her face, arms, and neck that she sometimes felt. She began to hope that she may have actually found a way to control this "horrible" problem. She opened her compact to take a look, and to her surprise, it had worked. Control *had* been the answer—she hadn't turned red. But then she pulled the mirror out just a little further and discovered to her alarm that she was soaking wet. She had sweated her way out of turning red, and she looked like she had just stepped out of the shower. As she practically sloshed her way out of the room, she noted that she had exactly what she had tried so hard to control—embarrassment.

We often ask clients to give examples of their own experiences where these kinds of things have happened. There are many rich and delightful stories told by clients but also some very painful stories about this paradox. One client reported that he was invited to a wedding that was to last three days. He was worried about feeling out of place with the people he didn't know, and he noted that his every effort was geared toward controlling his feelings of discomfort so that he could fit in. The harder he tried to control his discomfort, the more out of place he felt. His discomfort grew to such a great proportion that he started hanging out in his room so that he could work on getting his discomfort under control. As time passed and he couldn't make it work, he also grew angry and started to be upset with his wife and friends. It was soon brought to his attention that he was withdrawing and that he was making it difficult for people close to him to enjoy themselves. He left the weekend feeling more out of place than ever and reported that he also had a good dose of guilt and shame to go along with that feeling.

As another example, we once had a client report that she really wanted to seem intelligent to a new group of friends; she wanted to control feeling embarrassed by not saying "stupid" things or looking stupid. The more intelligent she tried to look, the less able she was to form coherent sentences, and she found that at times she couldn't even pronounce words correctly. She didn't want to feel stupid, and that's exactly what she got. Thank goodness she also reported that she could laugh about the strange way the whole thing turned out. As a therapist in this session, feel free to come up with your own examples, use the examples from this book, or have the client generate several examples. It is important to keep in mind that the message for clients is not to attempt to stop controlling or to control their controlling, but to simply observe how efforts to control can be paradoxical in nature. The only goal is to see this paradox— nothing needs correcting.

The Cost of Control

There are a number of metaphors that speak to the issue of control as the problem. These can be used to further demonstrate the point that if you don't want it, you've got it. Clients tend to connect to these metaphors in positive ways and often report that it helps them understand the ideas being conveyed. There are three metaphors that you may find useful at this point in the therapy: the quicksand metaphor (Hayes et al., 1999), the Chinese finger trap metaphor (Hayes et al., 1999), and the fighting-the-wave metaphor (Hayes et al., 1999).

The Quicksand Metaphor

Therapist: This situation is kind of like what happens when you fall into quicksand. Immediately, your mind tells you to get out. It may even tell you to panic because this is a life-threatening situation. So it kicks into gear and tells you to swim and push against the sand so that you won't drown. However, as we all know, the sooner you begin to fight against quicksand, the sooner it begins to suck you down. The more you struggle, the more you sink. And the faster you struggle, the faster you sink. Your mind says, "swim, swim, swim," and down you go, trying to get out of the situation. That is what this is like—the harder and the faster you swim, the quicker you sink. (*Pause and let this notion take hold.*) Now, does anyone know how to survive in quicksand? (*Allow clients to offer suggestions.*) That's right, you don't fight it. In fact, the way to survive in quicksand is to lay out in it, to let as much of your body contact the sand as possible. The more surface area that contacts the sand, the more likely it is that you will make it … Now what if this whole thing, getting through life with less suffering, is like that? The more you spread out and let it contact you, the more likely it is that you'll make it.

Here, clients will often say that this seems too hard, that letting go of swimming when it feels like you're going to drown is just too scary. You can continue to use the metaphor to work with the client on giving up control:

Therapist: So when your mind is telling you to swim, which it has, and you can feel yourself sinking, which you have done—right up to the edge of your nostrils—and one more stroke might put your nose below the sand, then what should you do? Let me remind you that you are drowning, metaphorically speaking, and in this one situation, swimming and struggling is the thing that makes drowning more possible. So should you take that stroke or try something new? What if the simple act of just stopping movement would make the difference?

Client: That is very scary, because it feels like you will drown.

Therapist: Yes, I know. But remember, you're already drowning. Could you feel scared and stop fighting if it meant that you would no longer drown?

Client: I suppose, but I'm scared.

Therapist: So let's just lay out in it, contact it without struggling, the feeling of being scared. Let's start there—no other place required.

Although a client may struggle with this new way of relating to internal experiences, the therapist remains in a compassionate stance. The therapist is willing to be with the client right where they are and is not making any requests for them to be something else, something more, something better or different.

Chinese Finger Trap Metaphor

Therapist: Do you know what a Chinese finger trap is? It's a small tube made of straw or a meshlike metal. There is an opening at each end of the tube where you can inset a finger quite easily, so that you could have an index finger in each end. But as soon as you try to pull your fingers out, the tube latches onto your fingers and prevents you from being able to escape. The harder you pull, the tighter the tube clamps down on your fingers, making it even more difficult to escape. Sometimes escaping emotional pain and difficult thoughts is like this. The harder you try to pull out of them, the harder they clamp down on you. Again, look to see, check your experience and see if this isn't so. In terms of the finger trap, if you push in with both fingers, rather than pulling away, you will notice that your fingers suddenly have more room to move.

An important point here is to have clients be clear that you are not trying to convince them of this situation. You want them to find how this has worked in their own experience. It is not the place of the therapist to try to force this notion on clients, but rather a time in therapy where the point can be made rather easily if clients can review their efforts to control internal experience across time. It can be helpful to talk with the client about how it is nearly as difficult to create emotions as it is to get rid of them. Asking the client to try to fall in love with the next person they see provides an example of this problem. The therapist can also say at this time, "Perhaps what this therapy is about is like pushing in and making more room for what's there, rather than trying to escape it." A useful suggestion when doing this metaphor is to bring Chinese finger traps to the session and actually have clients give it a try. They are relatively inexpensive and provide a nice nonverbal description of the process.

Fighting-the-Wave Metaphor

Therapist: Have you ever heard about how swimmers in the ocean can get caught in a current, get carried out to sea, and then try to swim against the current as a way to get back to shore? What happens is that the person gets tired and eventually drowns. The current is too strong and prevents them from going anywhere. It's as if they are swimming in place. The way to get back to shore when caught in the current is not to fight your way against the current but rather to swim with the current, parallel to the shore, until you can safely reach the beach. This might take a little longer and your mind will tell you that the beach is the other way, but if you ride the current, you will find your way to the shore.

We once worked with a trauma survivor who began to fear being outside. The possibility of being retraumatized and the accompanying fear and anxiety felt too overwhelming. She decided that she would organize her day more carefully so that she would only be in places where others could always see her. Yet, she found that the fear and anxiety would still arise; she worried that even in the broad daylight with others around, something bad could happen. She eventually decided that the way to control these fears was to remain close to home. She changed jobs and would only go out in the daylight and when others were around. With this new strategy for managing anxiety she was sure she would feel better. However, her fear and anxiety continued to haunt her; she just couldn't seem to shake the thoughts, feelings, and sensations about the trauma. She decided that she needed to try harder to make her environment even safer. She quit her job, went on unemployment, and stayed at home. Her husband did all the shopping and errands. Even still, she worried. Her fear and anxiety had not diminished even after all of this effort. She decided to close the windows and draw the curtains; she screened her phone calls and never answered the door. She believed that this would surely relieve her of her fear and anxiety. It didn't. She moved into her room, brought in the TV, closed the curtains, had her husband serve her, and only left the room to use the restroom. And there she waited for her fear and anxiety to go away, believing she was in the safest place to allow those feelings to subside, thinking that would be the place where she could finally get those feelings under control. She waited and waited, and fifteen years later she had not left the room. This is a true story of one person's struggle to control her fear and anxiety.

Control may seem to be the solution, but at what cost? We often ask clients what control has cost them, and usually it ends up that they have very narrow and inflexible lives. (Here you can reflect back on the homework exercise regarding the costs of being stuck and have clients elaborate on this as well as the costs of struggling against internal experience. Look to see if the costs are the same or different.) What have their efforts to make internal experiences go away robbed them of? We receive answers ranging from personal relationships, to golden opportunities, to simple dignity and a life well lived. Contacting these costs can also be quite painful. It can evoke personal regrets and wishes of having done things differently. This is a good time to remind clients about the person-in-the-hole metaphor, particularly how they were blindfolded when they fell into their hole and that they are not responsible for being there. However, they *are* responsible for what happens next. (We will explore the issue of responsibility versus blame more fully later in this chapter.) If sadness about costs shows up, we do not ask clients to try to rid themselves of these feelings either. We welcome them and talk about them as informative—perhaps they are a compass that will let the client know that they need to head in a different direction. You can do the following short tug-of-war exercise to further demonstrate the cost of trying to control:

Tug-of-War Exercise

This exercise (Hayes et al., 1999) can be done in both group and individual therapy as a nice demonstration of both the cost of control and the benefits of relinquishing control efforts. We have found it useful to physically act this metaphor out using a "rope" such as a jump rope, scarf, or belt. If you are using a belt as the rope, we do not recommend that you stand and suddenly begin to remove your belt. This can be a real trigger for clients with a history of childhood abuse. If you are using a belt, bring it with you into the session.

Therapist: *(standing and addressing the client)* There's an exercise we can do to make this idea more clear. Are you willing to do it with me? *(Client nods, and at the therapist's invitation, stands.)* Okay, I want you to pretend this is a rope and grab hold of it and hang on tight. Imagine that in between you and me is a fairly large, very deep hole. I'm going to hang on to this end so that we can play tug-of-war. Do you know that game? *(Client nods.)* Now the other part of this is that I am going to represent your PTSD *(or anxiety, fear, or whatever you're working on).* Okay? If you could give your PTSD an image, what would the image be? *(Client describes a large gray, bubbling blob.)* Think of me as this blob. I am your trauma memories, anxiety, or whatever you're struggling against, hanging on to the other side of this rope, and you've got that end there. Are you ready?

The therapist and client commence the tug-of-war, each (gently) tugging one end of the rope. When we do this exercise we put in enough effort to make the point but not so much that clients actually have to struggle to stand their ground or remain upright. After a moment, the therapist begins to point out certain aspects of this struggle to the client.

Therapist: It looks as though we could do this for quite a while. Would you say that's been true for you? Have you been fighting this blob, the memories of your trauma, for quite a while?

Client: *(with effort)* Yes! *(continuing to pull)*

Therapist: *(continuing to pull back)* Well, this doesn't seem to be working then. Can you think of another way to go?

Client: What do you mean?

Therapist: It looks as though this sort of struggle, pitting yourself against your trauma memories, doesn't make them fall down into the hole. There's no winning.

Client: There would be if you would just let me win.

Therapist: But how would that happen? I'm the gray blob, your trauma memories. I can't be erased; I'm here to stay. *(giving the rope a firm tug)*

Client: *(pulling back harder)* I don't know what you want me to do.

Therapist: Can you think of another way to do this game? One that doesn't involve tugging, since that strategy doesn't seem to be working?

(After pulling for a moment, the client suddenly drops the rope.)

Therapist: Ahhhh. That's interesting. *(letting the moment sink in)* Hmmm, no more struggle.

Client: Well, that seems obvious.

Therapist: But notice something. I'm still here. I haven't gone away. I am still the gray blob standing across from you.

Client: *(thinking)* True. But I'm not fighting you.

Therapist: That's right! And it even looks as though you could go somewhere else now that you're not so busy fighting me. Why don't you walk toward that window?

(As the client begins to walk toward the window, the therapist follows.)

Therapist: Look, I'm still here, but you're going where you want to go.

Client: *(with a smile)* But you're being annoying. I want to go by myself.

Therapist: *(picking up the rope and handing one end to the client)* Well, looks like we need to have a struggle over that. I'm the past, I can't be erased.

Client: No, I'm not going through that again.

Therapist: And you don't have to, if you're willing to let me be here. Go wherever you go, but I'll be with you.

Client: *(long pause)* Well … I'm not happy about it, but fighting you is worse. Where do you want to go?

Therapist: Ahh, now that's for *you* to decide.

Sometimes clients quickly arrive at the solution of dropping the rope; others require more time or even a few hints before hitting upon the idea. This a good group exercise, as group members are usually offering the client encouragement or suggestions—often someone is shouting "Drop the rope; drop the rope!" As with all the exercises and metaphors in ACT, once they have been experienced in session they can be repeatedly and effectively referred to as needed throughout the therapy.

Learning Control

So, if control is part of the problem, why do we humans continue to engage in this fruitless process? The answer is simple—because control works. It is important to let the client know that you are talking about *misapplied* or rigidly applied control when speaking of it as the problem rather than the solution (Hayes et al., 1999). You can also share it with your clients fairly straightforwardly, or you can ask them to participate as appropriate.

Therapist: It is the case that we can, relatively easily, control many things. We can control the temperature of a room, for instance, by simply changing the thermostat. We can control dirt on the floor by sweeping it up. We can control the way the furniture is arranged by simply moving it around. We can control garbage by throwing it away. In these instances, control makes sense. These are things that are occurring outside of the skin—in the environment. The distinction to make is based on what is controllable and how learning to control is misapplied to areas that can't be controlled (at least not in any long-lasting way). Perhaps in 95 percent of the world, the world outside of the skin, things can be controlled. However, for the other 5 percent of the world, the world inside the skin, perhaps control doesn't work. Control, then, is misapplied or rigidly applied to the domain of stuff that goes on inside the skin.

The therapist then points out several things about why we misapply control. First, we learn control by direct experience. That is, we have personally and directly manipulated the environment. Second, we also learn control by modeling. We watch others and it appears that they are able to control what is happening on the inside of their skin. Most therapists have observed clients who have wanted to cry, have felt as though they were crying, and yet are able to control the tears. Be clear, though—this does not mean that they have controlled the pain. In fact, they are most likely feeling pain—that pain that is leading to the tears and the pain of holding back the tears.

Third, people are also told, in a number of ways, that they should be able to control their internal states. Many control messages are out there in the culture and in our homes. For instance, Robyn's mom used to say, "Buck up little G.I. Joe," as a way to give her the message that she should control her feelings. Here, it can be helpful to generate a list with clients about all the different messages they were given that made them think it best to control what goes on inside. The list can range from popular songs like "Don't Worry, Be Happy" and "Big Girls Don't Cry" to verbal utterances at home like "Shut up before I give you something to cry about!" to more subtle messages such as disapproving looks from a parent when one becomes emotional. It is helpful to remind clients that their parents fell into the hole blindfolded too, which helps them consider that not only might their parents' ideas about control be flawed, but that they too are struggling. Other messages include sayings like "Get over it" or "Get on with it." By the way, these last two messages can be particularly difficult for trauma clients, as they can be interpreted as invalidating and as one more piece of evidence about how they are broken—not only did they have the trauma, they are also unable to get over it.

Lastly, control even seems to work sometimes when applied to internal events. There are a number of ways in which people have tried control and it seemed that it did work. Distracting yourself for a period of time, for instance, and finding that you did not think or feel about the trauma during that time, or using relaxation exercises as a means to calm the nerves and cast off stress—these can convey the message that control works. However, none of these kinds of maneuvers work as a long-term solution. There is never enough distraction and relaxation to make the painful events disappear. They almost always come back. If they didn't, the client wouldn't be in therapy. As the therapist, this is a good place to pay attention. The client will often be asking for you to help them "try harder" with these techniques, thinking that will be the solution. Don't be fooled—it is only a temporary fix.

Sticking Points for Clients

Although many trauma survivors will express concern about the concept that control is the problem, some will experience relief at the notion of letting go of trying to control all the time. The effort of staying in constant control of emotions and mind is exhausting. Letting go of this struggle can bring rest and a sense of liberation.

There have been times when we have worked with clients whose desire to gain control over their thoughts and feelings has outweighed any other desire, including living well. We have had clients state that the only thing they wish for at a fundamental level is good feelings and no memories of the traumatic event. Here, you have a couple of choices. First, you can work with clients on the paradox of control—the harder they try to control, the less control they will have. Second, if you confirm that control is truly what the client wants, then you might suggest that the client may need to look for the answers they are seeking in a different approach to life or through a different type of therapy. Finally, it's very helpful at this stage of therapy to clearly distinguish responsibility from blame. It can be the case that when trauma survivors begin to connect to this idea of control as the problem, they may also hear that they are to blame for what is happening to them. This is a good time to remind them about the person-in-the-hole metaphor, noting that they were blindfolded when they fell in the hole, that they were not responsible for falling in, but that they are now response-able to make things different in their lives.

Sticking Points for Therapists

Below, we briefly explore a few places where therapists can struggle when working on control as the problem. It is helpful to be aware of these issues during these sessions; however, they can also apply more generally throughout the therapy.

"Control" Language and Action

Therapists, just like their clients, are socialized to hold the notion that controlling internal experience is the goal of therapy and, for that matter, for "good" living. The language and action of control is built into many of the things that we do and say. You might catch yourself asking clients to move on or put something out of their mind or to stop thinking about the experience at hand. It can occur behaviorally by handing the client tissue at a time when experience is crucial—not all tears need to be wiped away. Engaging in these processes is a mistake. It gives a mixed message to the client regarding how to approach internal experiences. It is a relatively easy mistake to make and so initially requires a bit of vigilance, but working to avoid control language and action can be addressed with the client if a slip happens.

Excessive Control

When therapists use excessive control in their life in a way that is problematic, especially if it is distinguishable by clients, then it will be difficult for them to convey the heart of ACT. We have seen this in trainees and other therapists in a number of forms. One variation includes the need to be the perfect therapist, never making a mistake or showing personal emotion. This can show up in issues of right and wrong, needing to be smarter than the client, needing to look wise, or simply believing that you have the answer and the client doesn't. Another form includes simply not being willing to experience your own internal life more fully. The best way to implement ACT with others is to be willing to implement it with yourself.

Homework

Homework assignments should be copied and handed out to the client as appropriate. Two homework assignments are provided because control as the problem is sometimes covered in two sessions. If you complete control as the problem in one session and you feel the client can complete both homework assignments, feel free to assign both. Be familiar with the assignments so that you can answer any questions that the client might have. Ask the client to bring the completed homework to the next session for review.

HOMEWORK ASSIGNMENT 1: CONTROL AS THE PROBLEM

Instructions: Between now and the next session, complete an imagery exercise. Start this exercise by first finding a quiet place where you can have some time to yourself (make sure the TV is off and that you won't be interrupted by the phone or other people). Begin by closing your eyes or fixing your gaze on a spot on the floor or wall in front of you and by being mindful of your breath, as we have in our mindfulness exercises at the beginning of our sessions. Spend two or three minutes focusing on your breathing. After you have taken a few minutes to pay attention to your breathing, release your attention from your breath and think about a personal struggle that you have, a difficult emotion or thought or sensation. Give this struggle an image. Imagine its shape, size, color, character, and other details, just as we did in our last session. After you have formed the image, imagine it standing or floating before you. As you do so, see if you can just let it rest there without any effort to make it go away or come closer. Simply let the image be before you. Your job is to do nothing with respect to this image except view it. Allow yourself a minute or two to focus on the image. Then gently release your attention from the image and bring it back to your breath. Again, spend two or three minutes focusing on your breath and then gently allow yourself to return your awareness to the room. After you have completed the exercise, take a few moments to write about your emotions and thoughts in response to the exercise. Jot down what you observed or learned, whether it be negative or positive. Bring your notes to the next session.

Repeat the exercise a few days later, again spending time being aware of your breathing, and then reflecting on a struggle that you have. Give this struggle an image. Again, observe this image dispassionately, not trying to make it come or go but just observing it standing or floating in front of you. Write down your reactions to this second exercise, too. Describe any differences between the first and second exercise. Bring these notes to the next session also.

HOMEWORK ASSIGNMENT 2: CONTROL AS THE PROBLEM

Do the following mindfulness meditation exercise two to three times at home during the week for five minutes. Set a timer to help monitor your time. To begin, find a quiet place where you can practice this meditation without any interruption (turn off the television and radio, unplug the phone, etc.). Sit in a chair and place your feet squarely on the ground. Sit up in your chair so that your back is straight but not rigid. Make sure that your head feels square to your shoulders and place your arms in a comfortable position at your sides. This posture helps you to stay alert and focused. Begin by closing your eyes or by finding a place on the floor or in front of you on which to fix your gaze. Now turn your attention to your hearing. Notice what you hear as you sit in this room. Pay attention to every sound, shifting your attention to each new sound as it enters into your awareness. Turn all of your attention to hearing … If you find that your mind gets caught on a thought and pulled away from hearing, just gently notice where your mind went and then gently bring your mind back to sound … focusing on just listening … *Be* hearing … Focus on each sound as it moves into your awareness, letting it pass, and then focusing on the next sound that moves into your awareness … Be present to hearing. When you hear the timer ring, gently release your attention from sound and reconnect to the room by imagining it in your head or by looking around. Remember, practicing mindful awareness will help you to be more present to the moment and less engaged in the past.

Moving Forward

Once the solution—experiential control—has been established as part of the problem, then the work on finding an alternative to control can begin. Willingness as the alternative to control is introduced. Willingness is the place where acceptance comes to life.

CHAPTER 6

Willingness

God asks no man whether he will accept life. This is not the choice.
You must take it. The only question is how.

—Henry Ward Beecher

This chapter addresses one of the most challenging objectives of acceptance and commitment therapy—helping clients move into a position of willingness. By "willingness" we are referring to being willing to have the internal experiences of the moment without attempting to alter or escape them in some way. Willingness is therefore offered at this point in the therapy as the alternative to misapplied efforts to control internal experiences. We have found willingness to be a loaded issue in our work with trauma survivors, one that threatens to undermine the therapy. Clients often confuse being willing with the emotion of wanting something or with being okay with something (not having a negative reaction to it). The idea that they should somehow want their trauma or not be distressed by it is perceived as invalidating and impossible. As conceived in ACT, willingness is more of a stance one takes than a feeling; it is an active choice to have and hold whatever feelings are there rather than trying to create or be rid of any one feeling. Assisting clients to understand this distinction is an important part of the therapy. Additionally, while tremendous freedom lies within the concept of willingness, it can evoke fear in many if not most clients. This chapter will examine how to work with this and other challenges that can arise when establishing willingness as an alternative to control with trauma survivors.

Session Format (2-3 Sessions)

- Open with mindfulness

- Review prior session

- Introduce willingness

- Explore cognitive defusion

- Understand barriers to willingness

- Explore sticking points for clients

- Explore sticking points for therapists

- Assign homework: willingness

Opening with Mindfulness

As with the other treatment sessions, begin with a mindfulness exercise.

MINDFULNESS EXERCISE 1: BE-STILL MINDFULNESS
(Approximately 5-10 minutes)

Therapist: I would like everyone to start this exercise, as usual, by placing your feet squarely on the ground and sitting up in your chair so that your back is straight but not rigid. Assume the posture that we always take in these exercises. Let's begin by first noticing or paying attention to the fact that your body is actively sensing the environment. Notice that you can feel yourself sitting in the chair and you can feel your feet on the ground. Now, gently close your eyes. I would like you to place your attention at the tip of your nose and begin to notice the sensation of air moving in and out of your nostrils, ... paying attention to your breathing ... Allow yourself to just gently be with breathing, paying attention to the gentle, easy air as it passes in and out ... You may also notice the rise and fall of your chest. Be aware of the expansion and contraction—*be* your breathing ... If you become distracted by your thoughts, just take a moment to notice where your thoughts took you, notice where your mind went, and then, without judgment, let go and return your attention to your breathing. If you get distracted a hundred times, bring yourself back to your breath a hundred times. Now let's just take the next few minutes to focus completely on breathing. (*Allow a few minutes for focused breathing.*)

Now I would like you to turn your full attention to your body. Starting with your toes, scan up your body, following the scan right to the top of your head … Notice the position you are sitting in and the way your body feels in the chair. As you pay attention to your body, I would like to you to practice remaining perfectly still except the rise and fall of your chest as you breathe. You may notice that you have an itch or a desire to move. You may notice some discomfort, but your only task at this time is to notice those desires, discomforts, and itches without any effort to make them different. Stay still … Watch as your body and emotions and thoughts ask you to do something and notice too that you can remain perfectly still despite these requests. (*Allow time for clients to remain still.*) Continue to remain still as you notice the different sensations in your body. Also be aware that you do not need to react to sensations, you can simply observe them … You can simply watch them come and go. (*Allow time for clients to remain still. Then, continue with a few comments about being aware of the body while asking clients to remain still. Remember to remain still yourself as you guide the exercise. Some clients may have difficulty and will continue to move; you can have them practice this at home for shorter periods of time to help them see that they can observe body, emotions, and thoughts without reacting.*)

Now, releasing your attention from stillness, gently focus on just the rise and fall of your breathing … and then on your body and how it feels to sit in the chair. Notice the placement of your feet, your arms, and your head. Picture what the room will look like and, when you are ready, rejoin the room by opening your eyes.

MINDFULNESS EXERCISE 2: WELCOME ANXIETY
(Approximately 5-10 minutes)

Therapist: I would like to start this exercise just as we've started the others, making your posture alert but not stiff. Get comfortable in your chair … Gently close your eyes and begin by focusing your attention on your breathing.

Notice where your attention goes as you do so … For some it will go to your nose, for others it will go to the rise and fall of your chest. Spend these next few moments being aware of your breathing … Follow each breath as you draw it in and out. (*Allow a minute or two to focus on breathing.*) Now, as you remain aware of your breathing, following the in breath and then the out breath … I would like you to repeat to yourself, silently, on the in breath, "Welcome anxiety," (*you can also choose other emotion words that seem to fit*) and on the out breath "my old friend." So as you breathe in, say to yourself, "Welcome anxiety," and as you breathe out, "my old friend." Continue to repeat these words as you gently breathe. If you get distracted or caught by a thought, just come back to "Welcome anxiety, my old friend." (*Pause and allow a few minutes for clients to practice this mindfulness exercise; you might remind them of the words and of following the breath from time to time.*) Now, gently release your attention from the words and your breath and focus your attention on your body sitting in the chair, in this room. Picture the room in your mind's eye. When you are ready, rejoin the room by opening your eyes.

Upon ending the mindfulness exercise, take a few moments with clients to process the exercise. At this point in therapy, clients should be fairly used to doing mindfulness. You may want to keep in mind, however, that for some survivors of trauma, it is difficult to do these exercises and they may still be struggling. Be patient and have them practice as much as they are willing. With regard to the two exercises above, it may be helpful to talk about them for a brief period. In speaking to exercise 1, it is helpful to point out how the client can notice bodily sensations and yet choose not to respond to them. This matches well with being willing to experience, to just notice and choose. With exercise 2, some clients are caught off guard by the statements. We often hear expressions of surprise that are followed by recognition of the message contained in "my old friend." Again, welcoming anxiety is useful in establishing willingness.

Prior Session Review

Take a brief period of time to reflect back on the prior session and to check in with clients regarding their assigned homework:

■   Control as the problem imagery exercise, and writing about the experience

- Repeating the imagery exercise and writing about differences between the two times

- Mindfulness meditation: listening

Introducing Willingness

Those who have worked with trauma survivors understand the immense task these individuals face in attempting to reconcile the reality of what they have experienced. We are hardwired to experience emotions such as horror, fear, and shame as intensely aversive. Clients who have survived traumatic experiences know all too well how difficult these feelings can be, and they are intent on both ridding themselves of any remembrances of the trauma and making sure they never again have such an experience. These individuals can be threatened by the very concept of willingness, as though being willing to have one's internal experience raises the odds that one will encounter painful events. It can feel as though being willing is letting down one's guard, and this seems unsafe. In fact, being willing *is* about letting down one's guard, guarding being a control strategy that not only doesn't manage to prevent pain but serves as an impediment to living fully. However, asking clients to be willing to feel difficult emotions is not the same as asking them to engage in unsafe behavior. We are not asking the latter, and it's important to make sure clients understand this distinction.

As mentioned earlier, clients often misunderstand being willing as being the same as wanting something. We make it a point to discuss this directly:

Therapist: Let's say you notice that you're experiencing anxiety. Perhaps you are challenging yourself in some way and the feeling of anxiety comes up. Being willing is about noticing the anxious feeling and letting it be there, rather than engaging in various control or avoidance strategies. This doesn't mean you want to be anxious—who wants to be anxious? That would not be very natural. But willingness in this case means allowing yourself to have the feeling of anxiety at that moment without trying to change or escape it in some way.

Hands-On Exercise

One of the reasons the hands-on exercise (Hayes et al., 1999) is a powerful intervention is because it so graphically demonstrates the problem with control strategies (unwillingness) and the potential freedom of willingness. We have found that once we've done this exercise with clients, we can repeatedly refer to it as a quick and effective reminder of the problem of control and the possibilities in being willing. The dialogue below is preceded by the therapist asking the client's permission to touch the client on the hand (palm to palm)—this is, of course, very important when working with survivors of interpersonal trauma, especially as the therapist will sort of loom over the client during the exercise.

Therapist: I'd like to try something with you, would that be okay?

Client: Okay, sure.

Therapist: We're going to demonstrate something together. (*Therapist rises and stands before the client, holding one hand up in front of the client at about eye level.*) I'm going to ask you to put your hand up against mine, and then I'm going to press against it. Is that okay? (*Client nods. The therapist then places one hand against the client's and leans into it slightly.*)

Therapist: Now tell me something that you struggle with—an emotion.

Client: Fear.

Therapist: If you could give that fear an image, what image would you give it?

Client: It would look like a big black blob that is shapeless.

Therapist: Good. I am going to be that big black blob, the feeling of fear. Imagine that I am the blob, that I am your fear, and I want you to push me away.

Client: (*already tense*) Okay.

Therapist: Now I want you to do your best to push me away, to keep me off of you so that you don't have to have me.

The client then engages in pushing the therapist away, typically exerting a good deal of energy and concentration on the task. As the client pushes, the therapist matches the effort, leaning in more if the client pushes harder. It is of course important to be mindful of not injuring the client—many of the clients we see with PTSD have physical problems that need to be taken into account. This struggle is allowed to continue for a few moments more, and then the therapist eases off a bit while providing new instructions:

Therapist: Now I'd like you to keep your hand against mine, but stop trying to push me away. Just let your hand rest against mine, but don't push. Just let me be there, resting on your hand. (*The therapist now moves their two hands in a gentle circle, and then back and forth, demonstrating increased freedom of movement.*)

Therapist:	I want you to notice something. Would you say our hands are just as much in contact as before?
Client:	Yes.
Therapist:	So you're actually as in touch with me, with your fear, as you were before, when you were pushing so hard.
Client:	Right.
Therapist:	*(moving their hands gently again in a circle)* What else do you notice?
Client:	This is much easier.
Therapist:	That's interesting! It's easier even though our hands are still fully touching?
Client:	Yes, because, I'm not having to push.
Therapist:	So, even though fear is as much here as before, just letting it be here is much freer than trying to push it away. In fact, while your fear is as much here as it was before, it seems much more acceptable.
Client:	Yeah!

When conducting this exercise in group therapy, we have found it effective to ask other group members what they notice as the participating client just lets the therapist's hand be there. It is usually observed that the client seems more at ease and more aware of other things going on in the room. Often it's as though the client suddenly remembers that there are other people in the room, and can engage with them despite having a hand pressed against the therapist's (as the fear), while earlier all the client's thoughts and energies had been on the struggle.

Cognitive Defusion

Cognitive defusion, or the ability to recognize one's thoughts as internal phenomena versus literal truth, is essential to achieve a stance of willingness. As an example, consider the client who has the thought "I am a failure" and who is fused with that thought, meaning the client is not able to recognize it as simply a thought and instead buys it as being literally true. Such individuals are in a bind—either they must give in and be a failure, or they must somehow fix themselves such that they are not a failure and therefore okay. Clients can misunderstand willingness to have such thoughts as being the same as accepting them to be literally true, and they are justifiably upset at the idea. In addition, when these thoughts include cognitions about their emotional experience, such as "I can't have this feeling," or "This feeling is bad or unsafe," and so forth, they are now caught in the position of also having to fix these feelings in order to be okay. Finally, clients often have extensive histories of trying to overcome these experiences and associate this effort with fighting back and not giving in. For these reasons, clients who are unable to defuse from their thoughts often confuse willingness with resignation.

Along with these challenges, teaching clients to recognize thoughts as simply thoughts can be quite tricky, as this in itself requires thinking (the process of being fused with one's thoughts, making no distinction between thought and thinker). This is one reason experiential exercises form such an essential part of the therapy. In this section we will introduce exercises that directly tackle the problem of cognitive fusion. It should also be noted that many of the exercises and metaphors that will be introduced later in the therapy also highlight the concept of willingness.

Two Computers

We have found the two computers metaphor (Hayes et al., 1999) to be a straight-forward and effective way to help clients distinguish thoughts from literal truth, to "deliteralize" (defuse from) their thoughts. Here the focus is on helping clients to see their own programming. This metaphor resonates well for survivors of interpersonal trauma, particularly those who have experienced childhood trauma such as physical, emotional, or sexual abuse. Such individuals have been programmed to think very unhealthy things about themselves that they have assumed to be literally true. Recognizing that this is simply programming versus truth can be tremendously empowering, especially when later combined with self-as-context exercises (chapter 7) that promote the idea of an intact, unbroken self—that the client is not broken despite having experienced such painful programming. To illuminate this idea we have found it useful to draw (to the best of our ability) a representation of the concept on a large whiteboard. We typically do this in one of two ways. In one version we draw on one half of the board a figure sitting at a desk with a computer on it—the head of the figure drawn so that it is actually stuck inside the computer. On the other half of the board we draw the figure so that it is also sitting at a desk with a computer on it, but this figure is sitting and facing the screen at a more normal distance. Another version is to make an entire half of the board nothing but a computer screen, so that when looking at the board it's as though one is looking at a giant monitor. We put a salient phrase, such as "I'm damaged goods" on the screen. Then you would construct the drawing on the other half of the board as if one is looking at it from a greater perspective—one can discern not only the screen but the entire computer and keyboard as well. Both are graphic depictions of the difference between buying a thought (in other words, buying one's programming) and recognizing a thought for what it is—simply a thought (or programming).

Therapist: (*The therapist begins by drawing stick figures similar to the illustrations below or by printing out a copy of the figures, which are on the CD provided.*) We all have programming that starts almost as soon as we are born. This programming comes from a variety of sources, including Mom, Dad, friends, and life experiences that have led us to conclude various things about ourselves, others, and the world. It's as though someone is typing away at your keyboard all the time, programming away. Perhaps your third-grade teacher told you that you were a great storyteller, and so the rest of your life that was your programming—you believed you were a great storyteller. Or maybe someone told you that you were bad, and you have believed that for the rest of your life. Anything we experience goes into our programming. For example, when I was a kid I lost a relay race for our track team. I think this was in sixth or seventh grade. I was the anchor, and when it was my turn to go we had a good lead on the other teams. I started out fast, but then I totally pooped out. I can still remember the thoughts and feelings I had while, one by one, every other runner passed me up—feelings of panic, distress, exhaustion, and humiliation, thoughts of being a failure. To this day, if I'm out running and start to feel tired and winded, those very same feelings and thoughts come up. I start to feel panicky and overwhelmed. I have thoughts about how I "can't do it" and so on. That's because I've been programmed to have this reaction by that earlier event. We all are programmed by our parents, our families, our teachers and friends, our society, commercials, and so on—it can't be helped. However, we can help ourselves by recognizing our programming for what it is. For example, if I just bought the thoughts and feelings that come up when I'm running, I would think something terrible was

happening to me. Instead, I recognize this as a reaction that, while it may not be necessarily fun, doesn't reflect what is actually happening in the moment.

The problem is that we tend to buy our programming, like this person here (*pointing to the stick figure with its head inside the monitor*), so that we think it's literally true. We fail to see that programming is just that—programming, not necessarily truth. For example, imagine that this person with his head in the computer just had someone come up and press a button on the keyboard and the following pieces of programming showed up on the screen: "I'm no good; something's wrong with me." Then, instead of recognizing this as just words, just programming that has come up on the screen, he buys it as literally true. At that point, he *is* his programming. There is no separation between self and programming. From this position, it would seem he needs to start typing in new programming to get rid of the programming he doesn't like. However, what he learns is that this is nondeletable programming. Each time he hits delete, "delete" shows up on the screen as more of his program.

In this picture (*pointing to the second figure*), let's say the exact same thing has happened: someone has pushed a button that causes the same programming to pop up on the screen. He is reading the exact same words, "I'm no good; something's wrong with me," but he is able to see that these words are text on the screen, just part of his programming, and that in fact there are many, many words on the screen and that these particular ones have simply caught his attention. This isn't to say that this person doesn't have an emotional reaction to those words. Rather, he recognizes the thoughts and feelings for what they are—programming. He has just a little distance between himself and the words he sees on the screen. It is in this space, where one can see one's programming for what it is, that change can take place. That is, if you can view your programming rather than be your programming, you have created a space where choice is possible, a place where you can make choices that are about your life rather than about your programming.

Taking Your Mind for a Walk

The taking-your-mind-for-a-walk exercise (Hayes et al., 1999) is designed to help clients view the mind from a different perspective. This is a particularly effective exercise for clients who place high value on the mind, who have been taught that figuring it out is the answer. It provides an experiential demonstration of how the mind operates and that the constant stream of cognitions it produces aren't necessarily gospel truth—that in fact, they may be somewhat suspect. It also helps clients to see that even as mind stuff (programming) arises, they can take actions that are consistent with or directly opposite to what their mind has to say. Again, this points to one's choices being free from the mind's dictates. The following is an example of how this exercise is conducted in a group setting. If conducting individual therapy, the exercise is done much the same except that the therapist partners with the client.

Therapist: Everyone needs to pick a partner for this next exercise. (*The therapist partners with a client if there are an odd number of group members.*) What I'd like each pair of you to do is to pick someone to be the person, and someone to be that person's mind. For example, Lydia would be Lydia, and Chris would be Lydia's mind. Sharon would be Sharon and Stephanie would be Sharon's mind, and so on. (*Therapist waits for this to be arranged.*) Everyone ready? Does everyone know if they are the person or the mind? Good. Now, for the next five minutes I want each person to take your mind for a walk. Your job is to walk around the room, down the hall, around the building, doing whatever, while your mind follows along. Minds, your job is to do what minds do, just generate a constant stream of thoughts. As the mind, you need to say all these thoughts out loud, one right after the other. Persons, do not talk to your minds. This is not about having a conversation. Rather, you will just

walk about while your mind does its business. And persons, you cannot lose your mind. In about five minutes I'll ask you to switch places so that those of you who are now persons will become your partner's mind and you will continue to walk for another five minutes in your new role. Finally, all of you will walk alone for about five minutes, taking your own mind for a walk.

What ensues next is often a lot of hilarity, as clients somewhat self-consciously begin to move around, their minds in tow. If the therapist is paired with a client, it is helpful to be the mind first and to provide an example to the other pairs:

Therapist: *(following closely behind the client)* Okay, what do I do now? This is really stupid. I don't know what to do. I wonder what the point of this is? Maybe if I do something she'll stop talking. I'll just go down this hallway and get away from everybody. Yes, this is better … Actually, it would be easier just to keep on going and walk right through that door. Yeah, that's what I should do, just get out of here, open the door and keep going … Forget this therapy anyway, who needs it? I wonder what everyone else is doing? This must look pretty silly. Oh look, there's Stephanie and Sharon—they look like they're having fun; they're really laughing … I wish I was with them. What time is it? It must be getting close to five minutes by now. It's almost lunchtime. I'm hungry, wonder what's for lunch…

If the therapist is not paired with anyone, it can be helpful to assist the minds as they are following their persons, to momentarily take over as the mind to demonstrate, or to correct persons from having conversations with their minds. You might playfully say, "Never mind your mind." After five minutes the pairs switch places and repeat the exercise, and then after another five minutes each person walks alone. The therapist then calls everyone back into the therapy room and asks what this exercise was like for them. The following is a typical response:

Client: *(laughing)* She drove me crazy! I kept trying to walk away from her, but she just kept going on and on … I couldn't believe how well she knew me. She kept trying to get me to eat the doughnuts in the kitchen.

Therapist: What do you mean, "tried to get you"?

Client: She kept telling me how good they were, how no one would notice if one was missing, how one little doughnut wouldn't matter—she was terrible!

Therapist: And did you eat the doughnut?

Client: *(laughs)* No!

Therapist: But your mind was telling you to eat it.

Client: I know! But I already had one this morning, and I'm supposed to be watching my blood sugar.

Therapist: Are you saying that even though your mind told you to eat the doughnut, and even provided all sorts of reasons to eat it, you chose not to?

Client: That's right

Therapist: That's interesting, isn't it? Here your mind is doing what minds do, giving you all sorts of thoughts and reasons for whatever, and yet you still made a choice not to. In this case, you chose not to have a doughnut because you wanted to take care of your health. Here's another example: Laura, when I was your mind I told you to escape this stupid exercise and just leave the building. But you didn't. Instead you turned around and went back down the hallway.

Laura: Yeah, I couldn't believe you were telling me that because it's exactly how I felt! I felt really self-conscious and wanted to leave right then.

Therapist: But you didn't.

Laura: No, I knew that I needed to be here.

Therapist: So, even though you had the feeling of discomfort and the urge to escape, and even though your mind was telling you to leave, you didn't because you made a choice based on some larger goal. What was that?

Laura: What do you mean?

Therapist: Why didn't you leave?

Laura: Because I want to complete this therapy; I want to complete this program. I want to learn how I can live a better life.

Therapist: So even if your mind feeds you all sorts of different thoughts, you don't have to buy those thoughts. You can still make choices that are in line with your goals and values.

Laura: Yeah ... I never really realized that.

The dialogue shown above depicts a clinical opportunity that arose from clients doing something other than what their minds were telling them to do. That is, while the main point of this exercise is to help clients view their minds from a different perspective, they have learned experientially here that they can make behavioral choices despite what their minds are telling them. In this example, the therapist has also subtly introduced the concept of values, although this will be targeted more directly later in the protocol (see chapter 8). Some clients will do whatever their minds tell them to do during the exercise, inadvertently demonstrating cognitive fusion rather than clarifying the distinction between one's cognitions and one's self. The following exchange provides an example of how one might work with this scenario; in this example the therapist is working with a male client in individual therapy.

Therapist: In this exercise I'm going to play the part of your mind, and you are going to be you. That is, you are going to take me, your mind, for a walk. We can go wherever you want, down the hallway, around the building, whatever. As your mind, I am going to be doing what minds do, talking. I'm going to be giving you an endless stream of thoughts, but I don't want you to respond to me or try to talk to me. I'll just be busy producing thoughts as we walk around. Are you ready?

Client: So I just go somewhere and you're following me?

Therapist: Right. Are you ready?

Client: Sure, I guess. (*Hesitantly rises.*) So where do you want to go?

Therapist: (*regards client but does not respond to the question*) So I'm not sure what to do. I guess I'll ask her where she wants to go.

Client: (*laughing*) Oh, right. (*Starts walking around the room.*)

Therapist: So, I'm not really sure what do here, but I'll just start. Maybe I'll figure out something… (*as client hesitates*) I'm not sure where to go now. What do I do? She just keeps talking, but whatever…

This continues for awhile as the client moves about the room. Eventually he turns and heads toward the door.

Therapist: I'll try this now; I'm getting bored. (*Client reaches for the doorknob.*) Oh wait, I'll bet there are a lot of germs on this doorknob. (*Client pauses.*) I'll bet it's really dirty—think how many people have touched this door! (*After some hesitation, client opens the door.*) Man, it's really nice outside. Finally. We sure had our share of rain this year. (*Client continues down the front walk and starts to turn right.*) No! Don't go that way, go left. (*Client stops.*) Left is definitely the better way to go, trust me. (*Client turns left instead of right.*) I need to go a little faster I think. (*Client quickens his pace slightly.*) Actually, I should stop right now. (*Client stops.*) It's time to start again; I need to start walking now.

(*Client starts walking again.*) But not that fast. (*Client slows down.*) Stop! (*Client freezes.*) Jump up and down and squawk like a chicken!

Client: (*remaining frozen*) What?

Therapist: It's now time to jump up and down and squawk like a chicken—this is very important. I have to do this. I really need to do this right. I really need to be a chicken. (*Client laughs nervously and looks around.*) What am I waiting for? The time is now, no time like the present to be a chicken. (*Client laughs again, shakes his head, then turns and heads back in the direction of the office.*) But my mind really wants me to squawk like a chicken—my mind is going to be disappointed … Does my mind really think I'm going to do that out here on the street? No way. Wait, stop here. (*Client continues to head towards the office.*) Let's not go back. It's so nice outside. This hasn't been a very long walk … I think I'll just hum quietly to myself. (*Client is silent.*) I think a good thing to do would be to review the table of elements … Oh wow, that's a great looking shrub. (*Therapist continues in this vein as the client returns to the therapy room and resumes his seat.*)

Therapist: Okay, we're done. Thanks for being willing to do that exercise with me. What did you think?

Client: That was a trip!

Therapist: What do you mean?

Client: You're crazy!

Therapist: Your mind is crazy?

Client: You as my mind are crazy! There's no way I was going to do that, squawk like a chicken just because my "mind" was telling me to.

Therapist: But you were doing other things your mind was telling you to do—slow down, speed up, turn left…

Client: Yeah, that's true.

Therapist: So why that and not the other?

Client: I don't know … I didn't want to squawk like a chicken. I overrode my mind I guess. I wasn't willing to look ridiculous.

Therapist: You would have looked quite intelligent reciting the table of elements.

Client: (*laughing*) Oh brother.

Therapist:	And didn't you want to go right instead of left?
Client:	Yes…
Therapist:	Could you have still gone right even though your mind was telling you to go left? Like how you went ahead and touched the doorknob even though your mind was telling you it had germs on it?
Client:	Yeah, I could have … So I guess you're saying that I don't have to listen to my mind—I can do what I want.
Therapist:	And even what you don't want! If you chose to for some reason, you could have gone ahead and squawked like a chicken even though you had thoughts about not wanting to do it and fears about looking ridiculous.
Client:	So the mind is useless? That doesn't make sense.
Therapist:	The mind can be very helpful, but it isn't always your friend. The key is to notice that the mind does what it does, and that what it says to you isn't always literally true. It's important to know that thoughts are just that—thoughts.
Client:	I see. Yeah, I get it.

Eyes On

The eyes-on exercise (Hayes et al., 1999) is used to highlight the concept of willingness. It's effective in that it is certain to evoke a fair amount of discomfort in clients while presenting them with an opportunity to choose to be willing despite their discomfort. In individual therapy this exercise is done between the client and therapist; in a group setting participants are put into pairs.

Therapist:	For this exercise you will need to be in pairs, so everybody pick a partner and then sit in chairs directly across from one another. (*Therapist waits until this has been arranged.*) Great. Okay, now you need to scoot your chairs closer, so that your knees are almost touching.

The therapist continues to orchestrate this until everyone is thus positioned. Clients often demonstrate discomfort with this request by attempting to remain at a physical distance from their partners.

Therapist:	Good. Now I would like you to simply sit and look your partner in the eyes without speaking or otherwise trying to communicate. Just sit and

regard one another, and I'll tell you when the exercise is completed. Notice what comes up for you as you do this … anxiety, restlessness, boredom, judgment, wishing it was over, wanting to do it right, whatever—just notice and continue to look into your partner's eyes.

The therapist continues to guide the group, working to help them refrain from strategies aimed at alleviating their discomfort.

Therapist: *(as a pair of clients break into giggles)* Be present to what you're experiencing as you look at your partner. If it's an urge to laugh, just notice that urge and be willing to stay engaged with your partner. Notice all the ways you deal with being uncomfortable and choose to be willing all the same. Choose to remain engaged with your partner despite feelings of wanting to stop or escape. Just observe what you're experiencing while you look at this human being across from you.

In individual therapy, the therapist would partner with the client, providing the same initial instructions but then speaking only when necessary. It is important to allow for long moments of silence when possible, as the therapist's talking can also serve as a means to distract from what is being experienced. This exercise is not at all rushed; we typically allow three minutes to pass, or a little longer if it has taken a while for clients to cease avoidance strategies and engage in the process (don't overdo it; we rarely go beyond 5 minutes). When sufficient time has passed, the therapist ends the exercise and asks clients to relate their experiences. They typically express how much they wanted to laugh, or how uncomfortable they were.

Client: I wasn't sure which eye to stare at, the left, or the right. Then I started worrying about what she was thinking, if she could tell I was staring at only one eye…

Therapist: Did you want to quit looking?

Client: Yes! And then she started smiling, and I wanted to bust up laughing.

Therapist: Yet you were willing to continue with the exercise.

Client: Yes, it actually got better the longer we did it.

Second Client: I hated this exercise. I didn't get it.

Therapist: You noticed that thought and that feeling while you were doing the exercise? (*Note that rather than asking why or probing, the therapist remains focused on the point of the exercise.*)

Second Client:	Yes, I didn't see the point of this one at all.
Therapist:	How great that is then, that you chose to do it, that you were willing to do it even though you had hateful feelings about it and thoughts about not getting it. You were willing, despite all that, to go on.
Second Client:	*(somewhat reluctantly)* I guess so, but I did hate it.

In these examples, the clients can come to see that they can be willing to experience *and* engage in behavior, even under difficult circumstances. This will become particularly important when asking clients to engage values. Along with experientially demonstrating the concept of willingness, the eyes-on exercise also has the potential for an additional lesson, as demonstrated by this client's comment:

Client:	The most amazing thing happened! I was so uncomfortable I couldn't even look at Cheryl. I could tell she was, too. She would hardly even look at me—she kept looking at my ear. But then eventually we sort of settled into it, you know? And at some point I was just looking at this amazing human being. It's hard to explain ... Everything sort of dropped away and it was just me, a human, looking at another human, and I could tell she was doing the same. We were just totally connected—I almost started crying!

Such authentic connectedness is a profound experience, particularly with individuals who have survived a trauma. These clients often feel isolated by their experience, as though they are irrevocably marked as being different. They report feeling as though no one can possibly understand what they have gone through or how it continues to affect them. When the trauma includes childhood abuse, or when the client has low self-esteem for whatever reason, this sense of aloneness is even more heightened. It is therefore quite a significant experience to connect with another human being at an authentic level and to feel okay in the most basic sense.

Barriers to Willingness

At this point clients have been introduced to willingness as an alternative to control or avoidance. They have participated in experiential exercises that have provided a taste of how being willing allows for greater freedom, freedom to make choices despite what one is thinking or feeling. It would seem the reaction would be to jump for joy; however, clients can evidence reluctance or resistance for various reasons. Some seem to distrust that it can be this simple. Some seem reluctant to let go. The following section addresses some of the common barriers to willingness we have observed in clients with PTSD.

Confusing Willingness with Feelings

In the introduction to this chapter, we noted that clients can confuse being willing to have a feeling with wanting the feeling, which can then be perceived as an invalidation of their traumatic experiences. We note that being willing to feel a feeling doesn't mean that the client "wants" the feeling. A similar difficulty is when clients think willingness equals acceptance, which then equals forgiveness—constructs that open Pandora's box for survivors of interpersonal trauma.

Client:	*(angrily)* So you're saying that I should be okay with what happened to me? Just accept that I was raped?
Therapist:	Well, those are two different things. It seems clear that you are not okay with having been raped.
Client:	No!
Therapist:	Of course not. You will never be okay with being raped, because it was not okay and it will never be okay.
Client:	*(with confusion)* But isn't that what you are saying?
Therapist:	Were you, in fact raped?
Client:	Well yeah.
Therapist:	So you accept that as being true—you were raped. That acceptance isn't the same as being happy about it or wanting it. Accepting that it happened, and accepting your feelings about the fact that it happened, is not the same as feeling okay about being raped.
Client:	*(thinking it over)* Okay. I see the difference.

The following depicts an exchange that sometimes occurs during the discussion of willingness, depending on the client's learning history or religious and spiritual beliefs. The client in this case was severely injured in a car accident, the other driver being at fault.

Client:	You know, I've tried accepting. I know I'm supposed to forgive him, but I just can't. I get enraged just thinking about him.
Therapist:	You mean that you have tried to feel forgiving?

Client:	Yes, but I can't. Well, sometimes I think about how bad he probably feels, and how everyone makes mistakes, but mostly I'm just angry.
Therapist:	Willingness isn't a feeling. Feelings come and go. Even the feeling of forgiveness comes and goes—one day a person might feel forgiving, another day they might not. As meant in ACT, willingness is an active choice to simply have whatever feelings are going on in the moment—anger, forgiveness, fear, and so on—instead of trying to get rid of them somehow.
Client:	I wish I could get rid of them, though! I don't like being angry.
Therapist:	And have you tried that? Have you tried to get rid of your anger?
Client:	Yes, I've tried a lot.
Therapist:	And how well has that worked for you?
Client:	It doesn't work. I just stay angry.
Therapist:	Are you angry right now?
Client:	Yes, as a matter of fact.
Therapist:	Can you be willing to just have that anger in this moment? To just sit with those feelings here in the room with me?
Client:	*(pauses)* Yes, I guess I can.
Therapist:	Great.

Here, the client has confused willingness/acceptance with forgiveness. The therapist stays with having the client feel what he feels. It does not mean the client must forgive. The latter is a choice. We further explore forgiveness in chapter 9, providing examples of how to work on forgiveness if that is what the client chooses to do.

Confusing Willingness with Concession

Individuals with PTSD experience a great deal of pain. They have survived something horrific, the effects of which they feel to this day and throughout their lives. Prior to entering therapy, they have engaged in many unsuccessful attempts to make this different. Why then, would they be reluctant to embrace the possibilities of willingness? Therapists working with clients who have been victims of interpersonal trauma often speak of how some of these individuals seem to cling to the victim role. It is a paradox—these clients are clearly in a miserable place, and yet they seem to want to hang out there. Therapists often struggle with how to point this out without sounding invalidating to the client. We have found in the course of doing this work that the corpus delicti metaphor (Hayes et al., 1999) offers a powerful yet compassionate means to tackle this issue, one that clients are able to accept. When the therapist is presenting corpus delicti he should always take care that this is not about blame, but rather the cost of remaining the victim. The ensuing discussion can help clients shift into a stance of willingness and ultimately committed action (see chapter 9).

Therapist: Do you know the Latin phrase "corpus delicti"?

Client: (*client looks blank.*) No.

Therapist: Do you know the saying "Without a body, there's no murder?"

Client: Yes.

Therapist: *Corpus delicti* is Latin for "the body of the crime." It is also a legal term for the material evidence in a homicide, such as the corpse in a homicide case. Without the body, there's no murder.

Client: Hmm.

Therapist: Corpus delicti is often a very important concept for survivors of trauma.

Client: Really? How is that?

Therapist: For very understandable reasons, trauma survivors tend make sure there is a body for the crime, as a way to make sure there is evidence that something wrong has happened to them.

Client: What do you mean?

Therapist: If something bad happens to someone, if the person has been a victim of something terrible, the person seems to need evidence for this. It's as though this evidence is the only way to show that something bad has occurred, and if there's no obvious evidence, it's as though the thing never happened. The easiest way to do this is to be their own evidence.

Client: Their own evidence? You mean that I am the evidence for my assault?

Therapist: You were attacked and raped. You were injured physically and emotionally—this is not okay. It would make sense that you would want to somehow demonstrate its "not okay-ness" by being the evidence that something bad happened to you. Especially if you weren't listened to or were otherwise invalidated at the time of the trauma, it makes sense that you would need to show somehow that something terrible really *did* happen to you.

Client:	Hmm. (*thinking it over*) How have I been the evidence?
Therapist:	Well, what would you say? How do you demonstrate that you were hurt by the trauma?
Client:	Well … I started drinking right afterward, started fighting with my family…
Therapist:	How do you demonstrate it now?
Client:	(*slightly surprised but thinking it over*) Well, I have a lot of problems. I'm angry all the time and can't hold a job. It's hard for me to trust people, and I haven't been in a relationship for years…
Therapist:	How would you say that is the corpus delicti for what happened to you?
Client:	Well, I wouldn't have these problems if it hadn't happened.
Therapist:	So if you were able to be in a relationship one day, or if you weren't so angry, the assault didn't actually happen?
Client:	Well, no…
Therapist:	People who have experienced trauma often feel that if they continue on and live good lives, it's as though the trauma didn't happen, or that it wasn't really so bad. It's as though your perpetrator is sort of off the hook if you have a good life despite the trauma.
Client:	Yes! I get that. I do feel as though I need to keep saying "this was wrong!"
Therapist:	And in the meantime, life passes you by.
Client:	Yes. (*seems almost tearful*)
Therapist:	You know, what happened will never be okay. You know that, you know that what happened wasn't okay. Even if you went ahead and lived the most fabulous life, that wouldn't change, it wouldn't make what happened to you okay.
Client:	I see that. What's that saying, "Living a good life is the best revenge"?
Therapist:	Exactly.

The dynamic highlighted above can also be seen when working with individuals who experienced a trauma wherein someone close to them was killed. Combat veterans, for example, often struggle with feelings of survivor's guilt. As applied here, this can be conceptualized as needing to be the corpus delicti for their fallen comrades. We would work with this similarly:

Therapist: (*after introducing the concept of corpus delicti*) So if you have been the evidence for what happened over there in Iraq, how has that helped your fellow marines?

Client: I don't know that it has. I just feel like I didn't deserve to make it out of there when they didn't.

Therapist: So if you were to go ahead and live a good life, would that be dishonoring them somehow?

Client: No. (*thinking a bit*) Actually, they would probably want that.

Therapist: Do you think that you could ever forget what happened there?

Client: No way!

Therapist: Would living a good life make you think that what happened over there wasn't terrible?

Client: No, it was terrible. No matter what kind of life I had, that would be the case.

Therapist: It sounds as though you've been sacrificing your life, not living, for no purpose then. Is that okay with you?

Client: No, actually, it's not.

Sticking Points for Clients

We have discussed certain barriers that can arise when clients begin to consider the concept of willingness, such as confusing willingness with the feeling of wanting something, or needing to be the evidence that something wrong occurred. The following section addresses additional issues that can prevent clients from moving into a stance of willingness.

Moving Through Swamps

As early as 1941, social philosopher Eric Fromm wrote of the burden of freedom, a concept that also interested existentialists such as Sartre and Camus. The idea that we are truly responsible for our lives, including our identity, our behavior, and our choices, can be experienced as a frightening burden, and we often see this manifest in our work with trauma survivors. At this point in ACT, clients have difficulty continuing to blame the usual suspects (for instance, the trauma or uncomfortable thoughts and feelings) for the fact that their lives aren't working. Willingness in this sense is a double-edged sword. On the one hand, clients have tremendous freedom—by being willing to have whatever internal experiences are there at the moment, they can then choose to go live life despite their trauma and everything associated with it. On the other hand, clients are ultimately on the hook for how they live their lives. This can be particularly frightening for clients who do not have histories of living well. They are being challenged to give up all their reasons for not living well and move forward into the unknown. Clients typically demonstrate their fear of this by being unwilling—unwilling to have whatever feelings are present or unwilling to participate fully in the session, and so forth. This barrier will be addressed more fully in chapter 9, but in the meantime we work with it by continuing to present the client with the choice to be willing and encouraging them to simply have and hold whatever it is they are experiencing. We have also used the swamp metaphor (Hayes et al., 1999) as a way to help clients understand their dilemma and to choose willingness:

Therapist: It's as though you are in a swamp. You are in a swamp, and you want to get to the other side of the swamp. You can see your values and a life well-lived over there. You know that you want to get there, but the only way to the other side is through the swamp. Waiting for more information or until you feel more confident or less anxious won't get you there either. It requires willingness—willingness to take one step forward at a time even though you might get muddy in the process. If you aren't willing to get muddy, you will not move forward. Life is very much like that. Would you be willing to get muddy if it got you to the other side of the swamp?

Being Right

An additional sticking point for clients is the need to be right. As mentioned earlier, clients often desire some sort of validation that something shouldn't have happened or acknowledgment that someone else was wrong in what happened to them. Some clients will say that they can't get over it (live good lives) unless their perpetrator is punished or at least takes responsibility for their actions, even when clients understand that this reluctance has negative consequences for themselves as well. In this case, we frankly point out that they are apparently willing to sacrifice their lives in the service of being right. Clients are typically taken aback by this, and begin to consider whether they want to spend more years engaged in being right.

Sticking Points for Therapists

We have mentioned the importance of remaining rigorous with yourself when providing acceptance and commitment therapy. You must remain vigilant, looking for ways in which you might be inadvertently countering the objectives of this therapy.

Unwillingness

An obvious sticking point for therapists is not being willing themselves. In such cases it is inevitable that the client will receive control messages, either by observing the therapist's avoidance or by being directly told something by the therapist that supports avoidance. This is one reason why it is so key that ACT therapists practice willingness and conceptually agree with the theoretical underpinnings of ACT. In being willing to have whatever internal experiences show up in the therapy, and in being willing to allow clients to have whatever comes up for them during therapy, ACT therapists can then move through the protocol in an ACT-consistent manner. The willingness of the therapist is also one of those intangible factors that helps make a therapist particularly effective. That is, with willingness comes vibrancy and authenticity. Therapists who are willing to remain present in the face of uncomfortable feelings are able to connect more fully with what is happening in the room—and something real and powerful can then occur.

Homework

Homework assignments should be handed out to the client at the end of each session. Two homework assignments are provided as willingness is generally covered in two sessions (perhaps more). If you complete willingness in one session and you feel the client can complete both homework assignments, feel free to assign both. Be familiar with the assignments so that you can answer any questions that the client may have. Ask the client to bring the completed homework to the next session for review.

HOMEWORK ASSIGNMENT 1: WILLINGNESS

Instructions: Find some place in your life where you can be willing to engage in a behavior that you have put off for some time or a behavior that you don't do because your feelings or thoughts seem to tell you that you can't do it—that is, to be willing with your feet versus your feelings. This can be whatever you choose and can range in nature from a small action to a larger one. Some examples include the following: You want to isolate because you are feeling anxious, but you choose to be willing to feel anxiety and stay engaged, to not isolate. Or you want to call a friend and ask them to do something, but worry or fears of rejection are acting as a barrier. Instead choose to feel those feelings and make the call. Or you are angry with someone, but instead of just reacting, you choose to see what other feelings you might be having, like hurt. Be willing to feel those and then choose to do the thing that will be most helpful to you. Write a paragraph about your experience. Note what happened when you were willing and took action. How did things turn out?

HOMEWORK ASSIGNMENT 2: WILLINGNESS

Instructions: When we are unwilling to experience painful emotions and thoughts, we can get into struggles that keep us stuck rather than moving forward in our lives. We end up suffering over our pain. Imagine that it was 100 percent okay to feel pain, and that you didn't struggle with feeling it. Take a few minutes to let this notion take hold. Now write a paragraph or two about how your life might change if you were willing to feel your feelings and experience your thoughts. What would change? How do you think things would be different?

Moving Forward

Once you have established willingness as an alternative to control, you will want to help the client find a place where willingness is possible—where willingness can be fully engaged. This is done by exploring self-as-context. Willingness is possible when we are able to be in the moment—when we are able to connect to self-as-experience.

CHAPTER 7

Self-as-Context

I've been here all along!

—Jen, after completing the observer exercise

One of ACT's most unique and important contributions to the practice of therapy is its explicit emphasis on self-as-context. In this step of the protocol a distinction is drawn between one's self and the internal phenomena (thoughts, feelings, bodily sensations) experienced at any one time. Clients are helped to come into contact with the entity called the "self," to recognize the continuity of consciousness, and to observe (and accept) ever-changing internal experiences. One's "observer self" is then seen as the context within which other phenomena (content) comes and goes. We feel this concept is particularly powerful for individuals who have experienced trauma, providing them a way to acknowledge that something bad happened to them while not being defined by the event.

Session Format (2-3 Sessions)

- Open with mindfulness

- Review prior session

- Explore the power of self-as-context

- Examine trauma and the self

- Introduce the chessboard metaphor

- Introduce self-as-observer

- Discuss the concept of an intact self

- Explore sticking points for clients

- Explore sticking points for therapists

- Assign homework: self-as-context

- Moving forward

Opening with Mindfulness

As usual, each session begins with a mindfulness exercise. Not only does this help center and ready the client for the session, it also serves as practice for viewing internal phenomena from the perspective of the observer self. As clients progress through the protocol, the link between the mindfulness exercises and self-as-context can be made increasingly explicit.

MINDFULNESS EXERCISE 1:
RECOGNIZING MIND QUALITY MINDFULNESS
(Approximately 5-10 minutes)

Therapist: I would like everyone to start this exercise, as usual, by placing your feet squarely on the ground and sitting up in your chair so that your back is straight but not rigid. Assume the posture that we always take in these exercises, as it will help us to stay alert and focused. Let's begin by first noticing or paying attention to the fact that your body is actively sensing the environment. Notice that you can feel yourself sitting in the chair and you can feel your feet on the ground. Now, gently close your eyes. I would like you to place your attention at the tip of your nose and begin to notice the sensation of air moving in and out of your nostrils … Pay attention to your breathing. (*Continue with silently paying attention to breathing for about a minute.*)

Now I would like you to gently shift your attention to your mind's eye and imagine a place in nature like a garden or a park … perhaps a lake, stream, or mountain that you like to visit. Take some time to picture this place. Look around and notice all the sights and sounds there. Allow yourself to just be in this place. (*Wait about one or two minutes.*) Now imagine that, as you visit this place in nature, a swarm of gnats have come and are whirling around just above your head. They are flying this way and that. They make buzzing noises; some fly closer to your ear and sound louder, some rise high above your head at the top of the swarm and can barely be heard … And you know how it is that when you come across a swarm of gnats and you try to move away, they somehow follow? Well, that is what happens here. You step to one side and then the other, and that swarm still hovers over you. You may even try to run, yet still the swarm follows … See if you can take a minute and just let the swarm be there. Notice the buzzing but also notice that the gnats don't actually harm you. They just fly around, seeming to be a problem. They are very busy, but their busyness is really just a lot of noise and flying around. That's it. See if you can reconnect to this place in nature and just allow the swarm to be there. Stay with this place as gently as you can and invite the swarm to stay, allowing the swarm to do what it does … See if you can resist batting the swarm away, … gently remaining in this place of nature while also observing the swarm. Do the best you can settle into being aware and noticing the swarm. (*Allow a minute or two of noticing.*)

Now, gently releasing your attention from this place and the swarm, turn your focus to your breathing. (*Allow a few breaths.*) And then notice your body and how it feels to sit in the chair. Notice the placement of your feet, arms, and head. Picture what the room will look like, and when you are ready to return, rejoin the room by opening your eyes.

MINDFULNESS EXERCISE 2: FINDING-THE-CENTER MINDFULNESS
(Approximately 5-10 minutes)

Therapist: I would like to start this exercise just as we've started the others, making your posture alert while getting comfortable in your chair … Gently close your eyes and begin by focusing your attention on your breathing.

Spend these next few moments being aware of your breathing ... Follow each breath as you draw it in and out. (*Allow a minute or two to focus on breathing.*) Now, I'd like you to shift your attention to the area of your body that ranges from your hips to your shoulders. Focus on the area of your chest and belly. Narrow that attention further to find a place where you feel centered. Some of you may find it near your heart, and some of you may find it a little lower, closer to your belly or abdomen. Search for that place where you feel a sense of stability or a sense of slight heaviness—a place where your center of gravity seems to be located. As you focus on this place, see if you can allow yourself to just rest there. Spend time gently breathing into this center ... just being aware of this alive and stable place. (*Pause and allow time for clients to practice.*) If you find your mind drifting away, gently bring it back to this centered place, allowing yourself to rest there. Now, gently release your attention from this center and focus your attention on your body as you sit in your chair in this room. Picture the room in your mind's eye, and when you are ready, rejoin the room by opening your eyes.

Spend a few moments processing the exercise with clients. Exercise 1 may have caused a little surprise. Clients will comment that they didn't expect the swarm, and they didn't want it or like it. Here you can talk with clients about the nature of mind and how it can seem to be a swarm of activity at times and yet is still observable. Client reactions to exercise 2 range from a strong sense of connectedness to feeling unable to locate a center. In the latter case, you can work with the client in helping them to recognize this place as the observer, or perhaps talk about the center as the location of the soul if the client holds that belief. The point is to help the client locate a stable, centered place—a place of focus when getting centered is helpful.

Prior Session Review

Take a brief period of time to reflect back on the prior session and to check in with clients regarding their assigned homework:

- Being willing to engage an activity that has been put off and then writing about it

- Writing about willingness to experience thoughts and feelings

The Power of Self-as-Context

There are several significant advantages to viewing one's self as a context (Hayes et al., 1999). First, this viewpoint makes available the ability to experience various thoughts, feelings, and bodily sensations from a more helpful perspective. It is possible for clients to defuse from troubling thoughts and feelings when they can recognize a self that is more constant than or larger than such transitory phenomena. For example, rather than buying the thought that "I'm out of control; I'm going to lose it," the client learns to simply notice that thought (and associated feelings) from the stance of the observing self. From this stance of observation and acceptance, it is no longer paramount to fix or get rid of uncomfortable internal experiences.

A second advantage to operating from the perspective of self-as-context is that action is liberated from perceived control by thoughts and feelings. The individual is freed to make behavioral choices based on values, rather than in reaction to the thoughts or feelings they are having at the moment.

A third advantage is the reduction of suffering. While clients learn to accept without defense even very painful thoughts and feelings, the anxiety evoked by the belief that one shouldn't or can't have such thoughts and feelings is reduced. When seen as transitory phenomena, the potency of "negative" thoughts and feelings decreases, as they are no longer evidence that something is actually wrong or broken.

Finally, a powerful advantage to viewing one's self as context is the inherent supposition that that self, being larger than thoughts and feelings, has remained intact despite the trauma and the presence of even very disturbing thoughts, feelings, and bodily sensations. In our work with trauma survivors, we have found this realization to be one of the most powerful insights gained in conducting ACT.

Trauma and the Self

Despite the fact that selfhood is a fundamental aspect of being human, we have found that clients vary greatly in terms of the degree to which they endorse having a sense of self. There is often confusion regarding the distinction between consciousness and thoughts, and some clients struggle with identifying a self at all. We have found this latter problem to be particularly prevalent with trauma survivors. More specifically, many of the individuals we have worked with come to us with extensive trauma histories, including childhood physical and/or sexual abuse. Most of these individuals have a greatly impaired sense of self. Comments such as "I have no idea who I am" and "I'm afraid that under my anger there's nothing there" are not uncommon. In addition, many of the individuals we have treated fulfill diagnostic criteria for borderline personality disorder, a hallmark of which is an unstable sense of self. Those with less pervasive trauma histories may have more stable self-awareness but still seem to believe that the traumatic experience has irrevocably stamped itself upon their very personhood. Statements such as "I'm ruined" or "I'm not the man I used to be" are common.

The self-as-context component of ACT offers a clear gift to such clients. Not only does it help liberate behavioral choices from being artificially controlled by thoughts and feelings, it also helps clients recognize an intact self—*a whole self.* This is accomplished by direct discussion, by the use of metaphors, and with a series of experiential exercises designed to help clients access the observing self.

Playing Chess

A powerful way to help clients identify self-as-context is the chessboard metaphor (Hayes et al., 1999). For many of our trauma clients, this exercise is the most significant of any in the entire ACT protocol. We recommend using an actual chessboard as a way to make the concept introduced here more concrete and to maximize its impact. When doing group therapy, we will place the chessboard on the floor in the center of the circle of clients. We then begin to place the various white and black chess pieces on the board, explaining that they represent various experiences, thoughts, and feelings clients have had. We will often ask clients to give us examples of "good" and "bad" thoughts and feelings. As they call these out, we take a chess piece and place it on the board to represent that thought or feeling. As we continue, we group "bad" or uncomfortable experiences (chess pieces) together, making sure to include a particularly large chess piece or two as representative of their traumatic experiences, while "good" and comfortable pieces are also grouped together. We use the pieces to depict the struggle between "good" and "bad" thoughts, feelings, and so on, and to point out that there's no actual winning of *this* game. That is, just as history is additive (we can't erase our histories, our traumas), this board extends endlessly in all directions as an infinite plane, and as we go about life we are continuously picking up new experiences (demonstrated by adding pieces to the board). In the course of this demonstration, the client might suggest, "Just throw the bad pieces off the board!" In response, the therapist simply places another chessboard figure on the board to represent that strategy (that thought). We also point out how scary a chess piece is when you are so focused on getting rid of it. (We have been known to get down on our hands and knees and place our heads close to the figures—as if looking under a car—and peer up at the pieces from that vantage point. Clients can see how large pieces appear when viewed from that angle.) The therapist continues:

Therapist: We don't want these pieces. (*Therapist pointing to the pieces that are evaluated as bad.*) They are painful, and so we fight the good fight. Sometimes we devote our lives to trying to get rid of these pieces that can't actually be gotten rid of! How many of you can relate to this?

Clients are typically quite engaged in this exercise and clearly relate to the game of war between the good and the bad pieces. We point out that even the process of coming to us for treatment is yet another attempt to be rid of their trauma history—another piece on their board. We then ask, since it clearly isn't fruitful to engage in this battle that can't be won, if there is any other way to approach it:

Therapist: What if you weren't the content of those good and bad pieces? Keeping with this metaphor, is there anything else you could be besides the chess pieces?

Client: The player?

Therapist: Well, you could be the player. You could try to move these pieces around in an effort to win. (*Moves the pieces around on the board a bit.*) However, you can see that doesn't really change things—the player is still caught up in the game. We know that doesn't work. Which piece of yours has been successfully removed? (*Pauses for a moment.*) Can you think of anything else you can be besides the pieces or the players?

We try to have clients come up with the idea of being the chessboard, as an aha! moment. This seems to have greater impact than having the metaphor spelled out for them. We might pick up the chessboard and hold it in front of them at eye level, for example. Once they come up with the idea of being the board, we go on to emphasize several important points:

Therapist: Now that's an interesting idea, being the board. Notice how you would still have all the pieces but be free to go where you want to go. (*We walk around balancing the board at this point.*) What else do you notice about the board? (*We rap our knuckles against the board.*)

Client: It's strong and solid.

Therapist: Yes, it is in a sense solid; it is whole. Are the pieces the board?

Client: No.

Therapist: Right, but the board is in contact with the pieces. It is aware of the pieces ... It experiences the pieces. Is it invested in the game? Does the board care who wins?

Client: No.

Therapist: So from this space, from the place of being the board, can you see how it can hold all the pieces, experience them and yet not be them?

Client: Yes.

Therapist: And, again, the board is solid and free to move around … free to take a direction while holding all pieces.

Our emphasis on the durability of the board derives from an experience we had conducting ACT therapy with a young woman who had survived both military sexual assault and childhood physical and sexual abuse. After staring intently at the chessboard and pieces, she suddenly gasped and turned pale. Pointing to the chessboard, she exclaimed, "It's not broken! The board hasn't been broken by all the pieces!" This recognition of the self as a context that holds the pieces of experience, the traumas, the thoughts, the feelings, and so on, and yet somehow remains intact was a life-changing revelation for this client, as well as for the others in the group. This chessboard metaphor has particular relevance for abuse and sexual assault survivors who report an acute sense of being ruined or broken. This exercise helps them recognize that they are quite capable of carrying even the great burdens of such thoughts and memories without loss of self. It also is a good metaphor to use in exploring the concept of willingness. We emphasize that the chessboard is simply holding the pieces, not attempting to control them or rid itself of them in any way. In that sense the board is free to move in a valued direction despite the presence of even very difficult pieces. To further help the client contact and experience the sense of a solid, continuous "board level" self—a self that is larger than thoughts, memories, and so forth—we focus on helping them to contact this sense experientially by use of the self-as-observer exercise.

Experiencing Self-as-Observer

The observer exercise (Hayes et al., 1999) is used to help clients understand the self-as-context component of ACT. Rather than attempt to verbally explain the concept at this point, guiding clients through this exercise helps them to experientially increase their awareness of the observer self. Clients are gradually taken back in time through various experiences they've had as a way to highlight the ongoing consciousness that has been present throughout their lives. We conduct the exercise much as originally described by Hayes and colleagues (1999); however, because our clients have extensive trauma histories, we direct the exercise a bit more. Specifically, we gently guide clients to think about experiences other than traumatic events. While we are careful to maintain an atmosphere of acceptance throughout the therapy regardless of what shows up in the room, the objective of this exercise is to help clients contact the observer self. It is easy for clients at this point in the therapy to become embroiled in traumatic memories and risk missing the point of the exercise.

Therapist: (*at a slow, relaxed pace that provides plenty of time for clients to get settled and to access various memories*) I want you to close your eyes and get comfortable … Notice your breathing … Notice your weight in the chair … Notice any sounds you might be picking up in the room … Now think of an experience you had this morning—it doesn't matter what it was, just go with the first thing that pops up in your mind. When you have something in mind, raise your index finger so I'll know you've thought of something … Good. Now, thinking of this experience, see if you can remember what was going on around you at the time … What were you doing? … Where were you? … Was there anyone else around you, or were you alone? … Can you remember some thoughts you were having? … What were you feeling? (*Again, this is done slowly, with plenty of time between the various sensory memories clients are being asked to access.*)

Now I want you to think of something you experienced last week. Perhaps a conversation with a friend, some task you accomplished … It doesn't matter what it is, just whatever comes to mind. Raise your finger to let me know when you have it … Good. Now see if you can remember what was going on at that time … What were you seeing around you? … Can you remember some thoughts you had at the time? … What feelings can you recall having? … Can you remember any sounds you might have been hearing? … Can you see that the person having that experience last week is *you* … the same "you" that had the experience this morning? It is the same person who is hearing various sounds and having various thoughts and feelings right now. There is a *you* there that remembers that event from last week, the same you that remembers what happened this morning, the same you that is hearing me say this right now. Let's follow this out further.

Go back now to something that you can remember experiencing last summer. Take your time … Just think of something you experienced then, and let me know when you've got it by raising your finger … Good. Again, can you remember being in that situation? … Can you remember what you were seeing around you … the sound of your voice if you were speaking to anyone? … What you were thinking at the time? … Can you remember any of the emotions you were having? … Look around the memory and really see what was there, observe what you were experiencing … As you see this memory, notice that it is the same you having this memory as the you that had a memory from last week and this morning. A continuous you, a you that is sitting here right now doing this exercise with me.

Now let's go back to something that happened in high school, perhaps a particular class or a vacation. No rush, just allow your mind to go back there and let me know when you have it … Good. Now do the same thing; recall all you can about that situation … Where were you? … What was around you? … Take a good look inside this memory and, as you do, notice the continuous you, notice who is observing this memory. You were there then, and you are here now. It is the same you that was there last week, this morning, last summer. A you that is larger than any memory.

Now let's think of something that you experienced as a young child, perhaps a family vacation or a holiday, maybe an interaction with your favorite elementary school teacher … Good. Can you remember any feelings you were having at that long-ago time? … Any thoughts? … Can you remember being that person who was having that experience? That is the same continuous you, that being who had the other experiences as a child, last summer, and this morning, who has been aware that these things have been happening to you—the you that has been there all along and is sitting in this room right now hearing me say this.

You may notice that within the previous paragraph is an example of how clients with childhood traumas can be gently guided to think of a nontraumatic event. You might choose to do this so the client can remain focused on the point of this exercise, identifying the observer self, rather then getting caught up in traumatic content. However, first and foremost is the idea that even very painful thoughts and feelings that show up during the course of therapy are welcome. Should clients begin to experience traumatic memories, it is important to avoid sending messages that such phenomena need to be controlled or fixed. In such instances you can help clients to simply notice what they are experiencing and point out the continuous self that was present at the time of the trauma, during more positive experiences, and in the present moment.

After clients are guided to imagine various times in their lives, they are then asked to consider the many roles they have played as another way to recognize the observer self.

Therapist: (*continues*) Now let's shift gears a bit. I want you to think about the various roles you've had and currently have in your life. For example, think of your role as being someone's child, or someone's sibling. Now think of your role as parent … as neighbor … as friend. Think of your role as client … as citizen … as employee. (*Pause between these different roles to allow time for clients to formulate the roles in their minds.*) Think of how varied these roles are, and yet it's the same you, the same continuous you in all of them. There is a you there that is aware of these roles and, yet, is larger than these roles. (*Pause again.*)

Let's move on to another area, your body. Take a moment and think about how your body looked as a child. Were you tall? Thin? Short? Chubby? Picture how small your hands were … Now move forward in time, picturing your body as a teenager or a young adult … Notice what your body was like at that time … And now notice your body today … Think of how it has changed … Perhaps you have scars that you didn't have when you were younger, or maybe you've had an operation where some part of your body was removed … Maybe you have lost hair or gained weight. Notice how your body has changed across the years. (*Pause between different times of reflecting on the body to allow time for clients to formulate what their body looked like at that time.*) And even as you sit here, notice that your body is changing—cells are being repaired, food is being digested, oxygen is being fed to all parts of your body … As you notice all of these changes in your body, notice who is noticing … There is a you there that knows that this is your body now and that was your body back then. A you that is larger than your body … A you that has been there all along.

Some clients have a difficult time thinking about their bodies, especially individuals who have been sexually victimized. If it seems that a client or clients are reacting negatively to thinking about their bodies, make a comment that acknowledges this, such as "Some of you may even not like to think about your body, and yet you know it is there. Notice how you have evaluated your body across time. Sometimes you may have felt good about your body, and other times you may have felt bad, yet through all of those evaluations you knew that it was your body, just as you know it is your body now, in this room." Next, continue with a similar exploration of feelings, and then thoughts.

Therapist: (*continues*) Let's explore two more areas that may be a bit more difficult to see. Take a moment to notice what it is that you are feeling in this moment. See if you can describe it to yourself. Also notice that you have felt many, many emotions. Almost too many to list. Notice that your emotions at times have been high and that at times they have been low … Observe that you have had excitement and joy and sadness and anxiety … Notice that within these emotions you have experienced different levels of intensity … sometimes a great deal of anxiety, sometimes just a little, sometimes you have been laughing, and sometimes only smiling. Your emotions have been complex and difficult to describe, and then sometimes easy, not so complicated. As you notice all of these emotions, notice who is noticing: a you that has felt it all. A you that knows that these emotions come and go and come and go again. A you that is larger than your emotions.

And now let's take a look at one last place; your thoughts. Take a moment to notice that you are thinking … Notice that the things you think now may not be the things that you thought some time ago. Your thoughts have grown in complexity. You know things now that you didn't used to know, and you may have forgotten things you had once learned. Your mind is full of thoughts, shifting, refocusing, learning, remembering—thoughts are coming and going all the time. As you notice your thinking, once again notice who is noticing … There is a you there that experiences your thoughts and yet is not your thoughts. A you that is larger than any single thought. There is a you that is sitting here now, the same you that had those memories, the same you that plays those roles, the same you that is aware of your body, your emotions, and thoughts. A you that is larger than these things, an observer you—a continuous sense of you that stretches across all of these experiences and is larger than these experiences.

The client is then guided to reorient to the present moment and, when refocused, is asked to share what their experience was with the exercise. At this point we explicitly examine the concept of self-as-context, using elements of the just-completed exercise as examples of context versus content. It is important to directly ask clients whether they were able to identify with the observing self. When we conduct this exercise with groups, it is not unusual for at least one individual to state that they weren't able to contact a sense of self, particularly if they already suffer from impaired self-identity. The importance of the concept is apparent in the frustration and anxiety this provokes—such clients greatly fear they have no self. We have found it helpful to do immediate, in-the-moment work with these individuals:

Therapist: So, are you aware of yourself looking at me right now? (*client nods*) … You know that you are sitting there looking and listening to me? … Can you feel your own body weight in that chair? … Can you feel the temperature of the room? (*client agrees*) … Can you hear yourself answering me? (*client nods*) … Can you hear anything else in the room as well, like the hum of the air conditioner? … Can you catch any thoughts you're having? … Are there feelings you can identify? (*client says: "Yes, a little anxious."*) Are you aware of yourself speaking to me right now? … Okay, that person who is aware of all that, that is your observing self—the continuous you who knows what you are experiencing right now and what you have experienced in the past.

This strategy has proved effective even with clients with a very impaired sense of self. They typically evidence both relief and surprise that recognizing the self is that simple. Many rightly identify this as a core issue. Jen, the person quoted at the beginning of this chapter, had tears streaming down her face at the conclusion of the observer exercise. She could hardly contain her excitement as she exclaimed, "I've been there all along! All this time I've felt so lost, but I've been here all along!" This insight marked a major turning point for this client. We have also had clients with borderline personality disorder report spontaneously practicing the awareness exercise just described as they went about their daily lives, as a way to integrate and "get to know me."

Elements of this exercise can also be effectively used to center an individual who is dissociating. For example, someone who has been triggered and is reliving a past traumatic event can be quickly guided back to the present by reconnecting with the observer self:

Therapist: Are you thinking about what happened to you in the past? (*client nods*) Can you still hear the sound of my voice right now? (*client nods*) Can you actually say yes?

Client: Yes.

Therapist: Did you hear the sound of your voice just now?

Client: Yes.

Therapist: What other sounds are you hearing right now? Can you hear the sound of the ventilation in the background?

Client: Yes.

Therapist: Can you feel the arms of the chair you are holding? How would you describe what you're touching? As smooth or sort of rough?

Client:	Sort of smooth, I guess, and cool.
Therapist:	Are you aware that you are sitting in this room, with your peers beside you? Are you aware of their presence?
Client:	Yes. (*Client looks distressed again.*)
Therapist:	Did you have another thought just then about the trauma? (*Client nods.*)
Therapist:	So, now notice that you had that thought, and that some feelings came up with it, but that you're having other thoughts as well. There is a constant stream of thoughts coming and going, as well as sensations and feelings. For instance, can you feel your weight in that chair? Can you feel the temperature of the room on your skin? (*Continue in this vein.*)

Using this technique, we have seen even very distressed clients reorient to the present in only a couple of minutes. Several things are accomplished with this intervention: (a) clients are guided to connect with the observer self that is larger than the traumatic memory; (b) in so doing, they are able to view their traumatic memory from a different perspective and the memory itself is less frightening; (c) clients learn that thoughts are just thoughts—they come and go; (d) they learn that at any one time there is a host of stimuli that they are experiencing; and (e) it is pointed out that something (such as a trauma-related thought) just happened to have grabbed their attention. There is something extremely reassuring for clients about this quick exercise—a seeming relief that such experiences can be put into their proper place.

Many of the clients that we work with either check out easily or are sleepy, perhaps sedated due to medications. Under these circumstances, a longer eyes-closed exercise, which the observer self tends to be, can promote a quick nap. To reduce this problem and make sure that clients are engaged in the exercise, we will change the order and do two segments (regarding their body and roles) out loud and in an interactive format. For example, we will ask the clients to describe their various roles and notice the differences between them, or ask them to describe their younger bodies and the changes they have noticed. The wording is essentially the same as noted above. We then have them close their eyes and continue with memories, emotions, and thoughts.

The following metaphors and exercises can be conducted in subsequent sessions addressing self-as-context (we usually spend several sessions addressing this issue). They are designed to further help clients contact this sense of self-as-context as opposed to self-as-content.

Cargo Space

The box-with-stuff-in-it metaphor (Hayes et al., 1999) graphically demonstrates how private events—thoughts, feelings, and physical sensations—constitute content that is contained or experienced by the self. When doing this exercise, we typically grab a box of tissues and a wastebasket and put both in front of the client (or, when in a group setting, in the middle of the group circle). We then conduct the following exercise, being sure to relate the metaphor to the client's trauma history:

Therapist: Let's say for a moment, that you are this wastebasket.

Client: *(laughs derisively)* That fits.

Therapist: Yes, let's agree that you've had some bad things happen to you. (*Takes a couple of pieces of tissue, crumples them up, and tosses them into the basket. The tissues represent ongoing experience like thoughts, emotions, etc.*) What else comes up for you when something reminds you about your trauma?

Client: I get really anxious. I start sweating. (*Therapist wads up a couple of pieces of tissue and throws them in the basket.*)

Therapist: What comes up next?

Client: I start thinking I'm going to lose control. (*Therapist wads up a tissue and tosses it in.*)

Therapist: Then what?

Client: I try to distract myself. Sometimes I go shopping or I drink. (*Therapist crumples up several tissues and throws them in.*)

Therapist: What comes up with that?

Client: Shame—I hate myself. (*Therapist throws in a couple of tissues.*)

We typically engage in this exercise for a while as a way to emphasize the point and to create a big pile of tissues in the basket.

Therapist: (*throwing a final tissue in*) Isn't this interesting? All these pieces (*stirs around the tissues*) have to do with the first one. Instead of getting less important, the initial thought about the trauma got more important. The more you try to get rid of it, the bigger it gets! Even if we cover it up, it's still there, and since you're the basket, you know it's there. And if you are really determined not to have it, your life can become about covering it up, trying to squish it down, hide it away. (*pause*) But what if it's the case that you just hold these events? … Notice that the tissues are not the basket, they are just something the basket holds.

Anything the client says at this point is another tissue to be added to the basket. It is helpful to remind clients that history is additive, not subtractive. That is, history is unidirectional; we can only have more experience—even trying to remove a tissue is more experience.

This metaphor effectively demonstrates (a) that thoughts and feelings are content held within the self, (b) that control efforts are not only ineffective but add to the problem, and (c) that there is a cost to spending one's effort and energy on attempts to make unwanted thoughts and feelings go away.

Label Parade

Of course clients vary in their ability to grasp ACT concepts, and it is important to continually assess whether or not a particular idea has been understood. As your comfort level with the material increases, you will likely discover novel ways to make a particular point. For example, in working with a group of female trauma survivors who seemed to struggle with abstract concepts, we spontaneously created a labeling exercise (see also Walser & Pistorello, 2005) to further help delineate self-as-context. This exercise is similar to the box-with-stuff-in-it metaphor, but it helps to make the self-as-context concept even more personally relevant.

The labeling exercise can be done in individual therapy, but it lends itself particularly well to a group setting. Gathering a stack of index cards, a marker, and a tape dispenser, the therapist asks for a volunteer and sits across from the individual in the group or has the group member come and stand next to the therapist. The therapist hands the tape dispenser to a neighboring peer and then takes up the marker and prepares to write on an index card. The therapist also asks for permission to tape the cards to the client's body.

Therapist: Tell me something that you struggle with.

Client: My life sucks. (*The therapist quickly scribbles "Life sucks" on an index card, hands it to the group member with the tape dispenser, and tells this person to tape the index card somewhere on the participating client's body. This typically elicits some laughter from the group.*)

Therapist: What comes up for you when you have that thought that life sucks?

Client: It's not fair. (*The therapist scribbles "Not fair" on a new card and hands it to the client's peer, who then tapes it on the client. There is typically a sense of playfulness at this point in the exercise.*)

Therapist: What shows up right after "It isn't fair?"

Client:	My PTSD. (*Peer attaches card.*)
Therapist:	What comes up for you right after PTSD?
Client:	Something's wrong with me. (*Peer attaches card.*)
Therapist:	What comes up with "Something's wrong with me"? What follows right after that?
Client:	Fear, some sadness. (*Peer attaches two cards, which read "Fear" and "Sadness."*)
Therapist:	Then what?
Client:	Why can't I get over this? (*Peer attaches card reading "Why can't I get over this?"*)
Therapist:	What next? What feelings come up right after that?
Client:	Depression. (*Peer attaches card.*)
Therapist:	What shows up with depression?
Client:	I hate myself. (*Peer attaches "Hate myself."*)
Therapist:	What next?

Client:	I don't want to live. (*Peer attaches this card to the client. At this point there is typically a somber, heavy feeling in the room as the client and other group members get caught up in the content of what the individual is expressing. The therapist simply proceeds in a compassionate yet matter-of-fact way.*)
Therapist:	What follows right after "I don't want to live?"
Client:	Hating myself more. (*Peer attaches card.*)
Therapist:	What comes up after "Hating myself more"?
Client:	I don't know; it just sucks!
Therapist:	So we're back to "Life sucks." Is that how it usually goes for you, in a kind of cycle like this?

After highlighting this last point, the therapist then repeats the exercise with the other group members so that, in the end, there is a group of individuals covered head to toe in index cards. If one wishes to drive the point of this exercise home even further, it can be useful to have clients generate a list of positive internal experiences as well as those describing something they struggle with. For example, after engaging in the activity described above, we might ask clients to come up with a triumph, to think of something they are good at, or to relate a compliment they've received. We will then generate cards depicting the associated thoughts and feelings that come up around that initial idea as a way to again demonstrate the powerful yet transitory internal phenomena that are so quickly and easily evoked.

When we have completed taping on index cards, we then divide the group members into two groups and ask each group to stand in an opposite corner of the room. (This is an elaboration on the labeling exercise.) After allowing a few minutes to simply observe each other, we will ask one of them what they see when they look across the room at their peers. What we are pulling for here is the realization that the content on the cards is made up of just words, that the person standing there covered in index cards is not defined by the words on the cards, they are larger than all the content that is taped to them. The person is context, not content. In addition, if we only have time to label two clients, we have them walk around the group with their cards on, facing each person in the group and looking them in the eyes. We ask the group members to look back and notice, and then we continue to process the exercise as noted here.) Sometimes this realization is arrived at rapidly; at others it requires more guidance:

Therapist: So Karen, what do you see when you look across the room at your peers?

Karen: I see a bunch of women looking pretty silly covered in cards. There are a lot of cards!

Therapist: What else do you see?

Karen: (*pauses, thinks*) I just see my friends there. They're standing over there with all this stuff on them, but that's not how I see them.

Therapist: Are you saying that they're not that bunch of cards? That they are more than all that?

Karen: Yes! Those are just labels—it's not them.

Of course, this exercise may not always go so easily. In the ACT groups we conduct, we often look for volunteers who are likely to get the point of the exercise and model for the others in the group. The following is an example of a more challenging situation. In this case we had taped cards to only two members of the group, who were now in opposite corners of the room:

Therapist:	What do you see when you look across the room, Cheryl? What do you see when you look at Kristin?
Cheryl:	*(gazing fixedly at Kristin's cards)* I understand now why she wants to kill herself.
Therapist:	Why is that?
Cheryl:	Well, look at that! It's horrible! I wouldn't want to live either!
Therapist:	*(thinking rapidly)* What card are you reading that brings up that thought for you? *(Notice this choice of words—a subtle suggestion that thoughts are transitory and easily evoked, and that one has them, versus one is them.)*
Cheryl:	Well, that one that says "I'll never change" and that one, "I'll always be alone."
Therapist:	What feelings come up for you when you read that?
Cheryl:	Hopelessness.
Therapist:	Okay, good. Now, can you imagine if Kristin had a card that read "Tough stuff has happened to me, but I've never given up; I have always survived?"
Cheryl:	*(thinking)* What does it say again?
Therapist:	It says, "Tough stuff has happened to me, but I've never given up; I have always survived." What feelings do you think you would have if you were reading that card on Kristin?
Cheryl:	Well, I think I'd have a sense of hope.
Therapist:	Do you think that statement applies to Kristin?
Cheryl:	Yes, it's true—she has never given up.
Therapist:	Are there other strengths about Kristin that we could tape on her?
Cheryl:	Yes, like "I'm brave" and "I'm strong."
Therapist:	So there are a lot of things we could tape on Kristin, and some of them would bring up nice feelings, while others would bring up uncomfortable feelings. Does any one card define her?
Cheryl:	No, not just one.
Therapist:	Do all those cards define her?

Cheryl:	No. That's not who she is.
Therapist:	She's more than that.
Cheryl:	Yes, she's much more than that.

Along with learning the explicit self-as-context concept illustrated by the labeling exercise, clients have had the opportunity to experientially learn several key ideas. For example, they see firsthand how easily even very painful thoughts and feelings can be generated. It becomes clear how almost arbitrary this process is; that is, that positive thoughts and feelings can be just as easily recalled. In addition, the playfulness of the exercise creates a sort of therapeutic irreverence; the absurdity of being covered in cards depicting such painful content serves to help clients defuse from such content. And because at some point in the exercise clients are often pulled into the painful content of the cards, the therapist has the opportunity to highlight what happens when clients start buying their thoughts:

Therapist:	Did you notice that as you started buying what the cards said, you became more and more distressed? You started by laughing and having fun, and then you began to identify with what the cards were saying and became quite upset. Then a little while later, as we talked about a positive experience you've had and the thoughts and feelings that come up with that, you had a different experience—all this in a matter of minutes!

We also begin to work more directly with language, explaining the difference between having a thought or feeling and holding that thought or feeling to be true.

Therapist:	Just now during the labeling exercise, we saw what happens when we start to buy the various thoughts or feelings we are having as truth. Even though we all agreed that thoughts and feelings are just that, thoughts and feelings, and that we are larger than the content written on all those cards, we saw what happens when we start to buy into them. For instance, listen to the difference between "I am such a loser; I am so depressed" and "I'm having the thought again that I'm a loser; I'm having a feeling of sadness." One sounds terrible and hopeless, whereas the other reminds us that there is a self, *a continuous you*, who is having this experience but who is more than, larger than, those thoughts and feelings. Language is extremely potent—it has helped in many ways, and yet it can also be a problem. It is important to work with your language so that you remain in contact with the observer self.

From this point forward we gently correct clients when, while speaking, the[y] with their thoughts or feelings, and we correct ourselves as well! In fact, clie[nts] quite good at (and seem to enjoy) pointing out to us when we err in this way.

Programming

Once an ACT metaphor has been introduced, it can be repeatedly referred to as the occasion warrants. For example, we have found it effective to remind clients of the two computers metaphor (Hayes et al., 1999) at this point, as another example of the difference between buying and observing content:

Therapist: Remember the two computers we drew on the board? Where one person was right up against the computer, almost climbing into the monitor, and the other was sitting back reading the screen? Both might be reading the exact same text, "I am broken," but the one sitting back can recognize that those words are programming, content, whereas the other thinks the words are literally true.

The Self Is, and Remains, Intact

A second key concept in this component of ACT is the idea that the self (the self that is context, not content) is intact. That is, despite past learning, past traumas, negative self-evaluations, and so forth, the self is not broken and is inherently acceptable. Because this flies in the face of what most clients have been led to believe, the use of metaphors and other experiential techniques is particularly helpful in getting this message across.

At the conclusion of this section of ACT the following objectives have been met: (a) clients have been made experientially and explicitly aware of the observer self as the context within which private events come and go; (b) they have recognized the continuity of consciousness and that this consciousness is larger than the various internal phenomena they experience; (c) they have realized that the self is intact and capable of experiencing even very difficult thoughts and feelings; and (d) that if that is the case, one does not need to be rid of such phenomena in order to be whole.

Sticking Points for Clients

The two sticking points for clients discussed here mainly concern fusion. That is, clients remain fused with their minds and have difficulty taking the observer perspective.

Holding Too Tightly to an Identity

Occasionally clients will become so fused with the content of their minds that they fully hold that content as who they are. For instance, as mentioned earlier, the client identifies herself as a victim and she loses the distinction between having been a victim and currently being a victim, or the Vietnam Era vet sees himself "as Vietnam" rather than as someone who experienced Vietnam. Holding tightly to these identities can be costly. Often clients have lost contact with the fact that they have many identities, for example that of a mother or father, a son or daughter, a lover or friend, and these roles suffer as a result of the client clinging to a particular identity. Sometimes this manifests itself in complaints by others, who say things like, "For Joe, everything is about Vietnam, even breakfast." Here it is helpful to gently point out the costs of clinging to this identity while also acknowledging the importance of the history. For clients in this position you might have them do the homework assignment at the end of this chapter: Self-as-Context: Letting Go of Identity as a way to help loosen the grip. You also might try this same exercise in session and work through it with the client(s).

Missing the Point of Ongoing Experience

Some clients will have difficulty seeing that emotions and thoughts come and go; they connect to them as being more stable and ever present. It is most helpful for these clients to do present-focused work. Here you can have the client be aware of their body, thoughts, emotions, and sensations in an ongoing moment-by-moment process. Have them state out loud what comes into their awareness, for example "I am aware that I am thinking about this exercise, I am aware that I am uncomfortable in the chair, I am aware that I have an itch on my elbow." This exercise points to the movement of experience. It is not to say that an experience moves and then never returns—the client will have an itch again—but rather that each moment contains something different to be experienced.

Sticking Points for Therapists

The following are two particular sticking points that can easily arise for the therapist when dealing with self-as-context. As you read them, you will notice they are also challenges that can arise throughout the protocol, and it is important to be watching for them as you conduct the therapy.

Buying Your Own Identity

One pitfall for the therapist in doing this part of the protocol involves the belief in one's own self-concepts. For example, therapists may view themselves as professionals and may overidentify with this sense of self. This can show up in therapy in a number of ways, including taking a "one-up" position with the client (for instance, that the therapist knows best because they are the professional) or by letting strategies designed to maintain that identity interfere with therapy in some way (worrying excessively about what the client thinks of you, establishing your credentials, your intelligence, your ability, etc.). We recommend practicing mindfulness, doing the homework assignments, and holding your own identity lightly.

Buying Your Own Thoughts

This happens when therapists start to believe their own thoughts about the truth of the words used in this therapy or the words they are saying about a client's struggle. This is a bit of a tricky issue. Perhaps we can describe it with an example. We had a therapist in training who got caught in the content of being the board in the chessboard metaphor. He couldn't see that this description was also made up of words, a way of pointing to an experiential sense of being. He stated, "But isn't it true that I am the board?" Of course, the answer was "That is also a thought you are having." This can begin to take on the quality of feeling like you are falling backward in space and that there is no place to stand with respect to words at all. The therapist even stated, "I feel like I'm falling backwards." We simply asked him to notice that his feet were on the ground and that he was there, having that ongoing experience. The best solution for this issue is to remember that we and our clients are beings who are having ongoing experiences. Even when we think we have landed on something that must be true (because this therapy says so), remember, that is an experience too.

Homework

Homework assignments should be handed out to the client at the end of each session. Hand out one homework assignment per session. Two are provided because self-as-context is generally covered in two sessions (perhaps more). If you complete self-as-context in one session and you feel the client can complete both homework assignments, feel free to assign both. Be familiar with the assignments so that you can answer any questions that the client may have. Ask the client to bring the completed homework to the next session for review.

CLIENT HOMEWORK ASSIGNMENT 1:
EXPLORING SELF-AS-CONTEXT

Instructions: This homework assignment is designed to further help you contact self-as-context or connect with the self that experiences things like thoughts, emotions, and sensations as ongoing processes—as if they flow through you rather than being you. In this exercise, you will get practice being the observer self. Start by choosing two days between now and the next time we meet to do this exercise.

Day 1 _____

Day 2 _____

On each of these days, select three times throughout the day when you will pause for about five minutes and take the time to notice what you're thinking, feeling, and sensing. Write down these different experiences on the tracking sheet. Be descriptive and spend just a little time elaborating on these experiences. At the end of the third time, reflect back on all three five-minute periods and observe the differences between them. Take note of how your experiences changed throughout the day.

Once you have reflected on how your experiences changed throughout the day, prepare to do a five-minute meditation. Start with closing your eyes and reflecting back on these experiences. Spend time in the meditation noticing the you that had those experiences. Notice the you that was there continuously throughout those experiences. As you meditate, take comfort in the fact that you have been there all along—that there is a stable and continuous you that is aware of these experiences and knows that you are larger than these experiences. End the meditation by taking a moment to gently appreciate yourself for taking the time to contact this sense of self.

Write in your responses on the tracking sheet.

TRACKING SHEET

Day 1 **Time 1:**	**Day 2** **Time 1:**
Thoughts:	Thoughts:
Emotions:	Emotions:
Sensations:	Sensations:
Day 1 **Time 2:**	**Day 2** **Time 2:**
Thoughts:	Thoughts:
Emotions:	Emotions:
Sensations:	Sensations:
Day 1 **Time 3:**	**Day 2** **Time 3:**
Thoughts:	Thoughts:
Emotions:	Emotions:
Sensations:	Sensations:

Write a brief paragraph about your meditation experience on each day. What did you discover?

HOMEWORK ASSIGNMENT 2: SELF-AS-CONTEXT: LETTING GO OF IDENTITY

Instructions: This exercise is designed to further your connection with the observer self. Give yourself about thirty to forty minutes to complete this exercise. Find a place where you will not be interrupted, a place where you can have some personal quiet time while doing the exercise.

Read the following passage and then complete the writing and meditation.

Sometimes when we buy our thoughts or emotions, it is because we are holding on to a particular aspect of ourselves. It's as if we have linked ourselves to a particular identity, and we hold on to that identity as if there were no other way to view ourselves. For example, sometimes holding the identity of being a victim can become such a part of you that other aspects of yourself get lost. We can do this with many kinds of identities or self-concepts. You can have a self-concept as a professional, or as a strong person or a weak person, or as a doer of good deeds, or as a victim, a survivor, or a mom or dad, and so forth. The list can be long. From the observer perspective, all self-concepts or identities are to be held lightly—none of them to be taken as literally true. The aim of this exercise is to contact the sense of self that is larger than any identity. Start by writing a description of yourself as each of the identities listed below. Include what that identity would think, feel and look like:

- Your best self

- Your struggling self

■ Your _____ self (one of your choosing)

After you have a good description of each of those identities, find a quiet place to do a short meditation. As we have in session, take two to three minutes to observe your breath, allowing yourself to notice the breath as you follow it in and out. Then, gently shift your attention to your imagination and picture each of the identities that you have described, one at a time. As you picture each one individually, imagine what that image might say to you. Have that image say it as you practice just observing what is being said. After the image has said what you imagine it will say, imagine that you are holding a small version of the image in your hand. As you do this, say to yourself, "I hold this image lightly, as though I am a warm breeze holding a small floating feather. It is not me anyway." Do this with each of the images in turn. After you have gone through all of the images, say to yourself, "I hold these images lightly, like a warm breeze holding a small floating feather. They are not me anyway." Then gently shift your attention back to your breathing, taking two to three minutes to be aware of your breathing. Then return to the setting where you have chosen to do the exercise by gently opening your cycs.

Write a short reaction to the exercise.

Moving Forward

Once self-as-context is established and the client is in contact with the observing self (self-as-context), then freedom to make healthy choices is available. The client's experiences no longer need be the determiner of their path.

CHAPTER 8

Valued Living

The wisest men follow their own direction.

—Euripides

At this point in acceptance and commitment therapy, clients have arrived at an interesting place. Up to now they have been learning how to make room for their trauma histories, how to simply experience thoughts, feelings, and memories without engaging in unworkable control strategies. They have come to the important realization that, in fact, they are not slaves to their thoughts and feelings. All this begs the question "Now what?" If thoughts and feelings are simply phenomena to be experienced, if they are not in charge, then on what *do* we base our actions? Clients often convey a sense of being adrift at this point, all previous conceptions about what is needed in order to have a good life having been turned on their head.

The concept of valued living is introduced here as a foundation upon which to make one's choices, a direction in which to head. Clients can be helped to recognize their values and to commit to actions that support those values. The previous work regarding self-as-context plays a key role at this point. That is, the ability to understand that one can select values and make choices specific to those values entails the ability to defuse from thoughts and feelings. It is the self, that entity that is larger than such private phenomena, that ultimately gets to choose how one will live.

So why live according to our values? Because we can. Because by doing so we live lives of inherent value and vitality. We don't have to do this. In fact, each day we can make decisions based on how we are feeling, such as whether or not we're feeling loving, generous, or cranky, on whether or not we are feeling energetic or motivated. We could decide (and do decide) to base our choices on any number of things, and we give great reasons for why we do what we do. However, all these reasons don't amount to much when one looks back on a life without personal meaning. In our work with trauma survivors, we have found that clients' greatest source of regret and pain is about not having lived according to what is most important in their heart of hearts. In this chapter we will explore the concept of valued living and the strategies we have developed to help individuals with trauma histories acquire this key part of the ACT protocol.

Session Format (2-3 sessions)

- Open with mindfulness

- Review prior session

- Help clients identify their values

- Explore valued living

- Develop values and goals

- Examine values and trauma

- Explore sticking points for clients

- Explore sticking points for therapists

- Assign homework: identifying values

- Moving forward

Opening with Mindfulness

As in prior sessions, it is again useful to engage clients in mindfulness practice. Remember to get yourself and clients centered using techniques described throughout the book.

MINDFULNESS EXERCISE 1: COMPASSION MINDFULNESS
(Approximately 5-10 minutes)

Therapist: I would like to start this exercise just as we have started the others, making your posture alert while getting comfortable in your chair … Gently close your eyes and begin by focusing your attention on your breathing. Spend these next few moments being aware of your breathing … Follow each breath, becoming your breathing. (*Allow a minute or two to focus on breathing.*)

Now I would like you to shift your attention and spend a few moments thinking back on the struggle you have had with respect to your trauma and other painful events in your life … Notice how long you have been in a place of struggle … Notice the emotional battles and the desires to have it all be different … As you look back, also think about how much you have needed to be understood, accepted, and loved during these difficult times. (*Pause for a minute or two.*)

Now imagine that you are as large as the universe and that you have all of the capacity to hold these struggles, all the capacity to provide the warmth, acceptance, and love that was needed then and is needed now. Imagine that from this place of being as large as the universe, you could take a blanket of warmth and acceptance and wrap it around this struggle, letting it be what it is while holding it with compassion. Imagine this place for the next few minutes … Imagine that you can hold this struggle and be 100 percent acceptable and lovable. For these next few moments, you are whole. (*Pause and let the clients practice for several minutes; you may want to remind them that they have the capacity to offer compassion or take the stance of being whole any time.*)

Now, gently focus your attention on your body sitting in the chair, in this room … Picture the room in your mind's eye, and when you are ready, rejoin the room by opening your eyes.

Therapist: I would like everyone to start this exercise by placing your feet squarely on the ground and sitting up in your chair so that your back is straight but not rigid. Make sure that your head feels square to your shoulders and place your arms in a comfortable position at your sides. Gently close your eyes. (*Have clients focus on breathing for a few minutes as they have done in the past mindfulness exercises.*)

Now I would like you to turn your attention to your imagination. Picture in your mind a place that you enjoy going to, a place in nature that you consider beautiful and peaceful. It can be on a mountain, or next to a stream or lake, or in a park or backyard area. See if you can allow your imagination to make this place come alive. Notice all the colors and sounds that might be there. Think of this as your place of peace. (*Allow time for clients to formulate this image in their mind.*) Now that you can see this place, I would like you to hold this image while also attending to your breath. Imagine that you are sitting in this place and just breathing. Allow yourself to experience this place being full of breathing and noticing, observing all that you see. (*Have clients stay with this image and experience for a few minutes, letting them focus on both the image and their breath.*)

Now, releasing your attention from your breathing and this place, I would like you to gently place your attention on the image of this room and this group of people … and when you are ready, open your eyes.

Exercise 1 can be powerful in helping clients to bring compassion and acceptance to their experience. It can also bring up issues of nonacceptance and an inability to have compassion for their struggle. Work with clients to see if they can have even small moments of compassion. For instance, you might ask them to think of a time when they were in great pain, then ask if they are able to offer some kindness to that self who experienced that pain. It can be helpful to let clients know they can start with such a moment and then work toward growing this sense of acceptance. You may also ask how they would respond to another person who was having a similar difficulty and see if they can apply that response to themselves. In exercise 2, clients generally have a sense of feeling relaxed or at peace. However, they may also report being unable to connect to a place of peace during the exercise. Have the client work on finding this place by talking about a place where they have felt safe or peaceful in the past. See if they can use that as a reference for this exercise, even if only for short periods of time.

Prior Session Review

Take time to reflect back on the prior session and to check in with clients regarding their assigned homework:

- Exploring self-as-context

- Letting go of identity

Helping Clients Identify Their Values

As we have worked with individuals with trauma histories and PTSD, we have found that many of them have significant difficulty with the concept of values (for example, being a loving father, treating others with kindness, being honest). In general, it seems that such clients are particularly fused with long-held beliefs and self identities that impede the identification of values. For example, some combat veterans who have long evaluated themselves as being bad for things they have seen and done or who feel contaminated by their war experience struggle with giving themselves permission to have lofty values. Who are they to value loving relationships and being kind to others? Similarly, those with histories of childhood trauma seem particularly thrown when asked to identify their values. Their initial reaction is to worry that they won't be able to do it, or that what they'll come up with will be wrong or inferior in some way. Most of these clients are hesitant to aim too high, as though it is somehow presumptuous of them to have "big" values. We have noted that it frequently seems completely foreign for such clients to consider what *they* care about—an unsurprising reaction given that these individuals have extensive histories of being invalidated or even punished for voicing their wants, needs, and opinions

When developing the concept of values with clients, it is helpful for them to see that, in fact, they make many behavioral choices based upon values. For example, we might ask a group of residential treatment patients, "How many of you wanted to sleep in this morning? How many of you had thoughts and feelings about needing more sleep when the alarm went off?" Typically, every hand rises, after which we point out that, instead, they each got up at 6:30 a.m., went to the dining hall, and showed up for group on time—not because they were listening to their thoughts and feelings but because they were making choices based upon a larger value. Similarly, every time they come to group when they don't feel like it, when they take risks despite feeling fearful, they are making choices based upon certain values, such as to complete what they started, to learn, to create a better life for themselves. This dialogue helps clients to recognize some of their values, to see they are capable of making valued choices, and to recognize that these choices are not contingent upon the thoughts and feelings of the moment.

Choice Making

At this point in the therapy it is worthwhile to spend a little time on choice making. We mean something very specific here: the ability to choose simply because you can. Often clients feel that they have to have good reasons for why they make the choices that they do. We point out that choices can be made with or without reasons (Hayes et al., 1999).

Therapist: (*pretends to be holding two objects*) Imagine that I'm holding before you a Coca-Cola and a 7-Up. Which would you choose?

Client: The 7-Up.

Therapist: Why?

Client: Because I like 7-Up better than Coke.

Therapist: Why else would you choose 7-Up?

Client: Because it's lighter and crisper in taste.

Therapist: Great! Why else?

Client: Because I like the green color of the can.

Therapist: This is terrific! Why else might you pick 7-Up over Coke?

Client: Because the 7-Up doesn't have caffeine.

Therapist: Okay, great. We now have four very, very good reasons about why to choose 7-Up over Coke, right?

Client: Yes.

Therapist: Given all of those good reasons about why to choose 7-Up, could you still choose Coke? Could you take the Coke and drink it?

Client: Yes.

Therapist: Okay, here is the harder part. With all of your good reasons about why you can't live the life you value, such as you feel anxious, you have PTSD, and so on, could you choose things, regular activities, that are about your values even with all of your good reasons about why you can't?

Client: Yes, I suppose I could.

It is helpful at this point to remind the client that reasons are not causes of behavior. This concept can be further clarified by spending a bit of time with the client reflecting on how easily one can generate reasons and how little actual impact these reasons have on our behavior.

Providing Direction and Meaning Making

The what-do-you-stand-for exercise (Hayes et al., 1999) is designed to help clients identify what they value. Clients are asked to imagine their own funeral service and to imagine how they would like to be remembered. This, in turn, informs clients about what is most important to them. For example, if the client ideally imagines being remembered as a loving, supportive friend, that indicates that being a loving, supportive friend is something the client values. We begin the exercise by asking clients to shut their eyes and gradually become mindful of the present, where and how they are sitting, their breathing, and sounds in the room, and to notice emotions they are experiencing as well as passing thoughts. Once they are centered, we then move into the exercise.

Therapist: Now I'm going to ask you to imagine that you have traveled far into the future, so far in fact that you've reached the time of your death, and you are at your own funeral service. Imagine this time and place in the future. (*Be sure to provide adequate time for clients to evoke this image, as it is generally not what they were expecting.*) Now imagine the setting and allow yourself to make it as you would like it to be. Where would you like the service to be held? What would you like it to look like? (*This should be delivered at a slow pace, with adequate spacing between questions so that clients have time to evoke the images.*) Now, spend some time choosing who you would like to be there … Don't limit yourself by thinking of who is likely to be there or by evaluating who would and wouldn't want to come, and so on. This is about who *you* would like to have there. (*pause*) Who would you most want to witness this event? (*pause*) Let me know by raising a finger when you have someone in mind. Good. Now imagine that this person is getting up and speaking about who you were to them, how you impacted them, what they thought and felt about you, what they appreciated. It's very important that you give yourself permission to have them say what you would *ideally* like them to say about you. Not necessarily what you *think* they would say or fear they would say, but what you would most like them to feel or think about you. (*Provide ample time for clients to engage in this image.*) Now choose another person, someone else you would like to be at your funeral service, and again, have them talk about the things they value about you. Aim high! This is about how you would ideally like others to experience you.

The exercise continues like this for a while, providing clients ample opportunity to work through several scenarios. Another possibility is to be more directive in terms of who attends the funeral. That is, to suggest that the client's family be there, their partner, friends, and children, and perhaps coworkers and neighbors. Here's an example: "Now imagine that your partner is getting up to speak about who you were as a partner during your time here. Have her say whatever it is that you would like her to say, not what you think she would say." In this way, the client is guided through each of the other categories of individuals who might be present at the funeral. This doesn't necessitate going through each friend who is there; rather, have the client imagine a good friend and have that person stand and talk about the client. When this process is concluded, the client is guided to gradually reorient to the room and the exercise is processed.

Regardless of the careful directions described above, we find that many clients with trauma histories struggle with this exercise. In particular, they have difficulty envisioning how they would ideally like to be remembered. We have observed that many such clients remain locked into their histories and how they have been viewing themselves:

Client: I couldn't really come up with anything—my mom was there, but she never really had much to say to me. I didn't want my dad to be there … My sister might come if she had to, but we haven't talked since that big fight we had six years ago…

We have found that letting clients know the point of the exercise at the outset can mitigate this somewhat:

Therapist: This exercise is designed to help you discover what you care about, what matters to you. By giving yourself permission to dream, to aim high, to be bold, you will become clear on who you would really like to be in the world.

We have also done the following variation with success. Again, clients are guided through a brief centering exercise and then told the following:

Therapist: Now I want you to think about someone you admire—someone you have known, or someone you simply know of, who has had a meaningful impact on your life, someone you would like to be like. Raise your index finger when you have someone in mind … Good. Now imagine that you are at that person's funeral service. (*pause*) If you were to speak at the service, what would you say about this person? What did you most appreciate about them? In what ways would you like to be more like them?"

Although once-removed, this version of the exercise can help clients articulate values. For example, if they admire someone for being real or for making a difference, then being real and making a difference are values they hold. It is also possible to work with a client's experience during the what-do-you-stand-for exercise in such a way that values are eventually identified:

Therapist: You sounded sad when you were describing what you thought your children would say at your funeral. Why does that bring up the feeling of sadness? (*Note the wording of this last question subtly supports the idea of self-as-context versus fusing with the feeling of sadness.*)

Client: Because I realized they don't really even know me. I feel like I was a bad father—I was never around…

Therapist: If you could go back in time and do it all over again, what would you do differently?

Client: I would be a better dad!

Therapist: What would that look like, being a better dad?

Client: Well, I would have spent more time with them, been more involved with their lives … I would have listened more and tried to be more supportive.

Therapist: So, it sounds like being involved and supportive of your kids and being a good listener are values you have when it comes to being a dad?

Client: Yes, I guess so.

As seen in the above example, most of us do have values; we just don't always know that we do or what they are. Thoughts and regrets about past failures or disappointments are very salient—it's easier to stay fused with those sorts of evaluations than to see future possibilities. It is therefore useful at this point to discuss the concept of using values as a guideline for one's life.

Valued Living

As the term implies, "valued living" is about action, about behavior. It's not about reaching a destination; rather, it is about what will guide our choices as we move through life. The compass metaphor (Hayes et al., 1999) works nicely here (*dialogue continued from above*):

Therapist: Values are kind of like points on a compass. They point in a direction to follow. In this case, when it comes to your relationship with your children, your values can guide your behavior so that you can choose to listen better, to work toward being more involved in their lives. Regardless of where you've been in the past, regardless of what you have done or not done, those points on the compass remain.

It can be helpful to point out, in a concrete way, that the choices one makes ultimately define one's life:

Therapist: Just a few minutes ago you were expressing your sorrow over choices you have made in your relationships with your children. You know, we could be having this conversation five years from now, still talking about what a bad dad you've been. Or, you could choose to follow the points on your compass, making choices in the direction that points toward the sort of dad you want to be.

And:

Therapist: Imagine that it's five years from now, and you are looking back at the last five years. What do you think your life would look like if, more often than not, you made valued choices?

We have found that this latter statement seems to resonate with clients, perhaps because it helps them see how this abstract concept, valued living, would actually impact their lives. This sort of statement would not be offered earlier in therapy, however, as clients would likely use it as another control strategy: "Follow this strategy and your life will work out (you will feel good and avoid feeling bad)." Here, we're not focusing on how clients will feel in the next five years, rather on what they will do. In this way they can generally see how making valued choices could improve their overall quality of life in a meaningful way.

The compass metaphor also provides a way to address a common and potentially problematic reaction many clients have at this point in the therapy: When people fully grasp that their actions aren't constrained by even very difficult thoughts and feelings, they suddenly realize that this has always been the case. "You mean I could have been doing this all along?" is a frequent and poignant question. We address this as yet another experience to be had ("Thank your mind for that thought") and point out that the client could now make their life be about that (regret or remorse about missed opportunities), *or* they can consciously decide what to do from this day forward. We help the client see that values are not achievable in a final way, that they are not something someone fully acquires:

Therapist: Like the points on a compass, no one arrives at north or south. Rather, north and south are points to shoot for. Similarly, we don't arrive at "honest" or "loving," as though once there, there's no more to be done, no more need to be honest or loving.

Clients can be helped to see that if this is true, then it also follows that because they haven't always been loving or honest in the past, it does not have to mean anything about who they will be in the future. The question remains "What will you do with your life from this time forward?" It is important to note that in guiding clients as described above, we do not try to ameliorate feelings that arise, such as sorrow for time lost. These emotions are to be noticed and held, while still recognizing that one has the ability to make valued choices both now and in the future.

The headstone exercise (Hayes et al., 1999) is another way to help clients identify values. We ask them to imagine their own headstone and to think about what they would like it to say. We then discuss the meaning of this statement with the clients.

Therapist: Now I want you to close your eyes and get settled in your chair. Focus on your breathing … When you inhale through your nose, notice the sensation of air moving through your nostrils and filling your chest. Let the air out easily, and notice how you become a bit heavier in the chair as you exhale. Good. Now I want you to focus in on this question: "If you were, at some point far in the future, looking at your own

headstone, what would you like it to say? (*It is important to give clients plenty of time to think about this.*) Take your time; we have plenty of time … Just think about what you would like your headstone to say. When you have something, raise your finger so that I know you are done.

Another effective strategy is to do the headstone exercise by drawing two headstones on a whiteboard. On the first headstone write, "Paula [use the client's name or your own] was about…" Pause and then fill in the space; for example, "Paula was about making sure she didn't feel anxiety related to PTSD." On the second headstone do the same as above, but change the ending; for instance, "Paula was about being a loving mother." This demonstrates very clearly the concept of identifying values and the role choice plays in living a valued life.

Interestingly, in our work with trauma survivors this exercise does not evoke the same degree of self-deprecation described earlier. Perhaps it is easier (or feels less vulnerable) to express their thoughts about this than it is to acknowledge how they would like others to see them. Or perhaps the brevity and finality of the headstone statement pushes past such barriers and touches a central nerve.

Developing Values and Goals

In this phase of therapy, clients are provided with worksheets that help them identify their values (see the homework section at the end of the chapter on identifying values; adapted from Hayes et al., 1999) and they are asked to complete them before the next session. In filling out the sheets, clients identify values and goals regarding various life domains such as family relations, employment, physical well-being, and spirituality. As mentioned previously, clients with trauma histories often experience anxiety in regard to the topic of values, so it's important to emphasize that this assignment is not about having the "right" values.

Therapist: I'd like to you to spend some time thinking about your values before our next session. These values assessment sheets are designed to help you consider the values you might have toward all sorts of different areas in life. There isn't any right way to do this, and there are no right or wrong values—only you can know what you do and don't care about. Sometimes, though, it can be hard to figure out whether something is your value or someone else's, or if it's something you've been taught to value but you actually don't. For example, you might think that one should value getting an education, but in reality, that's not something you really care about. One way to help get at this is to ask yourself, "What if no one could ever know about this but me?" In considering this question, you are figuring out whether the value is yours or if it rests on something more external. For instance, if you're thinking that you value education and should go back and finish that college degree, ask yourself if you would still want to do that if no one else but you could know about it. If you find you still want that degree, you know that it really means something to you.

It is important to help clients make the distinction between goals and values:

Therapist: Whereas values indicate a general direction in which to head, goals are specific objectives you want to accomplish along the way. For example, let's say that you value being a good friend. What are specific goals that align with that value? Perhaps you decide that a goal will be to remember the birthdays of all your close friends and to call them on that day. Or perhaps you decide that you will let someone know how much they mean to you—that would be a goal that is in line with the general direction in which you're heading, that of being a good friend.

Clients are then given the values assignment. They are provided with both a clarifying values explanation sheet and a clarifying values worksheet (see homework section at end of chapter). We typically have clients work on these out of session and ask that they take their time in completing them. We also let our clients know that people often struggle with this exercise, and that this simply points to its importance. It can be helpful to work through an example in session.

Values and Trauma

It is useful to consider the concept of values in terms of its relevance to trauma survivors. That is, people who have seen or experienced something life threatening and horrible have a challenging task ahead—they must carry that burden for the rest of their lives. On top of that, a great deal of suffering comes from survivors' experience of having some of their values violated by the traumatic event. Often it's only when a value has been overturned by life that one becomes aware of it. For example, a trauma survivor who had served in Afghanistan experienced great distress over the fact that he "hated Afghans." On the one hand, he felt his feelings were justified in that he and his fellow servicemen had been under repeated attack by the Taliban and many soldiers in his unit had been killed. On the other, he felt guilt and shame about his hateful feelings. This client came to understand that while his reactions were understandable, he also held a basic value of being compassionate toward all human beings and that this value had been compromised in the war zone. It can be a tremendous relief for clients to realize that they can still have these values, that their values are inviolable. Just as one never *arrives* at being compassionate toward others, neither does one ever have to give it up.

As another example, a client described the terrible losses she had experienced as a result of being raped, including her sense of personal safety, trust in others, and, she reported tearfully, pride in being female. She said that she had always been proud of being a woman, but that the rape had left her with a profound feeling of shame in her vulnerability as a female. This client was liberated to realize (with the help of the chessboard metaphor among other self-as-context exercises) that, in fact, her femaleness was intact despite the rape, and that she was not broken, despite her feelings of shame. As we worked on the concept of valued living, this client got in touch with one of her core values—the right of women to be valued and treated with respect. This client went on to become a powerful advocate for the rights of women.

As can be seen in this example, there is an additional way in which the values component of ACT can be helpful to survivors of trauma. The values work can assist individuals who have experienced trauma to reconcile their thoughts and feelings about this with the realities of life. Consider the case of a father who witnessed his adult son being shot and killed in a random drive-by shooting. This client struggled mightily with his pain over the unfairness of this event, and his outrage over the fact that "people can't be safe on the street." On the one hand, he could acknowledge that life wasn't fair; on the other, his feelings were telling him this wasn't at all okay. In examining the concept of valued living, this client realized that although life wasn't fair, *he* could still value fairness, personal safety, and the safety of others.

Sticking Points for Clients

There are a couple of pitfalls for PTSD clients that can interfere with valued living. These include difficulty with finding value and meaning and continuing to wait for a particular outcome. We address these below.

Finding Meaning After PTSD

This chapter describes perhaps the most important piece in ACT therapy for the PTSD client. For many individuals diagnosed with PTSD, finding a life worth living may seem completely untenable. Connecting the client with the process of creation of meaning by living their values can have a powerful impact. We have had clients report that, although their anxieties may continue, living in new ways by making values-consistent choices has made all the difference. We focus on "mattering" (Hayes et al., 1999) as a verb and sometimes ask, "How will you spend your time mattering? About the trauma, or about your values?" Life can become about showing up and living with intention rather than waiting for small moments of "good" and "right" feelings as an indicator that life is worth living (Hayes et al., 1999). Guided by values, life is worth living as is.

Missing the Point That the Process Is the Point

It is possible for clients to miss the point of valued living entirely. That is, to approach living according to one's values as a task to accomplish (in order to be happy? be fixed? have everything worked out?) rather than as a way of life. This idea can be subtle yet insidious. Clients can sound as if they get it, and in fact think they are getting it, while in actuality they are madly hoping that at last they have the answer. This answer can, in fact, represent experiential avoidance at its best, and it is important to watch out for it. Here's an example, again with the client who had identified a value of being a good father:

Therapist: What do you mean by being a good father?

Client: It means doing everything I can to make my kids happy.

Therapist: Does that include letting them go bungee jumping with someone you don't even know?

Client: No! That's not what I mean. I mean doing things that help them, the things that children need.

Therapist: But it would make them so very happy to go bungee jumping.

Client: Yes, but…

Therapist: They might hate brushing their teeth.

Client: Okay, I get it. (*thinks*) I guess I value providing them with the basics—food, shelter, love.

Therapist: Why do you want to do that?

Client: Because that will make them happy—(*catches himself*) Shoot! (*laughs*) Because then they will be happy with me.

Therapist: And why do you want them to be happy with you?

Client: What do you mean? (*therapist waits*) Of course I want them to be happy with me!

Therapist: So let's say, in a given week, you provide food and shelter. You do this out of love, but darn it, for some reason they're unhappy with you. Do you stop?

Client: No, of course not.

Therapist:	But let's say that they're really unhappy with you, and that makes you pissed off and miserable. Your strategy, to feel good as a result of being a good dad, isn't working. Shouldn't you stop?
Client:	No, of course I'm not going to stop.
Therapist:	Well why not? Here you are, providing and loving and protecting, and you don't even get to feel good.
Client:	Because that's what dads do. That's what *I* do.
Therapist:	Because you live your value, providing and loving and protecting your children regardless.
Client:	That's right.

Sticking Points for Therapists

When we conduct ACT supervision, we frequently discuss the ways in which we as therapists get stuck. It is probably no surprise to you that when *really* stuck, therapists generally don't see it. We recommend that you keep the sticking points discussed throughout this book front and center as you conduct the therapy—if one seems particularly uncomfortable to look at, look harder.

For instance, a particularly tricky sticking point is getting caught in the idea of thinking right. We don't want therapists to get seduced into believing that there is a right way to do values and that clients must be convinced this is so. It may be the case that therapists share many values with their clients, but it may also be the case that clients have their own ways of doing things. For instance, as a therapist you may have a strong value about work and how one should engage in work. However, your client may have the value of "come what may" when it comes to work. If that is what the client chooses, then that is the right value for the client (even if you can see the possibility of negative consequences). Values are personal and need no defense. Similarly, it is easy to start to believe that this therapy is *the* therapy—now thank your mind for that thought!

Moving Forward

As they complete the values component of ACT, clients have begun to realize that nothing stands in the way of living a valued life: not feelings, not traumatic memories, not uncomfortable sensations or thoughts. In trauma survivors particularly, whose entire lives have been about needing to be repaired in order to live, this is a drastic shift that is full of possibility and freedom. Whether or not clients will choose to avail themselves of this freedom is another matter. For this reason, the concept of committed action becomes an essential part of the journey.

Homework

This first homework assignment is introduced in session and worked on with clients. Give clients additional sheets so that they may continue to work on clarifying goals and values outside of session. Additionally, this homework assignment is fairly large and can be revised and added to across multiple sessions. Be familiar with the assignment so that you can answer any questions that the client might have. Ask the client to bring the completed homework to the next session for review.

CLIENT HOMEWORK ASSIGNMENT 1: CLARIFYING VALUES

Instructions: The sheet you have just been given is a clarifying values worksheet. It lists different areas of life that are valued by most people. You may find that you have values in each of these areas, or you may find that you have values in only some of them. Focus on any area that is of importance to you. This worksheet is not a test to see if you have the "correct" values. Instead, work on describing the qualities that you would like to see be present for you in each area. Describe how you would like to treat people, including yourself, if you had the ideal situation. Feel free to elaborate and use additional sheets of paper.

To complete the values sheet:

1.   Describe your values as if no one would ever read this worksheet. Be bold.

2.   Rate the importance of this value using the following scale: 0 = not at all important; 1 = moderately important; 2 = very important.

3.   Describe several specific goals that could help you in terms of living each value. Choose goals that can be instituted regularly or immediately.

4.   Write down a thought or emotion that might prevent you from doing a specific goal.

5.   Write a short paragraph about what it would mean to you to live the value and what it would mean if you didn't.

Work through each of the life domains. Several of these domains will overlap. Do your best to keep them separate. Remember, a value is something that you can always be working on—it is your compass direction, not your outcome. We are not asking what you think you could realistically achieve or what you or others think you deserve. We want to know what you care about, what you would want to work toward, in the best of all situations. While doing the worksheet, pretend that magic happened and that anything is possible. Discuss this goals and values assessment in your next therapy session.

Clarifying Values Worksheet

Example:

1. **Value:** *I want to be a loving and gentle partner.*

    Importance: 2

    Goals: *1. Tell my partner that I love him; 2. Do kind things for my partner, like buy him small gifts that are a surprise now and then; 3. Honor his opinion; 4. Listen to him when he has a complaint and talk openly about it.*

    Thoughts and emotions that might prevent you from living your values: *Anxiety, anger, thoughts that my partner should tell me he loves me before I tell him that I love him.*

    Write a short paragraph about what it would mean to you to live the value and what it would mean if you didn't: *To live this value would mean getting more connected to my partner. However, that feels risky as I would need to be intimate. To not live with this value means I would continue to feel distant from my partner.*

Domains and Values

1. **Marriage/intimate relations values:**

    Importance:

Goals:

Thoughts and emotions that might prevent you from living your values:

Write a short paragraph about what it would mean to you to live the value and what it would mean if you didn't:

2.   **Family relations values:**

Importance:

Goals:

Thoughts and emotions that might prevent you from living your values:

Write a short paragraph about what it would mean to you to live the value and what it would mean if you didn't:

3.   **Friendships/social relations values:**

Importance:

Goals:

Thoughts and emotions that might prevent you from living your values:

Write a short paragraph about what it would mean to you to live the value and what it would mean if you didn't:

4. **Employment/education/training values:**

   Importance:

   Goals:

   Thoughts and emotions that might prevent you from living your values:

   Write a short paragraph about what it would mean to you to live the value and what it would mean if you didn't:

5. **Recreation/citizenship values:**

   Importance:

   Goals:

   Thoughts and emotions that might prevent you from living your values:

   Write a short paragraph about what it would mean to you to live the value and what it would mean if you didn't:

6. **Spirituality values:**

   Importance:

   Goals:

   Thoughts and emotions that might prevent you from living your values:

   Write a short paragraph about what it would mean to you to live the value and what it would mean if you didn't:

7.   **Physical well-being values:**

Importance:

Goals:

Thoughts and emotions that might prevent you from living your values:

Write a short paragraph about what it would mean to you to live the value and what it would mean if you didn't:

CLIENT HOMEWORK ASSIGNMENT 2: LOST VALUES

For this assignment, find a quiet place where you will not be disturbed. Take a pen and paper with you. Take a meditative posture and focus for a few moments on your breathing. Let yourself be gently aware of your breath for about two minutes. After a couple of minutes and while remaining in a meditative state, think back across your lifetime and gently review any values that may have been lost or pushed away as a result of your trauma. Notice any costs that may be associated with the losses, but be careful to remain nonjudgmental.

After this review, gently bring yourself back to the room. Now imagine that you could breathe life back into these values. Imagine that the gift of vitality has been given back to these values. Write a paragraph about these values and their importance to you. Be gentle as you do this exercise. Finally, make a list of two or three things for each value you have written about that you could do within the next twenty-four hours to bring the values back to life. Challenge yourself to engage one of these activities.

CHAPTER 9

Committed Action

There is no try, there is only do ... or do not.

—Yoda, *Star Wars*

In these last sessions of ACT, the focus is on holding internal experiences and moving in valued directions. By this time we have established with the client a sense of self that is larger than the content of mind and larger than the experiences of emotions and sensation. With willingness, self-as-context, and personal values in place, the client is free to move forward in chosen directions. In these sessions we further the work on choosing valued directions and add the notion of accepting responsibility for change. We focus on life as a process, not an outcome, paying particular attention to letting go of finish lines with respect to values while committing to goals regularly and with heart. We present the willingness question and bring it to life as a choice, focusing on disrupting the believability of perceived barriers to behavior change. Finally, in the last session we end with two very powerful exercises that bring the ACT protocol to a close. As a part of this process, we revisit earlier material that has already been explored as a means to tie things together for the client. You will notice some review, but we present the material here as we would in session. As this is the part of therapy where everything is tied together for the client, repeating key ideas can be quite helpful.

Session Format (3-4 sessions)

- Open with mindfulness

- Review prior session

- Tell the ACT story

- Regain values

- Identify remaining barriers

- Revisit willingness

- Explore commitments

- Ask the willingness question

- Explore sticking points for clients

- Explore sticking points for therapists

- Assign homework: committed action

- Moving forward

Opening with Mindfulness

This is a good time to further explore how clients are doing with their mindful practice. Take a little time to process any barriers that may be interfering with practice.

MINDFULNESS EXERCISE 1: WE ARE ALL IN THIS TOGETHER
(Approximately 10-15 minutes)

This exercise (Hayes et al., 1999) can be done in group or individual therapy. If conducted in individual therapy, you would adapt by having the client focus on you, the therapist, rather than the person sitting next to them, and then move on to the portion that begins with rising up out of the building. Before beginning the exercise with a group, have the clients look to their left and to their right just to be aware of who is sitting next to them.

Therapist: I would like everyone to start this exercise by placing your feet squarely on the ground and sitting up in your chair so that your back is straight but not rigid. Make sure that your head feels square to your shoulders and place your arms in a comfortable position at your sides ... Remember that this posture helps us to stay alert and focused. So let's begin by first noticing or paying attention to the fact that your body is actively sensing the environment. Notice that you can feel yourself sitting in the chair, and you can feel your feet on the ground. Now, gently close your eyes. I would like you to place your attention at the tip of your nose and begin to notice the sensation of air moving in and out of your nostrils ... Pay attention to your breathing. (*pause*) Now I would like you to gently expand your awareness to your body, noticing what you feel, sense, and hear. Be aware of the position of your body and all of the experiences it is having. (*pause*)

Now, gently expand your awareness to noticing that there is a person sitting to your right ... Be aware of that person, bring to your mind's eye what they look like, and notice that they are feeling and sensing too. Also notice that as you do this, someone is being aware of you. (*pause*) Now gently shift your attention to your left. Be aware of that person, bring to your mind's eye what they look like, notice that they are feeling and sensing too ... Also notice that as you do this that someone is being aware of you. (*pause*) Expand your awareness even further, so that it encompasses this whole group. Notice all who are here, each feeling, sensing ... struggling. (*pause*)

Now imagine that a part of you could float above this room and see this group of people from overhead ... Allow this part of you to rise further, passing through the ceiling and out of the building so that you are hovering above the building ... Now, using the best of your imagination, picture all of the people who might be in this building, notice that they too are sensing, feeling, experiencing, struggling, and that all are working on living. Now imagine that you could float even higher so that you could see the city below. To the best of your imagination, picture all the people moving about living their lives, feeling, sensing, fearing, loving, worrying, sleeping ... struggling. (*pause*)

Now travel out even further so that you can see the whole state, and again, to the best of your imagination, picture all of the people who might be there ... living, some thinking about not living anymore, some preparing to die, some loving, all thinking, feeling, sensing, worrying, wondering, struggling. (*pause*) Now imagine that you could float even higher so that you could see the whole of North,

Central, and South America. Again, imagine to the best of your ability all of the people ... living their lives, having feelings—some good, some bad—having anxiety, having love, growing, changing, hurting, crying, loving, and struggling. (*pause*) Now allow yourself to float even higher, out of the atmosphere, so that you are floating high above the earth ... You can see the whole earth ... Now imagine, as best you can, all the people living their lives, trying to live, having pain, having joy, having luck, having sorrow, all struggling. (*pause for a longer period*)

Now imagine that you are floating back toward the earth ... It is growing in size, and now you can see North, Central, and South America come into view ... Now float down even further until you see our state. Then continue on until you see our city ... and then float further until you are hovering right over this building ... Bring yourself back to hovering right over this group of people. (*pause*) Picture the person to your left ... who struggles too ... and then picture the person to your right ... who also struggles ... Then gently bring your awareness back to yourself, your body, your senses, your feelings and thoughts, and just gently note that we are all in this together. (*pause*) Now picture the room, notice the sounds of the room, and when you are ready, rejoin the room by opening your eyes.

MINDFULNESS EXERCISE 2: KISS THE EARTH WITH YOUR FEET
(Approximately 5-10 minutes)

This is a walking meditation and is a way to help clients get connected to mindfulness while in action. Have all the clients stand and then begin the mindfulness guidance.

Therapist: I would like everyone to stand for just a moment and focus on your breath. Be aware of your posture and how you're holding yourself. In just a moment we will begin to walk around the room, going wherever you like and taking care not to bump into each other. Also keep in mind that this exercise is done in silence. I may say a few things to keep us aware and focused on the present, but otherwise this is a silent exercise. As you walk, do so as if you were gently kissing the earth with your feet. The goal is to be mindful of each step, letting each one land with softness and with your full awareness. Go ahead and begin to walk around, kissing the earth with your feet. (*Have the clients move quietly about the room, being aware of walking for several minutes. You may say things like "If your mind has wandered away from being aware of walking, just gently bring it back" or "Feel your feet as you let them gently touch the ground; notice each movement.")* Now gently return to your seat, being mindfully aware that you are walking to your seat. (*Allow time for clients to arrive back to their chairs.*) Gently sit down and turn your focus to the group.

Prior Session Review

Take a brief period of time during this session to reflect back on the prior session and to check in with clients regarding their assigned homework:

- Identifying values

- Lost values

Telling the ACT Story

Telling the story of ACT therapy is a nice way to summarize and pull together the work that you have been doing together thus far. It can help clarify all the metaphors, exercises, and homework completed, while also helping clients to see where they have been and also where they are heading. The therapist might say something like this in one of the final sessions:

Therapist: So let's take a look at where we've been. If you recall, we started by listing all of the thoughts and feelings that you have struggled with and also by listing all of the ways in which you tried to make all those thoughts and feelings go away, lessen, be different. Remember? … What we found out was that all of those different strategies, even the good ones and the healthy ones, didn't quite cut it. If they had, you wouldn't be in therapy, you would just be using those strategies that worked … and you would be out there living your life. We talked about how these strategies were strategies of control—ways to try to control what you feel and think. They were attempts to practice that old saying, "out with the bad and in with the good." They were about having more good feelings, a better history, a different you—control. If you recall, we spent time talking about how control applied to the stuff that goes on inside your skin doesn't seem to work so well. But we noted that we want you to be in control of your life. Given this, we turned to the alternative to control—willingness.

We did a bunch of exercises that help to make willingness possible, including coming to see yourself as a context in which thoughts, feelings, and sensations occur rather than you actually being those things. We worked on helping you to see your self as a place where ongoing experiences occur, where they simply flow—to see there is a self there that can observe this flow. Remember the chessboard metaphor and that continuous you that stretches back across time? (*Client nods.*) Once we got connected up to that sense of you, we started focusing on your values and how they have been lost to the trauma and the fallout from the trauma. We also focused on how you can make choices that are about getting you realigned with these values, choices that are about getting your life back. Over these next couple of sessions we are going to work on bringing these choices to life. We will be working on committing to the actions that are necessary for you to engage in the process of your life.

Values Regained

During these last sessions we continue to focus on defining values, on describing goals that are in line with living those values, and on continuing to dismantle barriers that are about thoughts, feelings, memories, and sensations. In this process, outcomes from living a particular value begin to present themselves. Some are positive and rewarding; others may not be what was desired and may even be painful. The latter can drag clients back into the struggle in couple of ways.

Waiting for a Return

First, it is not unusual for the client to begin to more actively participate in regaining values, such as engaging with family members or submitting job applications. However, as the therapist you may note that clients sometimes link these actions to what others are doing in return. It generally takes the form of the client being upset because a family member (or job prospect) didn't respond in a way that the client was hoping for. It can come back into the therapy room as an "I told you so" or "I knew I was a failure" or "I knew this wouldn't work." It is helpful to remind the client that values can't be linked to how others might respond. They are freestanding and wholly chosen because the client can, not because the client is hoping to get something in return.

This said, it is often the case that when clients begin to live their values, good things do happen. We've had clients report a new feeling of openness given by a family member to an overture made by the client that brought about powerful reconnection. Clients have made a variety of bold moves, including leaving jobs that were harmful, starting jobs after years of unemployment, rekindling old friendships, confronting problematic people, taking walks in parks that were once scary, or shopping during the day when crowds were around. All of these and more have helped clients recapture what was lost.

In working with clients who get caught up in how others respond to the outcome of their efforts, we remind them that they are living *their* values, and we ask if they would choose it even if they didn't get what they wanted. The following dialogue represents how this might unfold. In this case, the client is referring to her value of having a loving relationship with her mother.

Client: So, I called my mom again this weekend, and I talked with her for a while. But, like always, I say "I love you" and there is silence on the other end of the phone. She just can't do it! By the end of the call she was criticizing me. I just can't seem to get her to love me.

Therapist: Seems pretty painful.

Client: Yeah. (*quietly*) I just don't know what to do to get her to love me.

Therapist: So I know you have been working on this value of having a loving relationship with your mother. But I can feel this deal in there where you have this value linked to her loving you back.

Client: Well, what's the point of living my values if all I get is criticism? What is the point of trying so hard if it just ends up being painful?

Therapist: (*gently*) I think you ask a great question. What is the point? I mean that: What is the point? Is the point to get your mom to say "I love you," or is the point to live your value of having a loving relationship with your mom? This is about you here. How do *you* want to do this?
… If you link this stuff to what you get in return, you will be right back to where you started—we just don't know what will happen if you live your values.

Client: Well, why do I have to do all the work?

Therapist: You don't. You don't have to do this at all. Maybe you will find that loving your mother isn't a particularly strong value for you. It is up to you. You get to pick this.

Client:	So are you telling me I'm picking my pain?
Therapist:	Not exactly … You are picking your value, and in this value, there is some pain. What do you think would happen if you could choose this value freely and not link it to what the outcome was … not link it to what your mother does in return?
Client:	I don't know how to do that. I can't imagine what that would be like.
Therapist:	It would probably be a bit of a challenge, because the thoughts of wanting your mom to love you will be there. But let's follow this out. It seems that you already know how to not be connected to your mom. You know that deal. All you have to do is do what you were doing in the past—nothing—with respect to this value, and you land in a place where you feel your mother doesn't love you anyway. That is, do nothing and you won't have a connection with your mom. So it seems either the value has to change or what you do has to change.
Client:	I can see that.
Therapist:	I'm wondering if you could observe the thoughts and feelings that show up when your mom doesn't do what you want, and still live this value—without a particular return on the value. That's not to say that at some point you wouldn't choose something different. But for now, given that this is the value you are choosing to work on, could you say "I love you" to your mom and be willing to experience what shows up when she doesn't say it in return? And maybe even be willing to accept where she is at with her inability to say "I love you" back?
Client:	I suppose I could, but I really want her to love me. I want her to say it.
Therapist:	I know it's hard, and you know what the other way looks like. Would you be willing to try it this way? See if some freedom comes from it?
Client:	I'll see what happens.

Following this exchange, the therapist and the client went on to talk about how the client could continue to engage in the value for as long as she chose. Some different strategies were explored, including writing letters, praying for patience and for her mother, talking to family members about wanting to heal the relationship, and focusing on forgiveness rather than being loved. You can see that the goals related to living one's values can be without number. Be creative and work with clients to generate many goals around these kinds of things.

It is important to note that we don't encourage clients to remain in relationships where there is no relationship or where harm is being done. Suppose, in the example above, that the mother never made any moves to reconnect in a healthy way with her daughter after the daughter had made multiple attempts. We may then work with the client to focus on how she can demonstrate being a loving daughter outside of that relationship. It may even include letting her mother go, letting her mother have her space with a recognition that the client would always be there should her mother change her mind.

Value as an End Point

A second way in which clients can misapply the concept of values is by seeking the outcome as a final destination. As described in chapter 8, this issue has been previously explored with clients. However, we have noticed that even at this later point in therapy we again bump up against the notion that the outcome (in other words, the value) is a place to arrive at. The *process* of values gets lost, and clients can seem surprised when they report that they have been working on a value and the desired outcome (such as connecting) didn't stick permanently. Consider a client who has a value of kindness and goes about his life doing kind things, and then something happens where he doesn't have kind feelings, or he has an upsetting encounter in the face of working on kindness. It is not uncommon for the client to suddenly throw the baby out with the bathwater, deciding that the value of kindness doesn't work. Some clients will expect that they will arrive at a place of kindness, or that they will feel better if they live their values, and they are subsequently surprised when this isn't the case. We present the metaphor of skiing (Hayes et al., 1999) to address this issue:

Therapist: Imagine that you can ski, or maybe in fact you do know how to ski. And imagine that every time you got to the top of the mountain and dropped off of the ski lift, you simply stepped into an elevator that returned you to the bottom of the mountain.

Client: Well, that wouldn't be very fun.

Therapist: No, it wouldn't. But what if this was the case? It would feel like a rip-off, wouldn't it? I mean, the point of skiing is to slide down the hill, to twist and turn, to go over moguls, to challenge yourself, to feel the air on your face, the speed of your motion, to breathe the air and feel your body working, right?

Client: Right.

Therapist: But the outcome is to get to the bottom of the hill. Right?

Client:	Yes.
Therapist:	So in skiing, it's important to get to the bottom of the hill. That is the goal, or outcome. The process of skiing is in doing the skiing; all that stuff that makes skiing fun and challenging, and hard and enjoyable, and so on. That's the important part, the process of skiing. What if values are like that? What if the important part is the process, not the outcome? Living your values is the challenging, fun, hard, enjoyable process of doing it.

We also remind clients that thoughts and feelings are transient, and that they may be buying a particular thought (for example, "I should feel good all the time because I am living my value"). As a therapist, you can talk with the client about this directly, noting again that the mind is tricky. We might say something about the mind being like looking through a pair of rose-colored glasses. Everything the mind sees seems to take on this color and is evaluated and responded to accordingly. When clients get stuck on the idea that living their values can be (or lead to) an outcome that is the answer, you can remind them that it is helpful to take off the glasses, even if only for a moment. This particular metaphor, in fact, can be useful throughout therapy. It helps to remind clients that while there is mind and its interpretations, there is also a self that is experiencing the mind.

Regaining values can be both wonderful and challenging for clients. They can vacillate between the excitement of bringing lost values to life and the pain of doing the same. Living one's values is not always easy, but it is what brings vitality to being.

Remaining Barriers

Completing unfinished business is the focus of this section. There are a few topics that can be particularly difficult for trauma survivors, and even at this point in therapy they may continue to be barriers to living values. These include forgiveness, concern about right and wrong, and clinging to conceptualized self.

Trauma and Forgiveness

Many trauma survivors struggle directly or indirectly with forgiveness and its meaning for them, as mentioned in chapter 6. Forgiveness is usually centered on forgiving others or on forgiving oneself for deeds committed against others or against the self. Additionally, it's a challenging and sensitive topic. From the ACT perspective, just as with all other thoughts and feelings, the thoughts and feelings that accompany forgiveness are there to be observed and held lightly while one also chooses and participates in personal values. With trauma survivors, however, forgiveness seems to be extra sticky in terms of being fused with the event. The therapist may want to spend an entire session or two working on this issue, depending on where the client is at with this matter. We do not impose the value of forgiveness on clients. However, should nonforgiveness show up in the course of therapy as a barrier to valued living, we help clients—particularly survivors of interpersonal trauma—distinguish forgiveness from conceding that what happened to them was okay. When working with clients on forgiveness, compassion and understanding are essential requirements.

There are several things that we do with forgiveness. First, we talk about the meaning of the word. Most people think of forgiveness as a feeling that comes along with telling someone that you forgive them for some action they committed. However, from the point of view of ACT, forgiveness is seen as an action, not a feeling. Forgiveness means to "give what went before the harm was done" (Hayes et al., 1999). In this sense, "giving" is an action. It may be the case that if the client offers forgiveness, they will feel a sense of relief, lightness, or peace and ease. These are often the feelings that come along with forgiveness. However, as with all feelings, these can come and go. Most of us have had the experience of forgiving someone and subsequently feeling good, only to realize moments or hours later that the feeling has passed and anger about the forgiven misdeed has arisen again. Now what do you do? The transient nature of these emotions is why it's most useful to talk about forgiveness as an action. The client can always choose to behave in a forgiving way as the feelings associated with forgiveness come and go. If clients are working on self-forgiveness, you might ask how they would be treating themselves if they had fully forgiven themselves for whatever it is they feel they have done.

In our experience, nonforgiveness and self-blame can range from self-destructive behavior, such as years of heavy drinking, painful isolation, and cutting oneself, to acts of hatred, including injuring others or observing war crimes and atrocities without taking action. Sometimes the self-blame is simply about not living the life the person would like to live. You may specifically ask the client, "If you were to give to yourself the life that went before the trauma, what would that life look like? What actions would you take toward yourself?" Clients generally come up with a fair number of responses to these questions, including such things as reaching out more, less or no isolation, no substance abuse, no cutting, not engaging in harmful relationships, being kinder and more gentle, and taking better care of themselves. Once you have compiled this list, it becomes clear what actions clients can take toward themselves in being forgiving. The following is an actual example of how this kind of forgiveness work might unfold in group session. In this case, the therapist is speaking to a war veteran following his explanation about an incident at age nineteen where he stood by and did nothing while viewing an atrocity. He was having great difficulty forgiving himself regarding his behavior.

Therapist:	This is a very painful event for you. I can see why it has haunted you for so long. That young self, that nineteen-year-old kid you once were, must have really been amazed and confused about what was happening.
Client:	He was completely shocked. And he was very dumb. He should have done something to stop this horrible thing.
Therapist:	*(very gently)* It makes sense to me that as you look back on it now, you wish he had done something different. That you wish he had taken a stand.
Client:	Yes, then I could still have my integrity. He ruined it for me.
Therapist:	We have talked about how history is not changeable and about how time only moves in one direction, but if you could go back and do something to help that kid, what would you do?
Client:	I would like to beat him up, whip him into shape … set him straight.
Therapist:	So you would really like to let him know how disappointed you are by harming him?
Client:	Yeah, maybe then he would have done something.
Therapist:	Maybe, but it's actually hard to say … We can't go back. And somehow beating that young kid up doesn't seem like the right answer. (*At this point the therapist asked for a volunteer from the group to stand about a foot or two away and in front of the client.*) Imagine that this person standing in front of you is you at the age that you witnessed this event … He is that nineteen-year-old kid. (*The therapist pointed to the group volunteer. At this point the client became very silent as the group member stood in front of him, simply watching him. After a short period of silence, the therapist again asked about the situation.*) What would you like to do?
Client:	*(hesitantly)* Well, I am feeling an urge to hug him.
Therapist:	Would you be willing to do that? (*The client at this time stood up and hugged the group member. Both became tearful and held each other for a few moments.*)
Client:	*(tearfully)* I never imagined that before, I never thought of that as the answer. I can see now what I can do differently.

The client in this interaction was experientially able to recognize an alternative to anger and nonforgiveness. These are the kinds of moments that move the client forward in the process of forgiveness. Again, we specifically talk about forgiveness being a process. We work with clients on the notion that they may be addressing issues of forgiveness as a process for a long time. But the key is to get the client off the hook. One metaphor that may prove useful here is to refer to the client as being like a worm stuck on a hook (Hayes et al., 1999). However, there is an additional worm on the hook, that being the person they are holding in nonforgiveness (this may also be the client; that is, the client could be both the first and second worm if the forgiveness work is in relationship to their own actions). In this metaphor, the client is on the hook first and the nonforgiven person is second, so that the only way for the client to get off the hook is to let the nonforgiven person off the hook first. This is an important distinction, particularly as it applies to suffering and anger. Often the person who is holding someone on the hook is the one who is suffering, not the person being held in nonforgiveness. Additionally, anger at this individual generally functions to harm the person who is angry— rarely is the target struggling over this or even feeling upset. You can ask the client if they would be willing to let the other person off the hook if it meant that they could get off the hook too. The crucial piece in terms of forgiveness is to remind the client that it does not have to be done in an all-or-none fashion, rather it can be done as a process. One could choose to work on forgiveness for long periods of time, moving in and out of the resulting feelings while remaining committed to the actions of forgiveness.

If it makes sense clinically, we will occasionally ask clients to engage in an exercise that is about forgiveness. The exercise has a gestaltlike quality to it. You ask clients to sit across from either you, an empty chair, or another person if in a group setting, and then to gently close their eyes for a moment and think of the person, whether it be themselves or someone else, with whom they would like to work on forgiveness. Then ask them to imagine what it is that they will be needing to forgive. We have learned that clients do not always select who we might expect them to (their perpetrator, for example). For example, they may choose someone who failed to protect them or who harmed them in other ways (for instance, painful relationships), or it can even be themselves. Once they have chosen the person and the misdeed, we ask them to open their eyes and begin to speak to the empty chair or the person as if they were talking to the one being forgiven. They are asked to say all that needs to be said in a process of forgiveness. If they are facing another person, for instance in a group, the other person is asked to listen with great intent and to hear all that is being said but not to interrupt the client. Once the client has said all that there is to be said, we ask them to sit and look into each others' eyes for a few moments. Finally, the exercise is ended by having them briefly process the experience. The listener is to remain in a nonjudgmental position. As noted, you can set this up as an empty chair exercise, or the therapist can take that role in an individual session. If you choose to use the empty chair, you would of course skip the request to look into the other's eyes. We have found this to be a powerful exercise that allows clients to say things that they have never expressed. Being heard by a focused listener also seems to have a freeing impact. We remind the client that this may not mean that they are off the hook, but that perhaps they have moved a little closer to the tip.

The ACT work here is not so much about defusion as it is about valued living. That is, the exercise described above is not especially designed to defuse clients from their mind; rather, it encourages them to be aware or become aware of how nonforgiveness may interfere with values. It may be helpful to point out to clients what their mind says about forgiveness as a way to get a little distance between the self and mind around this issue, but the heart of this work is geared toward living your values well.

Right and Wrong

Issues of right and wrong can be salient for most of us. However, they can sometimes play a larger role for trauma survivors. For instance, they can get caught in corpus delicti, as discussed in chapter 6. Less obvious or extreme issues of right and wrong can also be at play and can function to keep the client stuck by being barriers to committed action.

Clients can get caught up in right and wrong in a number of ways. They may have participated in failed relationships characterized by issues of who was right and who was wrong or may have practiced punishing others for deeds done, and so on. Punishment can take many forms, including shutting others out, giving the cold shoulder, frightening others, hiding out, or behaving inappropriately through violence or yelling. Each of these tends to be strongly linked to efforts to control internal experience. The control is usually centered on not wanting to feel sad or hurt. That is, if you look to see what is under the anger, you often find hurt feelings:

Client: I am right about this! He shouldn't tell me what to do. I am my own person and don't need him ordering me around.

Therapist: What happens when he tells you what to do?

Client: I get very angry and end up yelling at him. We get in a big fight and then don't talk to each other for a few days. Finally, we just get over it and act like it never happened.

Therapist: So what is the cost of this interaction?

Client:	*(aggressively)* I don't know. But whatever the cost, he doesn't get to tell me what to do.
Therapist:	Well, I can agree that you may not like it when he tells you what to do, but I am concerned about what happens when he does. You get angry and the two of you don't talk for a couple of days, right?
Client:	Right.
Therapist:	What if I could peel the anger back just a little and look underneath. What would I see? Is there some other emotion there?
Client:	*(thinking)* Well, I guess I'm hurt and a little scared. It's scary and painful to be ordered around. It's exactly what my dad did to me, and he was the one who abused me.
Therapist:	Here, we can do something. What would happen if you talked with your partner about the hurt or fear that you feel rather than getting angry? What if it was okay to talk about the original emotion?
Client:	That would make me too vulnerable.
Therapist:	Ah. *(playfully)* Another feeling to be avoided.
Client:	Yeah … and I know where you're headed.
Therapist:	Good. Would you be willing to feel hurt and vulnerable if it meant that you and your partner didn't get in yelling matches and then not speak to each other for days? You have told me that what you value is to have a committed and loving relationship with him. Could you choose to do this?
Client:	Yes, but…
Therapist:	What stops you?
Client:	I'm right about this.
Therapist:	Okay, let's say you are 100 percent right about this. Now what?
Client:	He better stop doing it, then.
Therapist:	But here you are in front of me, and you are the one who holds this value. How can you commit to it and mean it?
Client:	*(thinking)* I suppose I could feel the feeling and talk to him about it. But I don't like it! And I don't want to. It makes me look weak.

Therapist:	Thank your mind for that last thought, and remember that you don't have to like it or want it. But could you choose to do it if it meant living your value?
Client:	Yes, technically I could, but it would be hard.
Therapist:	Simple and hard at the same time…
Client:	Yeah.

At this point the therapist could work with the client on how she might talk to her partner and strategize about potential outcomes. Getting right and wrong out of the way can promote this interaction.

There are several other ways to address right and wrong. Keep in mind that we're pointing to the problem of being right as an impediment to a vital life. We want to create a place where the client is invested in letting go of being right because it is a barrier to living well.

Taking right and wrong off of the table can be truly helpful in getting clients to take action with respect to values. One of the more productive exercises in this area is the right-wrong game (see Walser & Pistorello, 2005). In this game, the therapist takes a stack of blank cards and holds them along with a marker. The therapist asks the client to sit directly across from him or her and asks if the client is willing to play the right-wrong game. This is a particularly powerful exercise in group therapy. Others tend to see the issue clearly and can recognize the places where the person playing the game gets personally stuck in being right. Once the client agrees to play, the therapist sets up the game. In the following example, the client is a highly critical woman who was verbally badgered and physically beaten by her father.

Therapist:	In this game of right and wrong, there are winners and losers. If someone is right, someone else has to be wrong. We will begin by focusing on what it is that you are right about.
Client:	Okay, I'm right about how stupid other people are; they should know better.
Therapist:	Okay, you're right, and I will represent those other "stupid" people. So I will be wrong. You get a right card, (*Writes "R" on a card and hands it to client.*) And I get a wrong card. (*Writes "W" on a card and places it in her lap. Client chuckles.*) Now, can you tell me more about how people are stupid?
Client:	(*somewhat forcefully*) Yes, they're rude, they don't consider others, and they don't think before they speak … In fact, I wish they would just shut up.

Therapist:	Okay, you're right. (*Hands client another "R" card.*) And again, me being those stupid people that should shut up, I'm wrong. (*Writes up and keeps a "W" card.*) But you know what I think? … I don't think people are stupid and that they should shut up. In fact, I think they should speak their minds, so I am going to be right and you can be wrong. (*Hands a "W" to client, keeps an "R" for self.*)
Client:	(*stubbornly*) Well, I don't agree with you.
Therapist:	Okay, you're right again and I'm wrong again. (*Distributes cards.*)
Client:	(*laughing*) Well, this is going nowhere.
Therapist:	You're right. (*Hands client an "R" card.*)
Client:	So, what if I say people aren't stupid?
Therapist:	(*playfully*) You're right again. (*Gives client another "R" card.*)

At this point the therapist can go on with the game for a while, talking with the client so each takes turns at being right and wrong. After a few minutes, the therapist concludes the game:

Therapist:	Okay, let's look to see what has happened. What do you have?
Client:	A bunch of cards that tell me I was right or wrong.
Therapist:	Did you win?
Client:	I don't know. I'd have to go back and count up the right and wrong cards to see if I won.
Therapist:	Suppose you have more right cards.
Client:	Okay, I win!
Therapist:	(*with emphasis*) You are right! (*Hands client another card with "R" written on it and takes a "W" card for herself.*)
Client:	Wait a minute, are we back in the game?
Therapist:	It would seem we are, if it's about who wins and who loses. Let's say we keep playing for another hour or two and then we count up the cards, then what?
Client:	We would be back in the same place.

Therapist:	(*playfully*) You're right! (*Starts to write a card while client laughs.*) So here is the deal. We can play this game, and it can go on forever. The problem is that it has costs. Some of the costs that you have mentioned include that people don't want to talk with you and they seem to keep their distance. That kind of heavy "being-right" evaluation and judgment puts people off. And can you see how your programming has come to life—this is stuff your dad said. (*Client nods in agreement.*) Now, what if we could take all of this right and wrong and set it aside (*taking all of the cards and setting them on a side table*) and we could instead zoom in on the value that you have about relating to people.
Client:	(*a little surprised and tearful*) I do want friends and perhaps a husband some day.
Therapist:	I know, and what if this content, this programming about being right, is getting in the way?
Client:	That wouldn't be good.
Therapist:	So when your mind says "stupid," could you notice that as your programming, observe it, and still do what works? Take those actions that are about bringing your value to life?

The therapist can then spend time with the client exploring specific actions that would be related to having friends and finding a partner. The game may need to be mentioned again from time to time, the therapist asking the client if the right-wrong game is happening again. If so, the therapist asks whether the client can set right and wrong aside and reengage the value. We do want to issue a word of caution when using this strategy in therapy: We have done this many times when it looks like the example given above; however, we have also done it when quite serious issues are on the table, such as extramarital affairs, leaving relationships, and problems with children. Should you choose to do this exercise under these circumstances, we recommend that you take the playfulness out of it and engage in the game with compassion and awareness of personal costs to the client. Even when tackling heavy subjects, the exercise can still be very powerful, offering clients a way to see how a focus on right and wrong has been interfering with solutions.

Working on this area doesn't mean that there are not times when clients are right about things. Certainly there are injustices in the world, including the trauma. The key is whether or not being right is a barrier. If you play to be right, then you are likely trading away your life.

Clinging to the Conceptualized Self

Many trauma survivors, like most people, cling to an idea of who they are. As noted, sometimes it looks like the identity of a victim, and sometimes like it looks like the identity of a survivor. There are many senses of self that get developed based on our ability to describe and then to assign that description to our own sense of who we are. Therapists, for example may have a conceptualized self called the professional self. Other senses of self may include the playful self, the child self, or the hurt self. Generally, we each have several forms of our own conceptualized self. (See observer self exercise presented in chapter 7; these forms are similar to the *roles* we all play as indicated in that exercise.) It is not necessarily problematic to have these forms of the conceptualized self. They can be useful in defining our activities, responsibilities, and so on. However, we and our clients can become so attached to these conceptualized forms of self that we lose ourselves to that identity. For instance, have you ever known people in your field who view themselves as their job? They have so identified with this sense of themselves that their professional self shows up wherever they go and rarely do others see another side. Additionally, it is anxiety provoking for these individuals to step out of this perceived self, so they are unwilling to do so.

This can also occur with trauma survivors to such an extent that they lose the larger picture of themselves and become similarly self-conceptualized; for instance, "I am victim" or "I am Vietnam" or "I am damaged [hurt, useless, afraid, and so on]." When clients cling to these conceptualizations too tightly, they become barriers to successful living. We have developed the following exercise to help clients gain a small bit of distance from their conceptualized self—just enough distance to choose their own values rather than what their conceptualized self would choose. We have learned that that self does not always know what is best for the client (or for the therapist).

The therapist asks the clients to pair up if in group therapy, or to directly talk to the therapist if in individual therapy. Each pair is to take turns describing several conceptualized selves. We usually choose four, as to do more can make the exercise quite long. These conceptualizations can range from the professional or working self to the victim self to the struggling self to the current self to the best self, and so on. You can formulate several of your own and also choose ones that seem to fit clients. Once you have chosen three or four, have each client describe each sense of self (using their imagination) in the following ways:

1. How does this sense of self dress and look?

2. How does this sense of self think?

3. How does this sense of self feel?

After each client has formulated the senses of self listed, have them prepare for an imagery exercise by sitting in the mindfulness posture in their seats. Have the clients close their eyes, then lead them through the following imagery exercise. You'll need to modify the exercise to reflect which conceptualized selves you worked with in the first part of the exercise.

Therapist: Allow yourself to breathe naturally as you think about the different senses of self that you just described. In your mind's eye, picture these four images standing before you … And now I would like you to focus on the first image, the image of you as your best self. (*Pause for a moment and allow the client to imagine this sense of self, then proceed.*) Now, as you see this self before you, notice your emotional reaction to this sense of self. (*pause*) What are your thoughts about this self-image? (*pause*) What would it mean to you if you could no longer hold this sense of self, if you had to let it go? See if you can hold this self lightly, like you might hold a butterfly in your hand. Now imagine that this sense of self is gently dissolving, and as you do, say to this self "I let go of you." (*pause*) Notice if you cling to any sense of this self, (*pause*) and see if you can let that go, too. As you do this, also notice that there is a you there hearing this in this moment, a you that has always been there. (*pause*) Now gently shift your attention to the image of you as your struggling self…

From this point forward, do the same thing for each of the conceptualized selves following the exercise as above. After you have gone through each self-conceptualization you can end the exercise by stating something like this:

Therapist: Now that you have focused on letting go of each of these senses of self, also notice that you are still here and hearing me say this; you are in the room in this moment … And that same you will, in just a few moments, be able to create another conceptualized self or return to the old ones just focused on. From this space, would you be willing, while holding all of your senses of self lightly, to choose what it is that you want your life to stand for, what it is that you want to live in playing out your values? Can you have compassion for these senses of self and their needs, remain open to them, but hold them lightly, like you might hold a butterfly in the palm of your hand … and choose your life? (*pause*) Now gently turn your attention to the room and this space, and when you are ready, open your eyes and rejoin the room.

There are a number of conditions under which you might choose to do this exercise; however, we generally use it for those who are fully fused with a conceptualized self that is interfering with living their values. The intention is, again, to help clients free themselves just a little from those fused places that remain barriers to vitality.

Willingness Revisited

We also continue to work on willingness at this point in therapy. Although it may seem like a simple concept, it is certainly not always easy to do. There are a lot of obstacles to being willing, not least of which are reason giving and emotions. Some clients will express concern about being willing and accepting the pain that may come along with this action. We let clients know that we are not asking them to experience pain for pain's sake. However, we are asking if they're willing to experience pain if it leads to effective action, if it leads to a more vital life. We use the Joe-the-bum metaphor (Hayes et al., 1999) to help illustrate the point:

Therapist: I would like you to imagine that you have purchased a new home and that you have decided to hold an open house. You are excited about the event, so you make flyers and decide to invite everyone in the neighborhood. You go around the neighborhood posting these little signs that say "all are welcome." The big day arrives, and everything is going well. You have a beautiful spread of food and drink, the place is all clean, and the guests are beginning to arrive. Everything is going well. Then you hear another knock at the door.

You answer and it is Joe the bum. And what you see is that Joe the bum looks and smells terrible. He hasn't bathed in months, his teeth haven't been brushed in who knows how long, he has sticks and bugs in his hair, his beard is ragged and long, and he has on worn and tattered clothes that are filthy. You say, "Not you, Joe" and begin to close the door so he can't enter. Joe says, "But you invited everyone. You said all are welcome," and he holds up one of the flyers that you posted around the neighborhood. You respond by saying, "I know, but I meant everyone but you, Joe," and you begin to close the door. At that moment, Joe gets a little a stubborn and places his foot between the door and the doorjamb so you can't close the door, and he says, "I'm not leaving. You said all are welcome." You try pushing a little harder on the door and Joe says, "I'm not going, and even if you close the door, I will go to the windows and knock. I'll go round back and keep bothering you until you let me in."

In your frustration and desire to get on with things, you agree to let Joe in, but only if he agrees to stay in the kitchen. You quickly rush Joe to the kitchen, close the door, and say "You stay in there, Joe." Whew! And you turn to rejoin the party. Just as you do, you notice that

Joe is coming out of the kitchen. So you turn again, place your hand on the door, and again say, "No, Joe, you stay in there." And again, you turn to leave, and guess what happens?

Client: Joe comes back through the door.

Therapist: Right! So what you figure out is that, in order to keep Joe in the kitchen, you have to butt your foot right up against the door and keep it there. Now, what's the problem with this scenario?

Client: Well ... I'm not at the party.

Therapist: Right! So here is the big question: Would you be willing to let Joe come to the party if it meant that you got to be at the party too?

Here you can talk with the client about the cost of not being willing. Unwillingness leads to loss of vitality and engagement. You can explore with the client if avoidance of difficult emotions and thoughts is worth the cost. You may even ask the client, "What stands between you and complete willingness?" This is a good time to remind the client that willingness is not a feeling and that it's not about wanting an unpleasant emotion. It's about being willing to let "Joe" be there so that *you* (the client) can be there too.

Choice also becomes important at this point. The only thing that really stands between the client and being 100 percent willing is the choice to do so. Workability is the key. The "why" of being is willing is because it *works* to do so, and workability is always linked back to values. That is, it works to be willing to experience if it also means that you get to live your chosen values.

The Character of Commitments

Making behavioral commitments and then following through can be the most challenging aspect of ACT, and yet this is the part that changes lives. For this reason, we spend quite a bit of time talking about the process of living values rather than the outcome of living them. We focus on the character of commitments in a number of ways. For some clients it works to talk about this issue by comparing it to a game (Hayes et al., 1999). It can be playful to make different choices in your life and see what happens. And the thing about games is that they are based on the notion that you need to be somewhere other than where you are. If you are playing the game of Trivial Pursuit, for instance, the goal is to get to the end of the game by following a set of rules about answering questions correctly and moving your piece forward until you reach the center. The game will continue as long as you haven't arrived at the center. Once you have arrived, the game is over. But there is always another game to play. Life is like that. The direction you take comes from making a choice that where you are *not* is more important than where you *are*. Most notably, it is not what's out there that is important—it's that you care about what is out there. The therapist can ask the client, "What game do you choose to play?" If clients respond that they can't decide, then they are playing the game of indecision. It has its own set of rules and outcomes. If clients are worried about making the wrong choice and so, like a child in a game of tag, decide they don't want to play because they might get tagged, then they are playing the game of not playing. This too, has a set of rules and consequences—ways to win and ways to lose. And we don't win every game we play. The therapist can ask the client, "What game are you playing now?"

For other clients we employ the use of metaphor to focus on the character of commitments. We often use the monsters on the bus metaphor (Hayes et al., 1999) to help the client remain in contact with the challenge, but also with the choice:

Therapist: Sometime this whole "living your values" thing can be like driving a bus. Imagine that you are the driver, and as you have gone along the bus route, you have picked up a number of passengers. Some of these passengers are easygoing and don't pose any threat. They take their seats and ride like good citizens. Other passengers look and act more like monsters. They are threatening and hairy and big and ugly. They make a lot of noise and never do what you tell them to. You try to ignore them, but it's too difficult.

Client: Why don't you just kick them off?

Therapist: Sure, sounds good. But what is the first thing you have to do to get them off of the bus?

Client: Stop driving.

Therapist: Correct. You have to stop … Plus, these guys are monsters—they are tough, and you can't kick them off. So you go back to driving, trying to pretend that they don't bother you until, at some point, one of them walks right up to the front of the bus and starts yelling in your ear, "Go left! I am not sitting down until you do." Now, you really don't like this monster, and in fact, you really want him to go away. So you agree. You cut a deal and turn left. But then another monster comes and tells you to turn left again, and the same thing keeps happening. What you find is that your world has gone from a whole city of driving to a small block of making left turns to make sure that monsters don't come up and yell in your ear. You see the deal here? The monsters get their way so that you don't have to experience them, but you know they are there anyway—you can still see them and hear them.

Client: Yes. But can't I just kick them off the bus?

Therapist: You tell me! Look to your experience and see—how many monsters have you successfully kicked off the bus?

Client: (*lamenting*) None.

Therapist: In fact, it's not possible to get rid of the monsters. As we drive through life we are constantly picking up these kinds of passengers, and because we can't erase history, they're on for good.

Client: I wish they weren't.

Therapist: Yeah … But, what if it's the case that the monsters can only come up to the little yellow line and make you look at them? What if that is the only thing they can do? Nothing else … You have to see them, you have to know that they are there, but that is all they can do. They can't rip the steering wheel out of your hands; they can't even grab you at all. All they can do is make you look at them, make you know that they are there.

Client: Hmm. Interesting.

Therapist: If this were the case, do you think you could keep driving? Driving in the direction that you want to go? … They can't cross the yellow line, and you can just keep on driving … where *you* want to go. You always have the choice to drive where you want to go, even if they stand right next to you and make havoc. Will you?

This metaphor can also be told as one big story without responses from clients. On occasion, in group sessions we have had the members have a little fun with acting the metaphor out (Walser & Pistorello, 2005). You can select a driver and a few monsters, such as the "anxiety monster" or the "worried monster" or the "angry monster." Have the driver move around in a circle with the monsters talking their parts, and remind the driver that no matter what the monsters say, he or she is in charge of the driving. At no point does the driver need to let go of the wheel, and if perchance it happens, remind the driver that he or she just needs to grab the steering wheel again.

We use other methods to try to get at the character of making and keeping commitments. The therapist can remind the client that making a commitment with respect to a value is like heading toward a large mountain. There are many paths to reach the top, and if you step off of a path—which all of us will do from time to time—you can just step back on again. It is important to remind the client that taking a direction with respect to values is always a matter of choice. Since choice is available moment by moment, the client can always choose to step back on the path and get realigned with values. Values are very active, whether they are lived in small ways or in large ways. We remind clients that there are a number of ways to set daily goals that are consistent with their values, and we also remind them that these goals don't need to be about shooting for the moon:

Therapist: It's important to take action with respect to your values, but let me remind you that you don't have to jump off of a building. You can jump off a chair. (*Sometimes we actually jump off of a chair to demonstrate.*) Or you can jump off a piece a paper. (*Lay a piece of paper on the ground and jump off the piece of paper, using the same motion as jumping off of the chair.*) But whatever you do … jump!

This nicely demonstrates how action can be taken. Working on small goals is still that … working. We also tell clients that there is no trying here (Hayes et al., 1999). We often have clients say, "Well, I'll try." Here, we demonstrate doing versus nondoing. We ask the client to try to stand up or pick up a pen or make some movement. As soon as the client engages in the behavior, we say, "Oops, you're doing it. We asked you to *try* to do it. Try again." Generally, the point is made very rapidly and the notion of trying versus doing is brought home.

The therapist can work with the client by focusing on the issue of workability. Does the commitment work in terms of the client's values? The therapist can have a discussion with the client about doing it because it works. You can talk with the client about how valued living is not about living up to someone else's standards (society, religion, parents); it is about living up to one's own standards, whatever they may be.

Finally, the therapist continues to work with the client on taking a direction as a matter of choice and about how that choice is freely made. It's really an act of faith. No reassurance can be given that will guarantee things will be different. We don't know what will happen if the client is willing to experience anxiety, or anger, or sadness. This is the process of life. However, we feel pretty confident about what will happen if they continue to focus on controlling emotion before values can be lived. We are clear that it will look pretty much like what they have been doing. We pose the following question to the client: "Would you choose a year of battling your internal experience or a year of being willing to experience what is there to be felt and to also live your values?" We've yet to have a client choose the former.

How clients spend their time mattering is essential, and the importance of making choices in this regard is brought home by the recognition that we have only this life and this moment. We often ask how it will be spent—by mattering about kicking monsters off of buses or by mattering about driving wherever the client would like to go.

The Willingness Question

During the last session we bring all the work that we have done down to a single question that embodies both acceptance and commitment. It is the core of the entire treatment: Out of the place from which there is a distinction between you and your ongoing experience, that place from which you can observe, are you *willing* to do that, observe, *and* do what works for you in the moment, according to your values? (Hayes et al., 1999).

We tell clients that this is the question that will never stop being asked. In session, we write this question on a whiteboard and explore it in terms of the title of the therapy: Acceptance and Commitment Therapy. The therapist can draw a diagonal line following the word "and," and then talk with the client about how the first half of the question represents acceptance. This is followed by directing the client's attention to the second half of the question and discussing how this represents commitment. During this time we are often talking with clients about how acceptance of self can be an act of love. From that place clients can operate on the basis that they are 100 percent acceptable and loveable and then go live out in the world, rather than having to be something else first. Self-acceptance is compassionate, and it is a "first you win before you play" kind of game. This message is conveyed with sincerity, warmth, and compassion. The basic stance of the therapist is that clients are held in esteem and viewed as capable of making vital lives for themselves.

After the discussion of the willingness question, we then move on to conduct two final exercises that continue to point to acceptance and commitment. The first is the child exercise (Hayes et al., 1999). In this example, we'll assume the client is female.

Therapist: We are going to do one last exercise that focuses on acceptance. It is a closed-eyes exercise and will last a little longer than some of the others that we've done, so you'll want to sit in a position where you are

comfortable but alert. (*Pause to allow adequate time for this to occur.*)
I would like you to close your eyes and take just a moment to focus
on your breathing, as we've done many times in the past. (*Allow the
client to focus on breathing for about a minute.*) Now I would like you
to search back through your memories to a time when you remember
feeling a little sad or lonely, perhaps when you were six or seven, maybe
a little older or a little younger. Picture what you looked like at that age.
Imagine how small your hands were and the type of clothing you wore.
Perhaps imagine yourself in one of your favorite outfits ...

Now, put yourself in the place of this child, as if you have become
that child and you are looking through her eyes. Look down and see
your small hands and the clothes you're wearing ... Now imagine that
you are going back to the place where you lived when you were that age.
If you can't picture your exact home at that age, choose one that you
can picture. Once you have the image, imagine that you are standing
before the home as that child. Imagine yourself walking up to the front
door of this place and reaching up to take the doorknob, turning it
to open the door, and stepping through. Look around and notice the
pictures on the walls, the furniture ... Notice how you have to look up
to see some things given how small you are ...

Now, I would like you to go to the place in this home where you
might find your mother or your mother figure ... the place where she
would hang out. When you have found her, notice what she is doing
... Look around and see the room. Walk up to your mother and do
whatever it is that you have to do to get her attention, so that she looks
you right in the face. Once she looks, from that place of one of your
early hurts, ask her for what you need ... Tell her what you need and
see if she can give it. (*Pause, allowing time for the client to complete
the request.*)

Now, gently pulling away from this interaction with your mother,
I would like you to go find your father or father figure ... Go to the
place in this home where he might hang out. When you find him,
notice what he is doing ... Look around the room and see what is there
... Now walk up to your father and do whatever it is that you have to
do to get his attention ... to get him to look you right in the face. Once
you have his attention, ask him for what you need in response to the
early hurt you've chosen ... Tell him what you need and see if he can
give it. (*Pause, allowing time for the client to complete the request.*)

Now gently leave your father and begin to walk in whatever
direction takes you to the front door ... When you arrive, reach up and
turn the knob and open the door ... Step through and pull the door

closed behind you. Begin to walk away from the house, head down the sidewalk or street ... and as you do this, notice that in the distance you see someone walking toward you, an adult. As you get closer, you realize that it's *you*. It is the adult that is you today. Go up to the adult you see before you and do whatever it is that you have to do to get her attention ... so that she looks you right in the face. Once you have her attention, from the place of hurt, ask her for what you need. (*Pause, allowing time for the client to complete the request.*)

Some therapists choose to end the exercise at this point. However, we add a bit more to the exercise to further the intended impact:

Therapist: Now imagine that you are leaving this scene, this scene of meeting the adult you on the sidewalk, and imagine that you are transported back to this very moment, to this room, this chair. You are now the adult that you know today. And now imagine that the little child, that you were just a moment ago, is standing right outside the door of this room. She is opening the door and stepping inside ... And now imagine that she is walking toward you ... She has come to stand right before you. As she stands there, give her your attention ... Look her right in the face and see what she needs. See if you can give it. (*Pause, allowing time for the client to complete the request.*) Notice if there is any withholding in you; check to see if you are resisting anything ... If so, see if you can let that go and give the child what she needs ... Now imagine that the child is climbing into your lap ... and imagine that she is melting into you, becoming a part of you. Now gently bring yourself back to the room, picture this place, and return when you are ready.

Once the exercise is complete, we spend time processing the experience. The exercise can be quite emotional, and you may need to allow some time for silence as clients reconnect with you or the group. Clients tend to have a range of reactions to this exercise. The overall response tends to be quite positive and moving. Most clients find value in being able to give to themselves what a parent could not. This giving usually is about love, acceptance, protection, hugs, kindness, being there, and so on. Clients will find great relief and power in this stance of self-acceptance and giving. Following this exercise, we have had clients say things like "That was amazing. I really can be there for myself!"

Some clients will report more difficulty with the exercise. For instance, we have had clients report that they were unable to see themselves as the child or could not find the home that they grew up in. In cases like these, we will spend time talking about what seems to be blocking the images. Often these clients will report that it seems too painful. It is important to work with this response from the perspective of willingness. You may ask if they are willing to experience pain if it is a means to self-acceptance, and *is* in fact acceptance. Other clients will report that they had a hard time doing the exercise because they had a negative reaction to the child. We have clients report that they wanted the child to go away or do something different. Generally, this is about not wanting the child to be vulnerable, feeling inadequate in terms of being able to help the child, or wanting the child to be able to make things different back then (such as protecting herself from abuse, standing up to a parent, running away, telling someone, etc.). We gently work with the client to contact the price of nonacceptance. The therapist may ask, "Does the child know that you are turning away? Can she tell that you are wanting her to be different, to be stronger, or whatever it is you are wishing she would do?" The answer to this question is most often yes. You can work with the client to find ways to approach the child. This may include, metaphorically speaking, simply letting the child stand before her or taking the child by the hand.

The therapist may also choose to do something a little more potent to help the client work on self-acceptance. For instance, we once worked with a client who was having great difficulty even "looking" at the child. She was quite stuck and really wanted to the child to be gone. Robyn, at that point, went over and gently knelt before the client and asked her to imagine that Robyn was her as a child. Seemingly without thinking, the client immediately reached out and took Robyn's hand. This moment held as the client began to weep. It was clear to everyone in the room that no words were needed. The process was ended by the client softly saying, "I get it. I can do this." This example demonstrates the power of experiential knowing versus verbal knowing. Regardless of what the client's mind was telling her, she was able to find compassion.

While some clients will report that their parents were able to give what was needed in the exercise (love, acceptance, etc.), others report that their parents were invalidating in some way. The therapist should acknowledge the pain of this situation and the difficulty of nonacceptance. Here it is important to ask whether, even though the parents could not give what was requested, the client's adult self was able to give the child what she needed. Again, most clients report that they were able to do what their parents could not. Occasionally, a client will report being unable to give what was needed. In this case, we ask the client if this is a repeat of what happened with their parents. We note how we sometimes unintentionally do the very thing that our parents did: turn away from ourselves, don't protect, don't offer love, and so on. Under these circumstances, the strategies just described can be helpful.

Finally, some clients will report that they had to make their imagination work hard because they were most likely to find their father outside the home, or that they couldn't remember a home. These are generally small issues. The therapist can ask if the client was able to stay with the point of the exercise. There is no need to spend time explaining. In fact, it's best not to, as you could end up derailing the exercise in favor of explanation.

Done well, this exercise can be one of the most profound and meaningful to the client. It is an experience that gives the client the opportunity to shift into a different relationship with the self—one that is loving, kind, and accepting. After processing the child exercise, we move directly into the stand and commit exercise (Hayes et al., 1999) as the final exercise for the group or individual session. This is not to say that you shouldn't continue to work with the group or individual; however, the components of the therapy have now all been completed, and all future work can based on this foundation.

The stand and commit exercise can be done in group or individual therapy. We will explain the process for a group, as the activities are the same for either form of therapy. However, with an individual the exercise involves working directly with the therapist.

Therapist: We have come to our last exercise, the piece that addresses commitment, just as the child exercise addressed acceptance. Before we begin this exercise, I would like us to form the group into a semicircle, leaving a space in the middle for a person to stand. (*Have the group place their chairs in semicircle all facing the same direction.*) In this exercise you will be asked to do three things. First, as an audience member, your role is to be connected to the person who stands before you, to offer yourself in an open manner, being willing to be present to the person who is standing and making the commitment. Second, as the person who is standing, you are to come before the group and stand. While standing, I would like you to silently make eye contact with each member of the group. Stay with them in this contact until you know you have been present with them, connected with them. Stay standing in one place, gently shifting your position so that you can stand before each member of this group. Keep moving from person to person, making eye contact, until one of the therapists lets you know that you are done. This may mean that you have to start at the first person again and move around the group a second time. Once you are cued to stop, the third thing you will need to do is take a small step forward and say what it is that you are going to be about in your life. Make a commitment to your values, saying as much as you like.

At this point you can ask one of the clients to come and stand before the semicircle, or the therapist can go first (a bit of modeling can occur in the latter case). If there are two therapists in the group, each should plan to take a turn, providing the instructions as the other participates in the exercise. Once the client or therapist has come to stand in front of the group, the exercise begins:

Therapist: Now take a moment to get connected to your group members. Look each in the eye at a pace that allows you to connect. Be present to them ... Notice any defenses or desires to defend that may arise, and see if you can let them go.

Helping the client to let go in this case might entail asking clients who fold their arms or hold their hands in front of themselves to let that go by unfolding their arms and dropping their hands to their sides. The client may smile or laugh, in which case the therapist would respond by gently asking the client to notice the response, to gently let that go also, and to be present to what is happening. Ask the client to stay with any emotion that is arising and let it be there for as long as it is there.

Therapist: See if you can gently connect, undefended, with each person. (*Therapist turns toward the group members.*) ... And group members, see if you can be here for this human being standing before you undefended.

Allow silence and time for the client to connect to each group member, occasionally dropping in comments about staying connected and about other group members having appreciation for the human being standing before them. Once the client has connected with each group member, have the client step forward and state their commitment to a value or values. If it seems the client is remaining defended and needs a bit more time in silent connection, have the client continue a little longer, making eye contact with members of the group. See if the client can get there. If they are unable to fully do it, the point is not to torture the client, but to be accepting of where they are. Have the client engage this part of the exercise a bit longer, before speaking their commitment.

Proceed through the exercise, doing the same as above for each client and each therapist. When everyone has finished, take a moment to appreciate the experience in silence, and then have the group members give thanks to each other for the opportunity to be present and whole.

At this point, we generally end the session without much processing. The exercise tends to speak for itself. We often ask, "Have we done our work?" The clients mostly agree, and the session is ended.

The End and the Beginning

In this last session it is recognized that although the therapy is coming to a formal end, it is just the beginning of accepting and living a vital life. From this point forward the client is able to choose something different than nonvitality and constriction—or those things that bring psychological and behavioral inflexibility. Once the client is clear that choice is always present, it is difficult to go back—one cannot unlearn this part. The question is now what choice will be made: one that enhances behavioral and psychological flexibility, or one that does not? Our wish for all of our clients is that open and flexible responses to themselves and others will be the beginning of a new and vital life.

Sticking Points for Clients

The issues described below are those that seem to commonly arise at this point in therapy. However, you will observe that the various sticking points mentioned throughout this book, as well as others you may discover, can appear and reappear at any point in the therapy.

For instance, as we come to the end of therapy, some clients will report that they do not feel quite ready to embark on living their values. The therapist works with such clients to help them see this struggle as consisting of more thoughts and feelings to be held with acceptance—as ongoing experiences that will come and go—and to take action. Clients can hold themselves up with not feeling ready, believing that they need to feel motivation or confidence before they can live. If you begin to do things, motivation will likely follow. Taking action is the key here. Jump, and feelings of motivation will come … and they will go and come yet again. It is better to take action than to wait to feel a particular motivation before doing so. If clients are waiting for motivation, they may be waiting a long time. Confidence is an action, too. It literally means "with fidelity, with trueness to oneself" (Hayes et al., 1999). So being confident is about acting with trueness to oneself.

Sticking Points for Therapists

The point made above, that clients' various sticking points can occur and reoccur at any point in the therapy, is true for therapists as well.

The Therapist Is Unwilling

We've talked about this in prior chapters, but we'd like to briefly reflect on the importance of working on your own willingness. It is very difficult to encourage clients to do this for themselves when you're not doing it. You will be a much more engaging and believable therapist if you, too, are willing.

Fear of Activating Trauma

As discussed with the observer exercise in chapter 7, therapists can have concerns about doing exercises that activate trauma memories, particularly if done in a group setting. For instance, in the child exercise, the concern is that the client will return to a childhood trauma as their "early hurt." This can happen; however, it should not be an obstacle to doing the exercise. The challenge for the ACT therapist is balancing the point of the exercise with inadvertent messages of control (avoiding trauma memories). The therapist can gently guide the client to a nontrauma memory (for instance, "Think of an early upset or hurt, not necessarily a traumatic event, but something that upset you"), even though, by this point in therapy, the client should be able to see the trauma for what it is—a memory (albeit one with many associated feelings, thoughts, and so on). Nonetheless, guiding the client might be done in favor of helping the client experience the main point of the exercise—to find compassion for one's self and to give what wasn't given (love, acceptance, etc.). It should be remembered, however, that in ACT the therapist always holds the position that the client is whole and capable of recalling painful memories. Should the client return to a trauma memory, and many will, we work directly on acceptance of that memory.

The Stand and Commit Exercise

Therapists, having their own internal experience, can get caught in wanting to do this exercise "right." This can look like not showing emotion, inauthenticity (smiling or looking proper and professional when feeling anxious), or seeming unwilling. Given that this is an experiential exercise, it is hard to describe this phenomenon in words, but we have seen it, and it is problematic. For instance, we once had a therapist trainee who, upon her turn to stand and commit, remained very poised, professionally moving through the exercise, timing her connection with each person so that it was equal across clients, and then choosing a commitment that was easy (one that she was already engaging in and which had proved to be no challenge). She rattled the commitment off like she was giving a professional presentation. Not only could we see right through it, the clients could see right through it too. She sacrificed authenticity, one of her stated values, for what appeared to be an attempt at professionalism. In the end it just looked like she was holding herself above the clients. She appeared problem free. This position is a mistake in ACT. We hold ourselves to be on the same plane as the client, struggles and all. It is important to just let yourself be with whatever is happening, letting go of defenses and being sincere in talking about your commitments. Participate, just as you are asking the client to do, openly and undefended.

Homework

Homework assignments should be handed out to the client as needed across sessions since this section may vary in length. Two homework assignments are provided; you can use them flexibly across sessions. Be sure both are completed by the end of the committed action session as that is generally the termination session. Be familiar with the assignments so that you can answer any questions that the client might have. Ask the client to bring the completed homework to the next session for review. No assignment is given at the last session unless it seems appropriate.

HOMEWORK ASSIGNMENT 1: COMMITTED ACTION

Instructions: During this next week, whenever a difficulty arises, I would like you to imagine that you have become your best, most compassionate friend. As this best friend, treat yourself as you would your best friend, in a way that is consistent with your values, with respect to this difficulty. Write about these experiences.

HOMEWORK ASSIGNMENT 2: COMMITTED ACTION

Instructions: Pick a day this week and "be your word"; that is, completely live your values. Do things purely because you have verbally committed to do so (for instance, go to the gym, eat well, make a call, pray, go see a friend). Write about your experiences.

CHAPTER 10

Therapist and Treatment Considerations

It is not our abilities that show what we truly are. It is our choices.

—Professor Dumbledore to Harry in *Harry Potter and the Chamber of Secrets,* by J.K. Rowling

In chapter 4 we explored how to begin ACT therapy by orienting the therapist and discussing the overall treatment and session strategy, how to structure sessions, and how to provide informed consent. In this chapter we examine the implementation of ACT more fully by exploring issues ranging from more comprehensive training in ACT to desired therapist qualities and therapist self-care. We also discuss application of ACT as it relates to different settings and decision making about who should be a client in ACT.

Chapter Objectives

- The first step: is ACT for you?

- Training in ACT

- Acquire core skills

- Desired therapist qualities

- Address vicarious traumatization

- Practice clinician self-care

- Recognize the importance of PTSD training

- Establish appropriate treatment setting and modality

- Explore the factors that affect treatment decisions

The First Step: Is ACT for You?

The first step for therapists who are interested in conducting ACT is to gain initial exposure to the therapy. This can be achieved independently by reading the ACT literature (see recommendations in the introduction and visit www.contextualpsychol ogy.org), by attending an ACT pre- or post-institute at one of the national conferences (see www.aabt.org or www.istss.org) or by participating in one of the regularly offered ACT workshops (see www.contextualpsychology.org). As mentioned, it is important for providers to discover whether or not they resonate with the philosophy and core tenets of ACT, because without this basic connection it is unlikely they will be able to adequately provide the therapy. ACT therapists are actively involved during sessions and hold themselves to be on the same playing field as the client; this is impossible to do well if the therapist does not relate to the material in a fundamental way. In addition, many of the core concepts of ACT are rather novel (or better said, not culturally supported) as compared to many current forms of therapy. If the therapist doesn't approach them with thoughtfulness and understanding, it will be difficult to adequately and consistently teach them to clients. A benefit to participating in an ACT workshop is that participants are presented with the metaphors and exercises in the same way they are presented to clients. Potential ACT therapists are thus able to experience ACT on a personal level and can better comprehend the experience of their future clients. It is our experience that therapists who participate in an ACT workshop can quickly discern whether they do or do not connect with ACT as an intervention they choose to pursue. Many ACT workshop participants report a fundamental shift in how they have been viewing human suffering, and that they wish to learn more about the theories behind ACT and how to implement the therapy as a result.

Getting Trained in ACT

Once you have determined that ACT seems to make sense and is a fit for you as a therapist, we recommend that you join, or if necessary establish, an ACT supervision group. We have found that a regular ACT supervision group, wherein more experienced ACT providers consult with newer ACT therapists, is quite effective. We have established two weekly supervisions, one in-person supervision and one consult for therapists who are unable to physically meet. You may also seek supervision from an ACT trainer either in person or by telephone. There are a number of other ways to stay regularly connected to training and the ACT community. One is to use the ACT listserv to read and engage in conversation about client issues, theory, and relational frame theory (RFT; Hayes et al., 2001). The therapist in training might also try e-mail discussions with fellow ACT travelers and an ACT expert, if possible. If, for some reason it is difficult to find an experienced therapist to work with, we also know of small groups of new ACT therapists who have formed to consult about their work with clients and to grapple with the theoretical underpinnings of ACT. Finally, we recommend reading the ACT books listed in the introduction; these are excellent resources, providing not only instruction in application, but also the whys of the therapy. One book that may be particularly useful is *Get Out of Your Mind and Into Your Life* (Hayes & Smith, 2005). This is a self-help book that walks the reader through the therapy and provides exercises that map the intervention. We recommend that you read through this book, doing each exercise and exploring it as intended—as self-help.

Although we recognize that it may not be available to many new ACT therapists, we nonetheless take this opportunity to present an optimal training model, one that we have been able to implement with good results:

1. Participate in a two-day ACT beginning workshop to get a sense of the therapy. (Later you may want to participate in an advanced workshop to further develop your ACT skills.)

2. Read the fundamental ACT literature (see the introduction to this book; visit www.contextualpsychology.org).

3. Observe an experienced ACT therapist conducting the therapy, either by sitting in on an ACT group or by watching training tapes.

4. Cofacilitate an ACT group with an experienced ACT therapist.

5. Conduct individual or group therapy solo while receiving weekly ACT supervision by an experienced ACT therapist.

6. Continue to participate in ACT peer supervision.

Again, the above model is provided as an ideal way to train new ACT therapists and is not intended to represent the only way to acquire competency in ACT. However, we have found that ACT consultation and supervision groups are crucial for new therapists—at the very least they provide the means to determine if what one is doing is in accordance with ACT principles. ACT consultation and supervision should reflect the key tenets proposed in ACT. That is, in order to effectively work within the ACT frame, therapists must be willing to have their own uncomfortable thoughts and feelings and be willing to relate to others in the group in an authentic and accepting way. When we work with supervisees, we take care to model this in our work with them and to present experiential acceptance as a core competency in ACT therapy (for a more detailed discussion of ACT supervision see Walser & Westrup, 2006).

Core Skills

The following is a discussion of the fundamental skills needed to effectively conduct acceptance and commitment therapy.

Understanding the Game Plan

In working with new ACT therapists, we have noted a phenomenon that can best be described as not seeing the forest for the trees. That is, some trainees seem to understand ACT concepts, such as self-as-context, control as the problem, and so on, but not how or why these pieces fit together. This shows up as uncertainty about how to proceed, especially when clients are not responding to the protocol exactly as anticipated. It is important that anyone conducting ACT understand what they are ultimately shooting for and the essential elements needed to get there. The following set of questions and answers works through these essential elements.

Question: According to the philosophy of ACT, what is the ultimate goal of therapy?

Answer: To help clients live a personally valued life.

Question: What does that mean?

Answer: It means to make choices, to *be*, in accordance with personal values.

Question: What enables clients to realize this and to choose actions that are in valued directions?

Answer: Realization that they are free to make these choices, regardless of what their emotions and/or minds are telling them.

Question: What do clients need in order to realize they have this freedom?

Answer: There are three central ideas that clients need in order to recognize that they have freedom of choice.

1. Awareness that internal experiences cannot ultimately be controlled and that misapplied control efforts can be quite problematic. This is needed for clients to cease engaging in nonfreeing, avoidant strategies. Creative helplessness and control as the problem address this issue.

2. Awareness that internal experiences do not need to be controlled in order for the client to be whole and fundamentally worthwhile. Self-as-context addresses this issue.

3. Awareness that if one is willing to have whatever internal experiences are there, one is freed up to make behavioral choices based upon what one cares about. Willingness, values, and committed action address this issue.

Another way to approach this is to develop a basic understanding of what each major ACT component offers:

1. *Creative hopelessness* helps clients to see that the strategies they have been using to eliminate unwanted thoughts and feelings are hopeless strategies. Trying to undo history or manipulate oneself into permanently feeling better cannot actually be achieved.

2. *Control as the problem* helps clients to see that attempts to control internal experiences don't ultimately work and may actually be part of the problem.

3. *Willingness* helps clients to see that as an alternative to control, they can accept whatever thoughts and feelings are in the moment, subsequently freeing themselves to make behavioral choices in valued directions.

4. *Self-as-context* helps clients to establish willingness by seeing that troubling emotions and thoughts don't need to be controlled or fixed—the client has a self that is both intact and larger than such transient phenomena.

5. *Values* helps clients to see that they have the freedom to choose what they will value in their life, the freedom to show up to a meaningful life on an ongoing basis.

6. *Committed action* helps clients to commit to behavioral choices that are based upon their values, which leads to an inherently meaningful life.

Once therapists have a solid grasp of the overall strategy in ACT, they can develop a treatment plan for clients and better guide the therapy. By understanding the function of each fundamental ACT component, the therapist can utilize various elements of the therapy as needed while working with particular clients.

Experiential Acceptance

The most important area of competency for ACT therapists is experiential acceptance. It is essential that ACT therapists be of the same mind with the basic philosophy of ACT, and that they thoroughly understand the function of experiential avoidance in trauma-related problems. As mentioned, to work effectively within the ACT frame, therapists must also be willing to experience their own emotions, sensations, memories, and thoughts as they arise. This requires awareness of personal efforts to control. One of the more common errors made by both new and seasoned ACT therapists is to support experiential avoidance that occurs in the course of therapy, either by avoiding something themselves (such as moving on quickly when an uncomfortable silence occurs); by inadvertently sending a control message to clients (for instance, suggesting or implying that their thoughts or feelings need to change or are wrong in some way); or by assisting them in avoiding something (for example, saying something to help clients feel less uncomfortable). It is fairly easy to make these kinds of mistakes, and the following example and explanation will demonstrate the sometimes subtle nature of this issue. This session occurred while trainees were observing:

Client: I am just tired of all of the problems I have. I want them to go away—I just need a break.

Therapist: It seems like that might resolve your struggles, getting a break … And sitting with that tired feeling itself even seems like a struggle.

Client: (*very pressured and loud and seemingly uncomfortable*) I just have such a hard time being understood. My mom doesn't understand me, my dad doesn't understand me, my friends don't understand me…

Therapist: I can feel the sense of tiredness in that too.

Client: (*with growing discomfort*) If I could only get people to understand.

Therapist: (*remains silent but focused on the client*)

Client: (*with more force*) What do I have to do to be understood?

Therapist: (*with a gentle hand gesture to slow down*) I wonder if we could slow down just a bit and notice what it is that you are feeling right now?

Client:	(*pressured*) I have to figure this out. I have to know how to make people understand me.
Therapist:	Again, I am wondering if we can just take a moment to notice what you are feeling? (*gesturing*) Slow down and notice.
Client:	And now here we are: I'm telling you I don't feel understood, and you don't understand me either!
Therapist:	(*observing that the client would like to have a conversation about nonunderstanding as a way to avoid emotion*) Notice the desire to run … (*softly*) Let's just breathe and be slow. (*Client and therapist sit quietly for a few moments and client begins to get tearful.*)

Following the session, one of the trainees began to question the intervention, suggesting that it would have been better for the therapist to tell the client with body language and kind words that she did understand or was working very hard to understand what was happening with the client. The trainee thought that the therapist had missed the opportunity to understand the client in some important way. What the trainee failed to see was the in-the-room avoidance of the current emotion. Talking about being misunderstood was a strategy to move away from painful experience. The client was working hard to get the therapist to engage in conversation as a way out of silence and feeling. The ACT-consistent move is to catch these forms of avoidance and respond accordingly by working on acceptance. If the therapist had done what the trainee suggested, both the client and therapist would have been caught in content, and they would have missed a wonderful moment to connect to experience.

Clients are besieged (as we all are) by countless control and avoidance messages. Just as an example, consider the endless array of advertisements pervading our culture, telling us on a continual basis that if we eat that, buy this, or look like that beautiful person we will be better off (happier). If we can just purchase that super-deluxe side-on mower, the sun will shine, the kids will play badminton on the lawn, and everyone will smile ceaselessly. Clearly the objective is to feel happy *all the time*. This is an impossible task for anyone, not to mention for individuals who have experienced and survived a trauma. Nonetheless, trauma survivors have doubtless been directly or indirectly told that they need to get over it or forget about it, and that something is wrong with them for continuing to be so affected by the past. The trauma survivors we have worked with certainly believe that something is wrong with them because they have failed to be happy. All this is to point out the formidable challenge facing the ACT therapist who boldly suggests that this entire happy agenda is an illusion and a dangerous one at that. The therapist must wholeheartedly endorse the notion that, broadly applied, experiential avoidance *is* problematic and that the way out of this fruitless, ever-happy endeavor is experiential acceptance. Otherwise the therapy will fall flat.

Assessing the Cost of Avoidance

ACT is a therapy that emphasizes the function of behavior. An important skill for an ACT therapist is to be able to discern how and when avoidance is at work in the therapy and in the client's life, and the costs of this avoidance. Focusing on this central idea will help therapists correctly and consistently deliver the therapy.

Mindfulness

It is important for ACT therapists to be able to be present—present to their own internal experiences and present to what is happening in the room with clients. Mindfulness, as discussed at length in chapter 2, is an effective way to help establish experiential awareness, which in turn paves the way for experiential acceptance. The ability to notice, observe, and sit with the various thoughts, feelings, and sensations that arise allows therapists to be keenly aware of what is happening in the therapy and better able to respond effectively. An ACT therapist uses such information to guide their work. For example, if observing a feeling of frustration, the therapist would turn their attention to how the frustration is functioning in the room.

Mindfulness is a skill that is developed through practice. The exercises provided throughout the book are offered as examples of how ACT therapists can continually develop their personal mindfulness. As mentioned, one gift of mindfulness practice is increased awareness of and contact with the observer self. Just like clients, therapists discover less need to defend themselves from uncomfortable internal experiences once they learn to view these from the perspective of self-as-observer. When less effort is made to stave off uncomfortable emotions, one is more open to feelings in general, including interest, excitement, and joy. The net result is an authentic and vital life, both in and out of the office.

Desired Therapist Qualities for ACT

This section addresses that nebulous but all-important aspect of any therapy—the intangible qualities that make up an excellent clinician. Of the many factors that come into play, compassion and authenticity are particularly important qualities in an ACT therapist.

The first of these, compassion, stems from the ACT therapist's awareness that the client's struggle is in fact similar to their own. Or rather, that humans struggle—the client struggles, the therapist struggles ... we all suffer. As a fellow human being, the therapist is in the same space with the client, and even though the therapist might know of another way to approach this dilemma, the dilemma itself is shared. Understanding and appreciation of this basic fact helps ACT therapists maintain a compassionate stance in the face of whatever shows up in the course of therapy. Resistance, manipulation, avoidance—these are all seen as futile yet understandable attempts to avoid suffering. In addition, our personal work with ACT and compassion is guided by the notion contained in the Latin meaning of the word "compassion." It means to "bear suffering." To "bear" is to accept or allow, especially without giving way. As it applies to ACT, the therapist accepts without giving way to the pain of the human in front of them. Finally, we consider the passion within "compassion"; we strive to bear this pain with passion.

Ultimately, in ACT, compassion is viewed as a choice. That is, compassionate thoughts and feelings may come and go, but the therapist chooses to *be* compassionate toward the client. This tenet guides the therapist when countertransference occurs, as it will in any therapy. The ACT therapist approaches such reactions to the client as additional phenomena to be noticed and held while continuing to pursue the goals of therapy in accordance with one's values as a clinician (to do well by the client, to do one's best as a therapist, to put the client's needs above one's own). An ACT therapist might, for example, have a strong negative reaction to something the client is relating (for instance, abuse of an animal) but would still choose to remain actively engaged with the client.

The above example brings up the issue of authenticity. That is, while ACT encourages authenticity versus artifice in both client and therapist, it does not insist that therapists should be authentic for authenticity's sake. Rather, authenticity is used in the service of other values, such as establishing trust, furthering the therapy, and so on. Consider if in the above example, the therapist were to exclaim (after hearing about the animal abuse), "That's horrible!" While such a thought might have indeed passed through the therapist's mind, expressing it as an act of authenticity does no service to anyone. However, if the client were to directly ask what the therapist thought about what the client had just shared, an inauthentic response (like "It's okay; I understand") would be unlikely to work. A more effective response might be something along the lines of "That's hard to hear about. I notice myself cringing inside. What is it like for you to share it?"

In order to be authentic, one must therefore be willing to have whatever internal experiences are arising in the moment. We have found this to be a challenge for new ACT therapists, particularly those in training or who are otherwise early in their career. The need to present as a together, confident, knowledgeable clinician (in other words, to avoid feeling anxious, insecure, and unsure) can be quite compelling. However, some of the most powerful moments in ACT arise from situations where such thoughts and feelings are very much present and the therapist is willing to claim them. Here's an example that occurred after Darrah had gradually become aware of a lack of engagement by the client and noticed her own sense of being stuck.

Therapist: What do you think is going on in the room here? I feel stuck and anxious about what to do next.

Client:	What do you mean?
Therapist:	I don't know. Something doesn't seem to be working today. I feel like I'm not interesting you today. Do you feel it?
Client:	(*hesitates*) No, it's not you...
Client:	It seems as though there's something heavy in the room, something unsaid.
Client:	Well … I guess I just don't feel like being here today.
Therapist:	Can you say more about that? Not wanting to be here?
Client:	I've had a really long day and my daughter is sick. I don't feel like working on anything … I'm tired, and I just feel totally stressed.
Therapist:	I see. You are having all these thoughts about your day and your daughter; you're having feelings of stress and anxiety, feelings of being tired.
Client:	Yeah.
Therapist:	And yet you are here! You chose to come despite having all these reasons why it's hard today.
Client:	Yes, but I didn't want to. I really feel like going home and just vegging.
Therapist:	(*very compassionately*) So here's the deal: In this moment, you can choose to be here fully, to be fully engaged in this session with me because you value what we're doing here, even with all this other stuff in the room. (*Pauses to let this sink in.*) Are you willing to do that?
Client:	Yes, I can do that.
Therapist:	Can you be willing to have all those thoughts and feelings you mentioned—to just let them be there and yet choose to be engaged with me?
Client:	Yes, I can … *I am.*

Here you can see how the Darrah's willingness to be open and present to her own sense of being stuck and anxious opened up a place for the two of them to work together. Had Darrah been unwilling to claim this experience (tried not to be anxious, or at least appear that way and as though she knew what to do), then it is likely that the therapy would have continued in a nonengaged fashion.

Vicarious Traumatization

A topic that seems to go hand-in-hand with treating PTSD is the issue of vicarious traumatization. Much has been written about the potential for individuals who are working with trauma survivors to be affected by what they hear (Naugle, Bell, & Polusny, 2003; Palm, Polusny, & Follette, 2004). While we do not know of any actual data assessing the degree to which ACT providers experience vicarious traumatization or any that compares these therapists with those providing other forms of therapy, we do know that ACT has been shown to reduce burnout in counselors who treat substance use (Hayes, Bissett, et al., 2004). It would seem, however, that providing ACT would actually be a protective versus a risk factor.

Consider the following scenario: A non-ACT therapist experiences horror, disgust, anxiety, and anger while listening to a client's account of being viciously raped. Driving home, she finds herself suddenly thinking about something the client said, a detail of the incident. She quickly tries to put it out of her mind but instead finds herself imagining the scenario, picturing her client being raped. Alarmed, she again tries not to think about it but nevertheless begins to fear that she is now going to be haunted by this image.

In that scenario, one can almost feel the initial thought building into a problem— one gets the sense that the therapist is now going to be engaged in a battle that ensures she will have what she is trying so hard to avoid.

Now consider this scenario: An ACT therapist has listened to her client relate a horrific account of being viciously raped, during which the therapist experienced horror, disgust, anxiety, and anger. Driving home, a sudden thought, a detail about the rape, enters her mind. She notices that thought and the feeling of anxiety that accompanied it. She does so from the stance of self-as-context; that is, rather than continue along in that line of thought, she is aware of her self that is having that thought (and others, and even more still). Aware of the self that is larger than such phenomena, she is in the present, where that thought is only a piece of her experience, not her entire experience.

In this example, it seems more likely the therapist will be able to put her experiences in perspective and remain in a supportive (non-burnt-out) position for her client.

Clinician Self-Care

Again, ACT is a profoundly compassionate therapy, and it rests on the premise that all humans are in this struggle together—that despite our shared desire to avoid pain, we nonetheless suffer. Accepting this fundamental idea provides one with a profound sense of comfort, a release from the "more, better, different" agenda under which we so often labor. In other words, more than simply knowing how to do the therapy, ACT therapists have an opportunity to view life and themselves from a perspective that is both comforting and vital.

In the previous section we proposed that therapists who operate within the ACT framework may be protected from some of the risks involved in working with clients with PTSD. Similarly, by working within the ACT frame, therapists are engaging in activities, such as mindfulness practice, that promote personal well-being. In helping clients treat themselves compassionately, therapists are building their ability to do the same. As therapist and client work together to view the self as context rather than content, both continue to increase their ability to simply notice rather than automatically buy uncomfortable thoughts and feelings.

In chapter 1, we discussed the role of language in human behavior and human suffering. As noted, we work carefully with clients to verbalize their experiences in such a way that distinguishes the self from the internal experiences of the moment. In following this principle, therapists avoid many of the pitfalls that can accompany trauma work, or any difficult therapy; that is, where most therapists struggle at times with discouraging thoughts and feelings, an ACT therapist will always be aware that these sorts of experiences are simply phenomena to notice and hold rather than believing them wholesale. An ACT therapist might mentally note, "I'm having the thought that I'm not a very good therapist," and see that thought as a passenger on their bus rather than being literally true. This takes the power out of the thought and also frees the clinician to carry on in a valued direction. Finally, we recommend that therapists adhere to their own personal values, taking care to balance work, play, family, and other aspects of life, as defined by their own choices.

PTSD Training

It is important that therapists working with trauma survivors acquire solid training in post-traumatic stress disorder. It is essential to understand the behavioral principles at work in PTSD (for example, conditioning and operant responding) and how the various symptoms of PTSD might manifest both in and out of session. It is also important to understand the wide-ranging manifestations of trauma exposure. These can range in nature from impaired interpersonal functioning (such as being unable to have sex following rape) to feeling disconnected from reality (depersonalization and derealization). Again, not all who suffer a trauma develop PTSD, and familiarity with the continuum of trauma-related symptoms is helpful to anyone working with trauma survivors. These, too, are often about experiential avoidance.

Exposure Therapy and ACT

In chapter 1, we mentioned that ACT is theoretically consistent with exposure therapy—the gold-standard treatment for trauma. It would be fair to say, in fact, that ACT is a form of exposure. It specifically endeavors to expose clients to difficult emotional and thought experiences while promoting efforts to remain present rather than escaping the feared experiences. Additionally, both treatment approaches are behavioral in nature and view pathological avoidance as the target of treatment. Exposure therapy, however, specifically homes in on clients' efforts to avoid trauma-related stimuli—anything that was associated (paired) with the trauma at the time of the event or that has subsequently become associated with the trauma. For example, a woman who was raped in the military might have initially sought to avoid anything that evoked that difficult memory, such as military bases, men in uniform, military gear, and so on, and over time the avoidance generalized to all men and crowds. Exposure treatment targets the original rape, and subsequently works to eliminate the client's need to avoid related stimuli by exposing the client to the memory and associated thoughts and emotions. ACT views avoidance as a more global and problematic control strategy, which certainly includes the avoidance of trauma-related stimuli, but does not limit treatment to only addressing the traumatic event(s).

The established exposure protocols for PTSD, such as cognitive processing therapy (Resick & Schnicke, 1993) and prolonged exposure (Foa, Rothman, & Hembree, 2006) involve guiding clients with the use of imagery to reexperience the traumatic event(s). A key element in this process is to help the client intentionally evoke the intense images, thoughts, physical sensations, and emotions present at the time of the event. This process is repeated until the client is desensitized to the traumatic material. That is, the traumatic account, while still inherently "not okay," loses salience—the client learns that he or she can revisit such memories "safely," that encountering associated trauma cues does not mean the event is reoccurring. In the above example, the woman in question would ultimately be able to encounter men without experiencing them as the original perpetrator.

Both ACT and the various exposure protocols help clients stop fruitless and problematic avoidance efforts, instead guiding them to intentionally turn and face that which they have been fleeing. A difference here is that ACT is about "having what you have," which might include, at any one moment, trauma-related thoughts and feelings, whereas exposure therapy intentionally heads into the traumatic material, with the goal being to evoke trauma-related memories and associated reactions. In ACT, a trauma-related thought or feeling is not intentionally evoked, but should such phenomena arise, they are treated as another experience occurring "inside the skin" and an opportunity for exposure. Clients are helped to simply hold such experiences, thereby learning (as in exposure therapy) that they can have such memories and associated reactions without incurring further injury. They further see, as in exposure therapy, that the control and avoidance efforts they have employed (and that led to severely restricted living) are unnecessary.

We have found that combining ACT and exposure therapy is a potent intervention for individuals with PTSD. We have had clients complete ACT and then move into exposure work, or they have received both protocols concurrently. We recommend either of these two strategies over first providing exposure therapy and then ACT. While there is no harm in the latter, we have found that ACT provides a base for effective exposure work. Specifically, the self-as-context component of ACT places clients in a particularly powerful position to head into even intensely difficult trauma material, because they are clear that they have a self that is larger than even such painful memories. Because ACT specifically targets control as problematic, clients understand why it behooves them to resist urges to avoid as they engage in the exposure work. We have found it effective to use ACT language in the course of the exposure work, such as reflecting back, for example, that they are "having the memory of their squadron being attacked, they are having the thought that they are going to die," thereby reinforcing the idea that the trauma is in the past, and that they are in the present with a self that survived it all and transcends such experiences.

Treatment Setting and Modality

ACT lends itself well to both individual and group therapy and has been successfully conducted in a variety of treatment settings (Bach & Hayes, 2002; Strosahl, Hayes, Bergan, & Romano, 1998; Walser et al., 2005; Zettle & Hayes, 1986). In terms of the relative merits of individual versus group therapy, we have not found either to be superior for conducting ACT. While clients participating in group therapy benefit from the active involvement of their peers, with ACT, individual therapy has this quality as well. As mentioned, ACT is an egalitarian therapy. Rather than holding themselves as experts or above the client, ACT therapists consider themselves to be on the same playing field as the individuals they see in therapy. The collaborative, peerlike feel of the sessions, combined with the numerous experiential exercises in ACT wherein both client and therapist are actively engaged, ensures an interactive, shared experience.

One thing to consider when providing ACT in a treatment setting such as a hospital, inpatient unit, or residential treatment program is the degree to which ACT concepts are in agreement or conflict with other treatments being offered to the client. For example, the client could be learning how to "sit with" thoughts and feelings in ACT and then learning they need to fix problematic feelings and thoughts in another group. Clients do notice this difference and inquire about it. We have dealt with this issue in a number of ways. First, we talk with the client about how completing thought records is another form of getting perspective on thoughts—being able to see their thinking. We also talk about how debating thoughts can be a form of deliteralization. Second, we talk about how ACT is based on a workability agenda. If at one time it works to deliteralize through a thought record, then do that, and if at another time it works to do a mindfulness exercise and just observe thoughts, do that. Workability is the key. In our experience, clients respond well to these explanations and work with various materials accordingly.

When pulling ACT into an existing treatment setting, we have found it helpful to educate all involved staff regarding the central ideas of the therapy and to offer more extensive training to those who are interested. The exercises and metaphors used in ACT tend to stick with clients, who will then subsequently engage in "ACT speak." That is, a client currently receiving ACT therapy might refer to certain terms or metaphors (like the "passengers on my bus" or "thank your mind for that thought") in the context of another group or program activity. Such comments can be indecipherable to someone not familiar with them (for instance, a therapist leading a psychoeducational group), when in fact, they may apply very well to the topic at hand.

To the extent to which other program curricula are consistent with ACT, the various ACT metaphors and exercises can serve to further other treatments. As mentioned, we have found that clients participating in ACT do particularly well in other treatments that evoke difficult emotions (exposure and process groups), and clients report that many of the ACT metaphors are very helpful to keep in mind when engaging in these other forms of therapy.

Factors Affecting Treatment Decisions

There are a few factors that the therapist may want to consider when making treatment decisions. We will address this in a question and answer format.

Question: Which clients are good candidates for ACT? When is ACT appropriate?

Answer: Generally speaking, clients are good candidates if emotional avoidance is a key problem in their lives. Additionally, if clients have been through multiple treatments or have had long-term difficulties, then ACT is an ideal intervention. From this perspective you can see how ACT fits nicely with clients who have chronic PTSD.

Question: Is it okay to do "ACT-light," and if so, when?

Answer: Yes, it is perfectly okay to do ACT-light. We often do this with clients who have not suffered a great deal (younger clients tend to fit this category) or with clients who fit into the category of the "worried well" (living fairly well but wanting to improve their lives). When doing ACT-light, it is helpful to do a very short and lean creative hopelessness session and to focus more on acceptance and values. It may also be the case that some clients are versed in acceptance and may just need exercises, metaphors, and values work to get them reacquainted with their vitality.

Question: Who is not a candidate for receiving ACT? When is ACT not appropriate?

Answer: If a client is requesting a particular type of therapy, such as CBT interventions that are straightforward cognitive therapy, it is most appropriate to honor those requests. In addition, if there are empirically supported treatments that are specific to a disorder, the therapist may want to implement those first. Dialectical behavior therapy (DBT) for borderline personality disorder is an example (Linehan, 1993). DBT followed by ACT has been found to be an effective treatment combination (Pistorello, 2005). If a client is actively psychotic or in the process of being hospitalized, then stabilization is the first order of business.

Question: Should you ever stop ACT before the protocol has been completed?

Answer: Yes, if the client is experiencing negative effects, e.g. the client is getting worse—not living their values and escalating strategies that are harmful.

Question: What if the client doesn't like ACT?

Answer: At no time do you want to force a client to do ACT—just as is the case with other therapies. Use your good clinical judgment to discern if not liking the therapy is a way to avoid experience or if ACT is truly a poor fit for the client. In the instance where the client says, "I don't like this because I have to feel things," it is important to work with the client on willingness in the service of valued living. The therapist might ask, "Would you be willing to feel things if it meant you got to have a better life?" The client can be reminded that the idea isn't to have pain for pain's sake but to choose willingness for the purpose of attaining values. Check to see if the comments about not liking ACT are avoidance in general, and see if the client is willing to have that thought and continue anyway. If you have clients who genuinely do not like the therapy, don't do the therapy. For example, Robyn recently had a couple of clients who sincerely wanted to learn how to control their emotions. She referred one to a therapist who was more experienced in the kind of techniques being requested, and she conducted a different, non-ACT therapy with the other.

CHAPTER 11

Clinical Issues and Assessment

Have patience with everything unresolved in your heart
And try to love the questions themselves.

—Rainer Maria Rilke

In this chapter we will briefly explore clinical issues related to different trauma populations and issues of comorbidity. We will also discuss the limits and meanings of acceptance. And finally, we will also address assessment of PTSD and ACT.

Chapter Objectives

■   Conduct ACT with particular trauma populations

■   Review comorbidity

■   Consider what and what not to accept

ACT and Particular Trauma Populations

It is important to note that we approach any particular trauma population from a unifying theory of how experiential avoidance and maladaptive responding functions in the development and maintenance of psychological problems. This approach to human functioning emphasizes the functional nature of behavior within a given context. As a principle-based approach, ACT is easily applicable to various trauma populations. Additionally, as therapists become more familiar with ACT, they learn to apply core ideas in an increasingly ideographic manner, tailoring the protocol so that learning is optimized. In this section we will briefly explore different trauma populations from an ACT perspective, emphasizing particular issues that are helpful to keep in mind when working with each group.

Interpersonal Trauma

It is well established that of one of the greatest risk factors for PTSD in both men and women is interpersonal trauma, particularly sexual assault (Breslau et al., 1998; Fontana & Rosenheck, 1998; Smith, Frueh, Sawchuck, & Johnson, 1999) and childhood sexual abuse (Briere & Runtz, 1987). It is thought that one reason for this correlation is the attendant experience of shame and stigma that occur with these types of events. Victims tend to feel tainted, even ruined by their experience. In addition, individuals who have experienced this sort of trauma are often operating within societal contexts that attach blame or other negative stigma to the victim, making recovery all the more difficult (DePrince & Freyd, 2002). Additionally, victims of interpersonal violence may be engaging in avoidance that leads to further difficulties. For instance, Kate Iverson (2006) suggested to us that victims of domestic violence may be avoiding in ways that contribute to inaction toward safety and other forms of valued living.

We have provided ACT therapy to many individuals who have PTSD secondary to childhood trauma, sexual assault, and domestic violence. In fact, many of the clients we've worked with have survived multiple traumas, such as childhood sexual abuse and additional trauma as adults. As we have introduced each ACT component in this book, we have detailed how certain metaphors and exercises might be experienced by such clients and have suggested ways to tailor certain exercises to address the unique issues that may arise in the course of therapy.

We feel that ACT has particular promise as a therapy with individuals who have survived interpersonal trauma. That is, while there are several exposure-based treatments for PTSD that reduce trauma-related symptoms, ACT additionally offers individuals a profound shift in their self-view. For instance, many clients who have survived childhood abuse have been taught from an early age that they have no value; their prevailing experience has been that of being broken, of being shameful and definitely not okay. Through ACT these clients begin to realize that they have a self that is larger than such experiences, a self that not only is intact but has always been so. We cannot adequately describe what this has meant to some of the individuals we have worked with, except to say that they regained their basic sense of worth.

Revictimization

Research shows that history of child sexual trauma is associated with retraumatization in adulthood (Cloitre, Scarvalone, & Difede, 1997; Follette, Polusny, Bechtle, & Naugle, 1996). Estimated rates of revictimization among adults who suffered childhood sexual abuse range from 24 percent (Mayall & Gold, 1995) to 65 percent (for males) and 72 percent (for females) (Stevenson & Gajarsky, 1992). Nonabused populations experience significantly less interpersonal trauma as adults (17 percent to 31 percent, Mayall & Gold, 1995, and Schaaf & McCanne, 1998, respectively).

Several explanations have been put forth regarding the phenomenon of revictimization. Survivors may encounter additional occasion to be victimized in order to master the original trauma (Levy, 1998); they may have learned maladaptive ways of relating to others and engage in poor coping, both of which increase their risk of interpersonal violence (Messman & Long, 1996); they may have lacked opportunity to develop a healthy self-identity and subsequently derive their value externally (their sense of worth depends on how others, even their perpetrators, perceive them; Chu, 1992); they may engage in numbing responses and dissociation that decrease their ability to perceive danger signals (Cloitre, 1998; van der Kolk, 1996); and they lack confidence in their own judgment, thoughts, and feelings, and consequently do not trust their ability to discern safe from unsafe situations. Each of these notions can be understood from the perspective of experiential avoidance. Mastering the original trauma, for example, implies a need to overcome some aspect of oneself and one's history in order to arrive at "mastery"—some place other than where the survivor is now. It denotes an insufficient self that must be overcome.

Similarly, dissociation, numbing, and other symptoms of PTSD can be understood as forms of escape from difficult histories, thoughts, or emotions. Individuals with a poor sense of self tend to turn away from their own experiences, making others' experiences more important. This is particularly pronounced in individuals who have been programmed to believe that their feelings are not truly what they are and that their purpose is to serve others (for instance, "You shouldn't feel that way," "You wanted this to happen," or "This is a secret that no one can ever know about"). Such encounters of invalidation and denial of experience have profound negative effects on the survivor's sense of self. These issues are common in the sexual-abuse survivor and may need extra attention during ACT sessions (as described in chapter 7). We recommend that therapists be quite patient with these individuals as they begin to regain their personal experience of emotion and establish a self-identity. From an ACT perspective, in-the-moment work (such as building awareness of internal experiences and self-as-context) is key with survivors of this sort of trauma.

Veteran and POW Populations

Veterans who have experienced captivity, combat conditions, or war-zone activity (including viewing dead and mutilated bodies, witnessing or experiencing extreme physical trauma) often talk about how their personal values were superseded by the conditions of war. Veterans who have participated in combat often report guilt over killing others or over doing nothing while witnessing the death of others, explaining that they would never engage in such behaviors under other circumstances. These individuals report having great difficulty in reconciling what they did and experienced with their personal values, such as being loving or kind. It is important to spend time on supporting the extraordinary circumstances of war and its realities—how what one is called to do may conflict with personal values. We then work with these clients on bringing their lost or surrendered values back to life. This is frequently necessary, as many veterans with PTSD seem to be stuck in the emotional dilemma of these lost values and experience numbing, disillusionment, or intense anger in response. We have talked with clients specifically about their value of honoring life and the cost of wasting or "killing off" this value, too. We remind them that resurrecting the life of human beings as a value includes giving life to themselves as well. That is, the real tragedy would be if yet another life, their own, was also lost to war. The therapist might ask such a client, "How will you honor this life, the one right here before me in this room?"

Terrorism and Natural Disaster

Large-scale disasters and acts of terrorism produce a number of psychological and emotional responses. Difficulties can range in nature from acute anxiety or extreme grief and depression to relationship problems and problems with work and daily functioning. However, most problematic reactions to these kinds of events, fortunately, resolve on their own (McNally, Bryant, & Ehlers, 2003) and are largely normal responses to horrific experiences (Walser, Ruzek, et al., 2004). Additionally, it is not uncommon for disaster and terrorism survivors to experience loss of concentration, loss of memory, anger, emotional numbing, insomnia, fatigue, and other effects that may actually function as experiential avoidance. Nevertheless, these experiences are quite natural and should not be understood to be problematic in the same way that long-term experiential avoidance is conceived according to ACT. Some avoidance in these circumstances is expected and even helpful, and it's only seen as problematic if it becomes chronic and impairs one's life in some way (in the form of PTSD, generalized

214

anxiety disorder, depression, relationship problems, etc.). In these cases, ACT can be applied as an effective intervention much in the same way as described in this book. In fact, ACT may prove useful to the estimated 9 to 37 percent of individuals exposed to large-scale acts of terrorism and natural disasters who will go on to develop PTSD (Breslau et al., 1998; Cao, McFarlane, & Klimidis, 2003; Kuo et al., 2003). Additionally, the development of PTSD is a significant risk factor for the onset of other disorders, such as depression and substance dependence (Breslau et al., 1997; Breslau, Davis, & Schultz, 2003). As reviewed in the section on comorbidity below, these secondary problems are often linked to emotional avoidance and play a role in continued suffering.

Lastly, living according to personal values can be of great help following a terrorist act or mass disaster. Individuals who survive these experiences often have lingering fears that interfere with their ability to move forward in their lives in important ways. For instance, it is easy to see why individuals would choose to stop flying in airplanes following the events of 9/11 or refrain from moving back to New Orleans after Hurricane Katrina. Although there is some reasonableness to these fears, the actual probabilities of these sorts of events happening to any one person are quite low, and the fear can come to affect quality of life (for example, a family is scheduled to vacation together and flight is involved, so they don't go). Making intentional decisions about *how* one is going to live following such events is both powerful and relevant. At such difficult times it is particularly essential to align one's choices with one's values.

Traumatic Loss and Grief

It is important to distinguish "normal" from problematic responses to traumatic events. The traumatic loss of a loved one is of course tremendously difficult, and the utilization of various strategies to cope with this is natural. However, the hallmark of complicated versus normal bereavement is an intractable nonacceptance of the loss. This is a natural fit for ACT therapy, which offers a way for individuals to honor their feelings for their loved one while reengaging in life. In ACT, individuals who have lost someone are not being told that they must first be rid of their feelings in order to move on. This is extremely important when such clients are likely to feel that this sort of moving on is akin to forgetting (and further losing) their loved one.

Working with the acceptance of grief and sadness over loss from an ACT perspective can dignify the process of loss. For instance, it has not been unusual for clients who have experienced loss to complain that they wished the pain and tears would go away. We work with clients on acceptance of these emotions, not only as continued practice in experiential acceptance, but also as an example of living one's values. We indicate to clients that the experience of loss points to the importance of relationship and connection. It is extremely powerful to explore with clients the possibility that these painful feelings of loss reflect their caring, that they in fact serve to honor and remember the individual who has died. The therapist might ask, "Imagine if you didn't feel the pain of this loss, imagine that you did not have the tears, what would that mean about the relationship? What would that say about how you experienced this person?" The therapist might also add that the client's experience can be seen as an indicator of what the client values (loving relationships), and in choosing to be willing to have these thoughts and feelings the client is honoring that value.

Comorbidity

As discussed in chapter 1, individuals with trauma-related symptoms or PTSD frequently suffer from co-occurring difficulties. In fact, many fulfill diagnostic criteria for disorders such as depression and substance abuse. While the range of difficulties is as varied as are people, certain problems are particularly associated with PTSD. This section addresses how to work with dually diagnosed clients from an ACT perspective.

It may surprise you to learn that, in fact, the use of ACT with clients who have comorbid disorders can actually simplify treatment. That is, rather than wrestle with how to address one issue (such as PTSD) and then another (substance abuse, etc.), both can be coherently conceptualized and addressed within one framework—experiential avoidance. Chapter 1 provided an argument for experiential avoidance as the unifying, pathological phenomenon underlying these disorders, and when viewed from this perspective, both the essential problem and the solution are clear. This is helpful for clients as well, who can easily become overwhelmed by their own lists of what is wrong with them. In ACT, clients see how drinking too much, overeating, overspending, pushing friends and lovers away, and feeling down are different manifestations of the same problem. In turn, the resolution of these difficulties is also much more clear and attainable: Stop avoiding or trying to control unwanted internal experiences and start to make choices in valued directions.

ACT and Depression

As discussed in chapter 1, an increasing body of research points to the role of experiential avoidance in the development of depression and shows that negative appraisal of internal experiences such as sorrow or loneliness can lead to avoidant strategies that increase both distress and behavioral dysfunction. Also discussed was how behavioral activation therapies, shown to be effective interventions for clinical depression (see Hopko, Lejuez, Roggiero, & Eifert, 2003, for a review), and ACT share the central therapeutic goal of moving the client from an avoidant to an action-based lifestyle. In ACT an individual with PTSD and comorbid depression would be guided to act despite the presence of depressive symptoms. Such behavior, particularly when done in the service of what the client most values, may actually lead to positive changes in the client's affective experience. However, as is so frequently mentioned in this work, that is not the point. Committed action *can* be counted on to significantly reduce the debilitating secondary effects of negative appraisal, inaction, and dysfunctional avoidant strategies.

A Word About Medications

It seems timely to discuss the issue of pharmacological aids and how this is addressed in ACT. The key to remember here is that ACT is about workability. That is, a significant number of the individuals we treat with ACT are taking some type of psychotropic medication, and this is considered problematic only if taking medication somehow serves as an impediment to living fully as valued by the client. While we might conceptualize the use of medication as an attempt to ameliorate a negatively evaluated internal state, we do not impose some value on the client around not relying on medication. However, if the use of a particular substance, including a prescribed medication, shows up in the therapy as a problematic coping strategy that serves as a barrier to something the client values, this would be included as a target of the intervention. At times, clients struggle with competing values. That is, a patient with bipolar disorder might have a value around doing things on their own and not having crutches and also one around self-care or holding down a job. In this case, the client might determine that self-care and holding a job require the use of medication. In a case like this, we would help the client see that the various thoughts or feelings that might come up around needing a pharmacological crutch are just that, thoughts and feelings.

ACT and Substance Abuse

The link between PTSD and substance abuse seems especially clear. Research has well documented the use of alcohol and other substances as being efforts to self-medicate (see chapter 1). In fact, it could be argued that the use of drugs or alcohol is the avoidant coping strategy of choice for individuals with PTSD—what better way (initially) to escape the troubling memories, thoughts, and feelings one is having? The notion that substance abuse constitutes an avoidance strategy should be fully addressed in the therapy. An effective approach is to help the client identify values that have been lost to the substance abuse and to work toward making choices that are more in line with those values (for instance, remaining abstinent so that their children are more willing to be in relationship with them). We feel ACT is an extremely powerful intervention for substance use disorders as it so clearly highlights the issue at the heart of the substance use (avoidance of negatively evaluated internal events) and offers clients the key (willingness) to escaping the vicious cycle of abuse. In addition, ACT has particular strength in preventing slips from turning into full-blown relapses. It is an oft-noted phenomenon that some of the tips and slogans found helpful in recovery (such as "there's no such thing as 'just one drink'") can also set the stage for relapse. Individuals who buy that sort of programming as literally true (programming that may have been largely workable) are in trouble if in fact they do have that one drink. In ACT, a relapse is seen as an example of falling off the horse—the solution being to get back on and continue in the valued direction.

ACT and Anxiety

Because PTSD is considered one of the anxiety disorders, it will come as no surprise that ACT lends itself nicely to the treatment of other anxiety disorders such as generalized anxiety, agoraphobia, and panic disorder. You can imagine the day-to-day experience of these individuals, who on top of trying to avoid anything and everything trauma-related are also burdened with avoiding anything that might bring up anxiety, period. It is not uncommon for such individuals to tell us that they have been literally hiding out at home for fifteen or twenty years. We treat these anxiety symptoms just as we do the other symptoms of PTSD, as (extremely uncomfortable) internal experiences that are to be noticed and held versus being reinforced by avoidant behavior (operant conditioning). We might assist clients by including specific references to these anxiety symptoms as we move through the protocol. For example, when doing the passengers on a bus metaphor with a client dually diagnosed with PTSD and panic disorder, we might include a panic episode as a passenger on the client's bus. We might ask such clients to notice when these uncomfortable internal events arise, and then to say to themselves, "Welcome anxiety, my old friend!"

ACT and Harmful Behaviors

The premise here is much the same as with the substance-use disorders. Urges to binge, purge, cut, overspend, and so on, are seen as various manifestations of experiential avoidance and are treated as such in the therapy. It's fascinating to observe how compelling "whys" are for some clients. That is, some clients seem to show great alacrity and skill in analyzing why they do certain things, such as "I noticed that every time my mom calls I go out and buy comfort food. Then I realized that I do this because I don't get what I need from her, so I go get stuff for myself." Such insight can easily pull both client and therapist off track, the cost being that they are caught up in content that is not about actual behavior change. Most providers can think of at least one person they've worked with who has become a professional client, endlessly examining the intricacies of why they are as they are while not changing their behavior in any meaningful way. ACT offers a way to get to the heart of this matter, as such self-analyzing is revealed as just another example of internal phenomena (thoughts, programming), and that one does not need to know the whys in order to make choices in valued directions. Many clients are thrown when we point out to them that asking why is another example of experiential avoidance (that "having the answer" is what they are needing in order to be fixed). This can usually be quickly addressed:

Therapist: So you're saying that you need to know why you spend so much so that you can stop doing it?

Client: Right.

Therapist: If I were to tell you I'd give you a free dinner with Johnny Depp if you were to stay within your budget, would you stop overspending?

Client: *(laughing)* You bet! I'd even make my own lunch every day!

Therapist: But I thought you needed to know why first.

Client: Well…

Therapist: So truly, if you were to never know another thing about why you overspend, could you technically stop overspending?

Client: Yes, I guess so.

Therapist: So it can't be about why. It's about choosing to not overspend.

In chapter 7 we discussed the potential benefits of introducing self-as-context to survivors of childhood trauma. This component of ACT holds similar promise for self-injurious behavior such as cutting. Individuals who engage in these sorts of acts often suffer from an impaired sense of self and are attempting to either feel something or escape from feeling something. ACT offers such clients a way to experientially access an *intact* self, a unique and powerfully positive aspect of the therapy.

ACT and Somatization

Here ACT offers the therapist a perhaps unexpected boost. That is, one of the main challenges therapists face in working with individuals who somaticize is balancing their awareness that the client's physical difficulties are largely psychological and their desire to avoid invalidating the client's experience of their symptoms. ACT circumvents this dilemma entirely. There is no need to disentangle "real" from psychologically-created difficulties. Both are viewed as experiences to bring willingness to. As clients increase their ability to accept uncomfortable internal experiences, it can be expected that symptoms of somatization would decrease; but again, from the ACT perspective even this is not required in order to live a valued life.

ACT and Psychotic Symptoms

If your client becomes actively psychotic or needs to be hospitalized, then stabilization is clearly the first order of business. However, it is important to state that ACT has been found to benefit individuals with even severe mental illness (Bach & Hayes, 2002). The idea of willingness as applied to psychotic symptoms might seem counterintuitive; however, we point to the movie *A Beautiful Mind* as an accessible example of how this might be usefully put into practice. In the movie, inspired by the true story of Nobel Prize–winner John Forbes Nash Jr., Dr. Nash ultimately discovers that his best friend, along with this friend's daughter and another character, are in fact visual hallucinations—intricately constructed delusions he has apparently had for many years due to undiagnosed schizophrenia. After an extensive and debilitating period of being on various psychotropic medications, Dr. Nash decides to go off his medications and deal with the hallucinations in a different way (again, we are not advocating that individuals with schizophrenia go off their medications). In short, he stops fighting his hallucinatory experiences and just lets them be (willingness), having come to realize that although his experience of them is real, they are not literally real, and therefore he does not have to react to them or heed what they have to say (defusion and self-as-context). Dr. Nash chooses to return to his academic work with his hallucinations right alongside him (valued living and committed action). This is a powerful example of one individual's refusal to be defined by his internal experiences, choosing instead to live a life according to his values.

One of the clients we worked with, who was compliant with his prescribed medications, struggled mightily with PTSD-related visual hallucinations that came to him at night. This client would be just dropping off to sleep (or he would be sleeping only to be startled awake) when he would suddenly find several people in his bedroom, visual hallucinations of several people he had accidentally killed (the source of his PTSD). (It should also be noted that this individual's culture supported belief in ghosts and hauntings.) This client was understandably terrified of going to sleep and would go to great lengths to either avoid falling asleep or to sleep uninterrupted, both involving the use of a lot of substances. An amazing shift occurred for this client during the course of his work in ACT. Shortly after completing the willingness portion of the therapy, during which he tackled the possibility of being willing to have even these experiences, the client reported, clearly amazed and somewhat tearful, that he had an incredible thing happen to him. He explained that he had been just dropping off to sleep when the dreaded hallucinations once again appeared beside his bed. This time, instead of covering his head, he turned to them and said, "Well, hello again. Nice to see you." He reported that instead of being terrifying, the figures no longer looked angry. He said he told them that if they didn't mind, he was going to sleep, and that is what he did.

What and What Not to Accept

Given the nature of some of the above traumas, it is important to include a brief clarification about acceptance and what is and is not acceptable. We use the term, "acceptance" as it applies to acceptance of internal experiences. We do not support acceptance of harmful behavior such as violence or otherwise dangerous situations. In fact, we actively work with clients to get out of or remove these kinds of problems from their lives. Occasionally, we have to make this distinction for clients who have suffered harm at the hands of others. Clients will sometimes ask if we are asking them to just accept being poorly treated, for example. We very clearly state that this is not the case and that, in fact, we want them to take action that increases their ability to be safe and harm free.

Assessment of PTSD and ACT

There are a number of assessment tools that are useful in diagnosing trauma and associated difficulties. The following sections will focus on diagnosing PTSD and assessing associated symptoms, how to assess and monitor progress in the particular areas of change targeted in ACT, ways to assess mindfulness, and how to evaluate the overall effectiveness of the therapy.

Assessment of Trauma and PTSD

The Clinician Administered PTSD Scale (CAPS; Blake et al., 1995) is the recognized gold standard for diagnosing PTSD. It is a thirty-item scale for assessing frequency and intensity of the *DSM-IV* symptoms of PTSD. It has three main subscales: intrusion, avoidance, and hyperarousal, with additional items to assess social and occupational functioning, global PTSD symptom severity, and response validity. The PTSD section of the Structured Clinical Interview for DSM-IV (SCID-II) can also be used for diagnostic purposes. Other sections of the SCID-II (such as substance abuse or depression) can be used to evaluate comorbid current and lifetime disorders. The SCID is a well-established diagnostic interview and has been used in numerous psychosocial and biopsychosocial research studies (First, Spitzer, Gibbon, & Williams, 1995).

Two good assessment instruments for symptoms of PTSD that do not require a clinical interview are the PTSD Check List (PCL; Weathers, Litz, Herman, Huska,

& Keane, 1993; Blanchard, Jones-Alexander, Buckley, & Forneris, 1996) and the Trauma Symptoms Checklist-40 (TSC-40; Elliot & Briere, 1992). The PCL is a self-report measure assessing symptoms of PTSD. Respondents are asked to consider each symptom with respect to a stressful event. This instrument provides information regarding symptom intensity, as well as lending support for a diagnosis of PTSD. There are two methods of supporting a diagnosis of PTSD with the PCL (Weathers et al., 1993): The cutoff-score method, wherein a PCL cutoff score greater than 50 indicates a diagnosis of PTSD; and the symptom-cluster method, wherein a symptom item rating of "moderately" or higher (a score of 3 or more on a 5-point scale) indicates endorsement of that symptom. Individuals are subsequently diagnosed with PTSD if they endorse one or more cluster B (re-experiencing) items, three or more cluster C (avoidance/numbing) items, and two or more cluster D (arousal) items. Example items on the PCL scale include "Repeated, disturbing dreams of a stressful experience from the past," "Avoiding thinking about or talking about a stressful experience from the past or avoiding having feelings related to it," and "Feeling irritable or having angry outbursts."

The TSC-40, another self-report measure, evaluates symptomatology in adults that has arisen from either childhood or adult traumatic experiences. It has six subscales that can be reviewed for multiple purposes: anxiety, depression, dissociation, sexual abuse trauma, sexual problems, and sleep disorders, as well as a total score. Individuals taking the assessment are asked to report how often they have experienced the different symptoms listed in the past month. Some of the symptoms listed include headaches, insomnia, sexual problems, loneliness, trouble controlling your temper, and feelings of guilt, for instance.

The Post-Traumatic Cognitions Inventory (PTCI; Foa, Ehlers, Clark, Tolin, & Orsillo, 1999) is a thirty-six-item measure of cognitions believed to underlie the pathology that can arise after a trauma. Respondents indicate the degree to which they agree or disagree with particular trauma-related thoughts using a 7-point Likert scale. The PTCI shows good sensitivity and high specificity in identifying individuals with and without PTSD in a traumatized sample (Foa et al., 1999). However, if this instrument is being used to assess an ACT intervention, it is suggested that the clinician also include a question about the client's ability to see the thought as a thought or about the degree to which the client believes each of the thirty-six cognitions on the instrument. Currently, the instructions read, "Please read each statement carefully and tell us how much you agree or disagree with each statement." The client then reports on a Likert scale ranging from 1 ("total disagreement") to 7 ("totally agree"). Example statements include: "I have permanently changed for the worse" and "I am a weak person." By adding an instruction that assesses the degree to which the individual believes the thoughts (for instance, "Please rate the degree to which you believe the following thoughts, even if they continue to occur"), the therapist can disentangle whether the client does or doesn't have the thoughts, or if they simply don't buy into them.

The instruments described above help therapists monitor the various symptoms associated with PTSD. However, it should be noted that from the ACT perspective, therapists and researchers may not always see large reductions in symptoms as measured by these instruments. In other words, clients may continue to report feelings of anxiety, but if they are now able to accept anxious feelings when they arise, making valued choices instead of allowing the anxiety to become a barrier, ACT has been successful. We recommend that therapists and researchers use other measures that evaluate quality of life and/or ask other assessment questions that evaluate taking new actions in life. For instance, we had a client whose value was to create better relationships with her family—relations were strained due to her PTSD. Yet she lived in a different state as a means to avoid any issues or problems with them. During the course of therapy she had been phoning her family and reestablishing connections. She reported that things were "bumpy, but going well." By the end of therapy she had chosen to move back to her hometown. General assessment strategies do not get at these kinds of changes (things like phoning, moving, reestablishing connections). It can be very helpful to track these issues as assessment of change. See the section on assessing committed action below.

Assessment of Experiential Avoidance and Acceptance

It is useful to assess the degree to which clients endorse experiential acceptance and avoidance, as this is viewed as the central issue in individuals with PTSD. Because these are the main targets of ACT, such measures also provide information regarding how well clients are progressing (or not) in this area. The Acceptance and Action Questionnaire-2 (AAQ-2; Bond & Bunce, 2003) arose directly from the development of ACT and as such is the only measure specifically assessing experiential avoidance and acceptance as conceived in ACT (gauging greater psychological flexibility). It is a self-report measure that focuses on emotional avoidance, cognitive fusion, and inaction. Respondents report on a 7-point Likert scale the extent to which each statement applies to them. Items include "It's okay to remember something unpleasant," "My painful experiences and memories make it difficult for me to live a life that I would value," "I'm afraid of my feelings," and "My painful memories prevent me from having a fulfilling life." The measure is scored so that higher scores indicate greater acceptance or psychological flexibility.

It may be useful to know that there are a number of disorder-specific versions of the AAQ. For instance, McCracken (1998) validated the Chronic Pain Acceptance Questionnaire (CPAQ), which was developed by changing AAQ items to focus specifically on pain. McCracken found that acceptance of pain was associated with lower pain intensity, less pain-related anxiety and avoidance, less depression, less physical and psychosocial disability, more daily uptime, and better work status. Other studies have shown that the CPAQ is a better predictor of disability and adjustment than simple pain ratings (McCracken & Eccleston, 2003; McCracken, Vowles, & Eccleston, 2004). Gregg (2004) developed a version of the AAQ for use with individuals who are receiving treatment for diabetes. A high experiential avoidance score on this measure was found to predict poor treatment response. Gifford and colleagues (2004) have shown similar results for individuals attempting smoking cessation. Finally, a version of the AAQ is being developed for use with individuals who have PTSD. Katie Brachen has taken a lead in this effort and several colleagues, including Robyn, are involved in this effort. We look forward to this version being published soon.

Assessment of Avoidant Thoughts and Cognitive Defusion

The AAQ described above measures cognitive defusion to some degree (for example, "My painful memories prevent me from having a fulfilling life" rated as not true). However, other instruments more directly assess avoidance and cognition, including the White Bear Suppression Inventory (WBSI; Wegner & Zanakos, 1994) and the Automatic Thoughts Questionnaire (ATQ; Hollon & Kendall, 1980). The WBSI is a self-report questionnaire that assesses thought suppression; that is, the degree to which individuals wish or believe they can successfully avoid a thought (Wegner & Zanakos, 1994). Respondents use a 5-point Likert scale to report the extent to which each of fifteen statements apply to them, with higher scores indicating increased desire to suppress troubling thoughts.

The Automatic Thoughts Questionnaire (Hollon & Kendall, 1980) assesses the frequency of certain automatic thoughts that may have occurred over the past month. The ATQ taps into four aspects of automatic thoughts: personal maladjustment and desire for change, negative self-concepts and negative expectations, low self-esteem, and helplessness. Respondents report the extent to which each thought occurs using a range of 1 ("never") to 7 ("always"). In order to measure the ability to defuse from thoughts (versus simply the presence of thoughts) ACT researchers Zettle and Hayes (1986) added a "believability" scale (creating the ATQ-B) that assesses the degree to which respondents buy into their thoughts (for example, "If this thought occurred to you now, how believable would it be?"). In a small randomized, controlled trial comparing ACT to cognitive therapy, these researchers showed that ACT produced a greater reduction in believability but not frequency of depressogenic thoughts than did cognitive therapy, and that this in turn correlated with greater gains made by clients in the ACT treatment condition. Additional studies have also shown that ACT has a positive impact on cognitive defusion as measured by the ATQ-B (Walser et al.,

2003) with individuals diagnosed with PTSD, and to date has shown an effect for defusion as measured by a decrease in believability of problematic thoughts.

Assessing Mindfulness

There are two mindfulness measures that may prove useful when conducting ACT. The Kentucky Inventory of Mindfulness Skills (KIMS; Baer, Smith, & Cochran, 2004) is a thirty-nine-item self-report measure designed to assess one's general tendency to be mindful in daily life. This measure targets four areas of mindfulness skills: observing, describing, acting with awareness, and accepting without judgment. The "observe" items include paying attention to internal and external events, the "describe" items focus on one's ability to place sensations, thoughts, and feelings into words. The "act with awareness" items assess one's ability to engage in activity with undivided attention, and the "accept without judgment" items refer to making evaluations about one's own experiences. The KIMS has been found to have high internal consistency and adequate-to-good test-retest reliability (Baer et al., 2004)

A second mindfulness measure is the Mindfulness Attention Awareness Scale (MAAS), developed by Brown and Ryan (2003). This fifteen-item measure assesses the presence or absence of attention to the present moment with questions such as "I find it difficult to stay focused on what is happening in the present" and "I do jobs or tasks automatically without being aware of what I am doing." Research using the MAAS has shown it to be a reliable instrument (Brown & Ryan, 2003).

Assessing Committed Action

One of the most important areas to assess in terms of ACT is that of commitment and action. The fundamental problem for individuals with PTSD is that they are not living the lives they would like to be living—they have become inactive in terms of a number of important values. Assessing how clients are doing with respect to their values in various areas makes sense when doing ACT and also demonstrates whether or not the treatment is effective for particular clients. The Valued Living Questionnaire (VLQ; Wilson & Groom, 2002; Wilson & Murrell, 2004) is a twenty-item assessment instrument that measures both the importance of a particular value as well as the degree to which the value is being realized in the individual's life. Ten different domains are assessed: family (other than marriage or parenting); marriage/couples/intimate relations; parenting; friends/social life; work; education/training; recreation/fun; spirituality; citizenship/community life; and physical self-care (diet, exercise, and sleep). This instrument is a useful clinical tool in guiding both clinician and client with respect to target values. However, we most frequently use the Values and Goals Worksheet that follows. It is a second measure that assesses: a) the client's personal definition of their values, b) action steps related to achieving greater degrees of success in living those values, c) internal reasons as to why the values are not being lived, and d) degree to which value is currently being lived. This assessment can be used throughout therapy.

Ideally, you would have the client do a thorough values and goals self-assessment, completing a worksheet for each of the following domains (plus any other domains the client would like to add): family, intimate relationships, parenting, friendships, work, recreation, health, community, and spirituality. One of the goals of therapy is to increase the degree to which the value is being lived.

Values and Goals Worksheet

Please complete the form below by stating a single value, listing action steps related to that value, and describing thoughts or emotions that might interfere with taking the action steps. Please rate the degree to which you are currently living your value by using the following scale: 0 = not living it at all; 1 = living it a little; 2 = moderately living the value; 3 = living the value most of the time; 4 = completely living the value.

Value	Action steps	Internal reasons (thoughts, emotions)	Degree to which value is being lived
Example: 1. Lead a spiritual life.	*Pray on a daily basis.*	*1. Forgetting to pray* *2. Feeling anger at God*	*2*
2.			
3.			
4.			
5.			
6.			
7.			
8.			
9.			
10.			

Several of these assessment instruments may be used throughout therapy to track the client's progress. The WBSI and AAQ, for example, are relatively short instruments that can be given to clients on a regular basis. Clients can also utilize daily diaries, such as the following form, to track both emotional willingness and action as they relate to valued living. These daily dairies can be kept within easy reach and filled out on a regular basis. Additionally, they can be tailored to specific issues if desired.

Daily Diary

Please complete the following sheet on a daily basis for one week . Briefly answer each question. Begin by filling out the first three columns. Later in the day, complete the last two columns. Bring your diary to discuss in session.

List one value that you intend to live today.	List goals that support that value.	Describe any potential emotions or thoughts that may get in the way of your goals.	Did you complete your goals? What was the outcome?	Describe any reactions to your experience of either living or not living your value today.
Example: *Kindness*	1. *Say hi to neighbor.*	1. *Fear that the neighbor will not say hi back.*	1. *Yes. Neighbor said hi.*	1. *I liked it. It was nice to connect with my neighbor.*
	2. *Treat myself with a 10-minute relaxation exercise.*	2. *Thoughts about not deserving to get a treat.*	2. *No. I didn't give myself time to relax today. Too rushed.*	2. *I felt worse about not giving myself the treat. I have difficulty being kind to me.*

List one value that you intend to live today.	List goals that support that value.	Describe any potential emotions or thoughts that may get in the way of your goals.	Did you complete your goals? What was the outcome?	Describe any reactions to your experience of either living or not living your value today.

Evaluation of treatment should generally target the following three areas:

1. Changes in ACT processes (as discussed in the preceding sections);

2. Changes in frequency of the client's value-oriented actions (also discussed in preceding sections); and

3. Client acceptance of the treatment.

The degree to which clients accept or are satisfied with the therapy can be assessed using instruments such as the Credibility/Expectancy Questionnaire (Borkovec & Nau, 1972; Devilly & Borkovec, 2000). This measure assesses the extent to which clients view a particular therapy package as credible and whether change can reasonably be expected. Clients also report the percent improvement they believe will occur by the end of treatment. Finally, client acceptance of treatment can be obtained by regular verbal feedback from the client about the degree of helpfulness/usefulness the treatment provides.

Conclusion: Opening to Vitality

We have only begun to imagine the fullness of life.

—Denise Levertov

It is our hope that ACT will bring a new vitality to survivors of trauma who have suffered, encountered loss, and moved away from that which is so important—a personally valued life. In our own experience, ACT has been a powerful and promising therapy. We also recognize the importance of science and we take time to address the science behind ACT here. As scientist-practitioners, we are very invested in the science of psychology and the understanding of human behavior. In this conclusion we provide a brief overview and speak to both the scientist and the practitioner.

Our Science Side

One of the main reasons that we have gravitated to ACT is due to both its core philosophy and its basic research foundation. ACT emerged from a wing of behavior analysis based on a philosophy of science known as functional contextualism (Hayes, 1993). This orientation conceptualizes psychological events as products of an ongoing process involving the whole organism, which includes its history and current context. "Contextualists" are much more interested in the function of behavior than the form of behavior. For example, contextualists are interested in the "why" of someone isolating (e.g., avoidance of emotional experience), rather than a description of the isolation (e.g., stay at home and watch television). Additionally, ACT focuses on workability. A question we regularly ask is: How does this behavior function in this context and is it workable according to the client's stated value? This way of understanding human behavior guides the treatment and helps to considerably broaden the focus of change (e.g. change is not focused just on feeling better or eliminating a problem, but on how well life is being lived in a variety of settings, circumstances, and relationships). The other piece that draws us to ACT is that it is based on a comprehensive program of basic research investigating human language and cognition, relational frame theory (RFT; see Hayes et al., 2001 for a review). Finally, we are drawn to ACT because of its broad applicability. This principle-based therapy can be used effectively with a wide variety of psychological problems and in a number of settings with different populations. ACT and RFT are not just technologies; they reflect an interactive approach based on a theory and set of principles that can be traced all the way from basic research to applied settings (Hayes, Strosahl, Bunting, Twohig, & Wilson, 2004).

ACT is considered to be one of the "third generation" behavior therapies that have been defined by Steven Hayes (2004, pp. 5-6) in the following way:

> Grounded in an empirical, principle-focused approach, the third wave of behavioral and cognitive therapy … tends to emphasize contextual and experiential change strategies in addition to more direct and didactic ones. These treatments tend to seek the construction of broad, flexible, and effective repertoires over an eliminative approach to narrowly defined problems, and to emphasize the relevance of the issues they examine for clinicians as well as clients.

In our own work with ACT we have been keenly interested in its scientific support. This interest lies not only in its effectiveness for PTSD but in its potential for alleviating human suffering in general. As discussed earlier in this book, one of the central goals of ACT is to reduce experiential avoidance—a key player in the creation of human suffering. An increasing body of research points to the role experiential avoidance plays in PTSD, including findings that show increased psychological distress with increasing experiential avoidance (Boeschen, Koss, Jose Figueredo, & Coan, 2001; Polusny, Rosenthal, Aban, & Follette, 2004; Rosenthal, Rasmussen Hall, Palm, Batten, & Follette, 2005; Ulmer et al., 2006) and the tendency for combat veterans with PTSD to inhibit emotional responses (Roemer, Litz, Orsillo, & Wagner, 2001). Other studies that have investigated thought suppression (Guthrie & Bryant, 2000; Shipherd & Beck, 1999), suppression of intrusions and worry (Steil & Ehlers, 2000), and emotional numbing (Litz, Orsillo, Kaloupek, & Weathers, 2000) have also lent support to the experiential avoidance model of PTSD.

In our own pilot study (Ulmer et al., 2006), we found similar results as well as additional evidence that experiential avoidance is directly linked to symptomatology. This study involved piloting ACT as a treatment for male and female veterans who were participating in residential rehabilitation programs for PTSD. As it was a pilot, there were a number of limitations, most notably the inability to randomize participants or to control for other therapeutic interventions (i.e., ACT was only one of many interventions offered to program participants). Nonetheless, we used specific assessments designed to target conceptual themes in ACT (e.g., AAQ, WBSI—see chapter 12 for more information on these measures) and found important statistically significant outcomes worthy of further exploration. For instance, experiential avoidance and suppression were significantly associated with pretreatment increase in trauma symptoms. We learned that experiential avoidance and suppression decreased significantly from pre- to post-intervention. Additionally, improvements in the measures of increased acceptance and less suppression were predictive of positive outcomes, including a decrease in trauma symptoms, less depression and anxiety, and a decrease in dissociation and automatic thoughts. They were also predictive of improvement in social openness and hope for the future. We also found that subjects had an increased ability to take action in the face of difficult emotion (Walser et al., 2005; Ulmer et al., 2006).

Lynn Williams (2006), one of our Australian colleagues, also conducted a study using ACT with Vietnam-era veterans who suffered from PTSD. She compared ACT as a full treatment to ACT with the self-as-context component removed. She found that all veterans had decreased symptoms (as measured by the PCL-M; see chapter 12 for more information on this measure) and increased ability to be mindful (as measured by the KIMS; again, see chapter 12). Additionally, the group who had received all of the ACT components in treatment had greater improvement on the KIMS subscale measuring to "allow and accept without judgment" internal and external experiences and had better maintained reduction in avoidance symptoms than the group with self-as-context removed. Certainly, controlled studies are needed, but we are encouraged by these findings. We intend to further pursue our research endeavors, adding on to the small but growing body of literature that supports ACT as an effective treatment for trauma (Batten & Hayes, 2005; Orsillo & Batten, 2005).

Anecdotally, we have had many clients tell us about the circumstances of their "new" life—one that is values based and full of vitality. We have heard countless stories of trauma survivors taking action in important ways. For instance, we have had clients report reconnections with long-lost family members; ventures to public places that were previously adamantly avoided; increased ability to manage stress and other life problems under difficult circumstances; ability to face previously avoided activities, such as searching for employment; and re-engaging in social activities, church, and other spiritual endeavors. Some participants even began to do things that they had never planned to do, such as making public appearances to support treatment for women who have been raped.

Finally, it is important to recognize that the ACT intervention processes and outcomes have been investigated in a number of other areas. ACT has been evaluated with both individual and group psychotherapy formats and with a variety of patients and lengths of intervention (Hayes, Pankey, Gifford, Batten, & Quinones, 2002). To mention a few of these efforts, ACT studies have found a decreased rate of rehospitalization for individuals with positive psychotic symptoms (Bach & Hayes, 2002; Gaudiano & Herbert, 2006); a significant reduction in depression and decreases in depressogenic thoughts (Zettle & Hayes, 1986); large reductions in obsessive-compulsive disorder without use of in-session exposure (Twohig, Hayes, & Masuda, 2006); that ACT is a superior intervention to a control condition in the treatment of polysubstance-abusing opiate-addicted patients (Hayes, Wilson, et al., 2004); and that ACT promotes greater rates of smoking cessation at one-year follow up (Gifford et al., 2004).

ACT has also been found to significantly decrease workplace stress while improving psychological health (Bond & Bunce, 2000) and produces greater decreases in stigmatization of clients by therapists and greater decreases in therapist burnout than an educational control (Hayes, Bissett, et al., 2004). Finally, ACT has been found to produce generally more effective clinicians as measured by client outcome (Strosahl et al., 1998). A more extensive review of ACT research is available (Hayes, Masuda, Bissett, Luoma, & Guerrero, 2004) and we encourage interested readers to take the opportunity to become familiar with this body of literature.

Honoring Those We Have Worked With

We have spent years listening to the stories of trauma brought to therapy by the men and women in our practice. At times we wonder if we will ever reach a time when we will be unable to hear one more story of trauma. And yet, to our amazement, we never seem to get there. We believe it is our work with ACT, both personally and professionally, that has allowed us to retain our commitment to serving this population. But even more importantly, it is the human beings we serve, who finally reach a place of acceptance—a place of wholeness—who ultimately energize our work.

Late one night while cloistering ourselves away in a noisy hotel to work on this book, Darrah found herself searching through sets of poems and prayers for inspiration to press on after working many long hours. She read one out loud that seemed to fit our wish for the trauma survivors we work for:

> In spite of everything I still believe
> That people are really good at heart.
> I simply can't build up my hopes on a foundation

consisting of confusion, misery and death.
I see the world gradually being turned into a wilderness,
I hear the ever-approaching thunder, which will destroy us, too,
I can feel the suffering of millions, and yet,
if I look up into the heavens,
I think that it will all come right,
that this cruelty will end,
and that peace and tranquility will return again.
In the meantime, I must hold up my ideals,
for perhaps the time will come
when I shall be able to carry them out.

—Anne Frank

Being

It has been noted that the field of psychology has made significant shifts into the realms of mindfulness and acceptance (Hayes, 2004). Perhaps ACT and other acceptance-based therapies are the result of an inevitable maturation process. That is, the ideas of acceptance and mindfulness have been around for a long time. They reflect age-old Eastern wisdom earned the hard way. Over time, we Westerners have also come to realize that "putting your mind to it" doesn't always work, that some things are to be had, regardless of how much we don't want them. Perhaps our relatively youthful culture is simply catching up to the rest of the world. However, there is tremendous strength to Western optimism, to our sheer determination to be in control of our lives and to have them be good. ACT brings the best of these worlds together, and the result is powerful indeed. As individuals who are actively engaged in this work, we observe our own evolution as we learn to accept what is to be accepted and to make choices in accordance with our most dearly held values. We look forward to what comes next, while showing up to being.

Perhaps we should warn you that being familiar with this technology can be a pain. For example, we find ourselves at this point hoping that you feel satisfied with what you have found here, excited about the possibilities of this therapy, and encouraged that you can begin to use this powerful intervention in your own practice. However, thanks to the knowledge we have gained in doing this work we know that you "have what you have," and that we must be willing to sit with our own anxiety about these things. We leave you then, with thanks for your willingness to learn more about this approach, and with real appreciation for our shared interest in this field.

Best,

Robyn & Darrah

References

Allen, S. N., & Bloom, S. L. (1994). Group and family treatment of post-traumatic stress disorder. *Psychiatric Clinics of North America*, 17(2), 425-437.

American Psychiatric Association. (2000). *Diagnostic and Statistical Manual of Mental Disorders* (4th ed., tex rev.). Washington, DC: Author.

Bach, P., & Hayes, S. C. (2002). Use of acceptance and commitment therapy to prevent the rehospitalization of psychotic patients: A randomized controlled trial. *Journal of Consulting and Clinical Psychology*, 70(5), 1129-1139.

Baer, R. A. (2003). Mindfulness training as a clinical intervention: A conceptual and empirical review. *Clinical Psychology: Science and Practice*, 10(2), 125-143.

Baer, R., Smith, G. T., & Cochran, K. (2004). Assessment of mindfulness by self-report: The Kentucky Inventory of Mindfulness Skills. *Assessment*, 11, 191-206.

Batten, S. V., & Hayes, S. C. (2005). Acceptance and commitment therapy in the treatment of comorbid substance abuse and posttraumatic stress disorder: A case study. *Clinical Case Studies*, 4(3), 246-262.

Beddoe, A. E., & Murphy, S. O. (2004). Does mindfulness decrease stress and foster empathy among nursing students? *Journal of Nursing Education*, 43(7), 305-312.

Blake, D. D., Weathers, F. W., Nagy, L. M., Kaloupek, D. G., Gusman, F. D., Charney, D. S., et al. (1995). The development of a clinician-administered PTSD scale. *Journal of Traumatic Stress*, 8(1), 75-90.

Blanchard, E. B., Jones-Alexander, J., Buckley, T. C., & Forneris, C. A. (1996). Psychometric properties of the PTSD Checklist (PCL). *Behaviour Research and Therapy*, 34(8), 669-673.

Boeschen, L., Koss, M. P., Jose Figueredo, A., & Coan, J. A. (2001). Experiential avoidance and posttraumatic stress disorder: A cognitive mediational model of rape recovery. *Journal of Abuse and Maltreatmet*, 4, 211-246.

Bond, F. W., & Bunce, D. (2000). Mediators of change in emotion-focused and problem-focused worksite stress management interventions. *Journal of Occupational Health Psychology*, 5, 156-163.

Bond, F. W., & Bunce, D. (2003). The role of acceptance and job control in mental health, job satisfaction, and work performance. *Journal of Applied Psychology*, 88(6), 1057-1067.

Borkovec, T. D., & Nau, S. D. (1972). Credibility of analogue therapy rationales. *Journal of Behavior Therapy and Experimental Psychiatry*, 3, 257-260.

Breslau, N., Davis, G. C., Peterson, E. L., & Schultz, L. R. (1997). Psychiatric sequelae of posttraumatic stress disorder in women. *Archives of General Psychiatry*, 54(1), 81-87.

Breslau, N., Davis, G. C., Peterson, E. L., & Schultz, L. R. (2000). A second look at comorbidity in victims of trauma: The posttraumatic stress disorder-major depression connection. *Society of Biological Psychiatry*, 48(9), 902-909.

Breslau, N., Davis, G. C., & Schultz, L. R. (2003). Posttraumatic stress disorder and the incidence of nicotine, alcohol, and other drug disorders in persons who have experienced trauma. *Archives of General Psychiatry*, 60(3), 289-294.

Breslau, N., Kessler, R. C., Chilcoat, H. D., Schultz, L. R., Davis, G. C., & Andreski, P. (1998). Trauma and posttraumatic stress disorder in the community: The 1996 Detroit Area Survey of trauma. *Archives of General Psychiatry*, 55(7), 626-632.

Breslin, F. C., Zack, M., & McMain, S. (2002). An information-processing analysis of mindfulness: Implications for relapse prevention in the treatment of substance abuse. *Clinical Psychology: Science and Practice*, 9(3), 275-299.

Briere, J., & Runtz, M. (1987). Post sexual abuse trauma: Data and implications for clinical practice. *Journal of Interpersonal Violence*, 2(4), 367-379.

Brown, K. W., & Ryan, R. M. (2003). The benefits of being present: Mindfulness and its role in psychological well-being. *Journal of Personality and Social Psychology*, 84(4), 822-848.

Burpee, L. C., & Langer, E. J. (2005). Mindfulness and marital satisfaction. *Journal of Adult Development*, 12(1), 43-51.

Cao, H., McFarlane, A. C., & Klimidis, S. (2003). Prevalence of psychiatric disorder following the 1998 Yun Nan (China) earthquake: The first 5-month period. *Social Psychiatry and Psychiatric Epidemiology*, 38(4), 204-212.

Carlson, L. E., Speca, M., Patel, K. D., & Goodey, E. (2004). Mindfulness-based stress reduction in relation to quality of life, mood, symptoms of stress and levels of cortisol, dehydroepiandrosterone sulfate (DHEAS) and melatonin in breast and prostate cancer outpatients. *Psychoneuroendocrinology*, 29(4), 448-474.

Carroll, E. M., Rueger, D. B., Foy, D. W., & Donahoe, C. P. (1985). Vietnam combat veterans with posttraumatic stress disorder: Analysis of marital and cohabiting adjustment. *Journal of Abnormal Psychology*, 94(3), 329-337.

Chu, J. A. (1992). The revictimization of adult women with histories of childhood abuse. *Journal of Psychotherapy Practice and Research*, 1, 259-269.

Cloitre, M. (1998). Sexual revictimization: Risk factors and prevention. In V. M. Follette, J. I. Ruzek, & F. R. Abueg (eds.), *Cognitive-Behavioral Therapies for Trauma* (pp. 278-304). New York: Guilford Press.

Cloitre, M., Scarvalone, P., & Difede, J. (1997). Posttraumatic stress disorder, self- and interpersonal dysfunction among sexually retraumatized women. *Journal of Traumatic Stress*, 10(3), 437-452.

Cohen-Katz, J., Wiley, S., Capuano, T., Baker, D., Deitrick, L., & Shapiro, S. (2005). The effects of mindfulness-based stress reduction on nurse stress and burnout: A qualitative and quantitative study. *Holistic Nursing Practice*, 19(2), 78-86.

Davidson, J. R., & Fairbank, J. A. (1993). The epidemiology of posttraumatic stress disorder. In J. R. Davidson & E. B. Foa (eds.), *Posttraumatic Stress Disorder: DSM-IV and Beyond* (pp. 147-169). Washington, DC: American Psychiatric Press.

DePrince, A. P., & Freyd, J. J. (2002). The intersection of gender and betrayal in trauma. In R. Kimerling, P. Ouimette, & J. Wolfe (eds.), *Gender and PTSD* (pp. 98-113). New York: Guilford Press.

Devilly, G. J., & Borkovec, T. D. (2000). Psychometric properties of the credibility/expectancy questionnaire. *Journal of Behavior Therapy and Experimental Psychiatry*, 31(2), 73-86.

Dimidjian, S., & Linehan, M. (2003). Defining an agenda for future research on the clinical application of mindfulness practice. *Clinical Psychology: Science and Practice*, 10(2), 166-171.

Eifert, G. H., & Forsyth, J. P. (2005). *Acceptance and Commitment Therapy for Anxiety Disorders: A Practitioner's Treatment Guide to Using Mindfulness, Acceptance, and Values-Based Behavior Change Strategies*. Oakland, CA: New Harbinger Publications.

Elliott, D. M., & Briere, J. (1992). Sexual abuse trauma among professional women: Validating the Trauma Symptom Checklist-40 (TSC-40). *Child Abuse and Neglect*, 16(3), 391-398.

First, M. B., Spitzer R. L., Gibbon, M., & Williams, J. B. W. (1995). The Structured Clinical Interview for DSM-III-R personality disorders (SCID-II), part I: Description. *Journal of Personality Disorders*, 9(2), 83-91.

Foa, E. B., Ehlers, A., Clark, D. M., Tolin, D. F., & Orsillo, S. M. (1999). The Post-Traumatic Cognitions Inventory (PTCI): Development and validation. *Psychological Assessment*, 11, 303-314.

Foa, E. B, Rothman, B. O., & Hembree, E. A. (2006) *Prolonged Exposure Therapy for PTSD: Emotional Processing of Traumatic Experiences: Therapist Guide*. Oxford: Oxford University Press.

Follette, V. M., Polusny, M. A., Bechtle, A. E., & Naugle, A. E. (1996). Cumulative trauma: The impact of child sexual abuse, adult sexual assault, and spouse abuse. *Journal of Traumatic Stress*, 9(1), 25-35.

Fontana, A., & Rosenheck, R. (1998). Focus on women: Duty-related and sexual stress in the etiology of PTSD among women veterans who seek treatment. *Psychiatric Services*, 49, 658-662.

Gaudiano, B. A., & Herbert, J. D. (2006). Believability of hallucinations as a potential mediator of their frequency and associated distress in psychotic inpatients. *Behavioural and Cognitive Psychotherapy*, 34, 497-502.

Gifford, E. V., Kohlenberg, B. S., Hayes, S. C., Antonuccio, D. O., Piasecki, M. M., Rasmussen Hall, M. L., et al. (2004). Applying a functional acceptance based model to smoking cessation: An initial trial of acceptance and commitment therapy. *Behavior Therapy*, 35, 689-705.

Gregg, J. A. (2004). A randomized controlled effectiveness trial comparing patient education with and without acceptance and commitment therapy for type 2 diabetes self-management. Unpublished dissertation, University of Nevada, Reno.

Gunaratana, B. H. (2002). *Mindfulness in Plain English* (updated and expanded ed.). Summerville, MA: Wisdom Publications.

Guthrie, R., & Bryant, R. (2000). Attempting suppression of traumatic memories over extended periods in acute stress disorder. *Behaviour Research and Therapy*, 38(9), 899-907.

Hayes, S. C. (1993). Analytic goals and the varieties of scientific contextualism. In S. C. Hayes, L. J. Hayes, H. W. Reese, & T. R. Sarbin (eds.), *Varieties of Scientific Contextualism* (pp. 11-27). Reno, NV: Context Press.

Hayes, S. C. (2004). Acceptance and commitment therapy, relational frame theory, and the third wave of behavioral and cognitive therapies. *Behavior Therapy*, 35, 639-665.

Hayes, S. C., Barnes-Holmes, D., & Roche, B. (2001). *Relational Frame Theory: A Post-Skinnerian Account of Human Language and Cognition*. New York: Plenum Press.

Hayes, S. C., Bissett, R., Roget, N., Padilla, M., Kohlenberg, B. S., Fisher, G., et al. (2004). The impact of acceptance and commitment training and multicultural training on the stigmatizing attitudes and professional burnout of substance abuse counselors. *Behavior Therapy*, 35(4), 821-835.

Hayes, S. C., Follette, V. M., & Linehan, M. M. (2004). *Mindfulness and Acceptance: Expanding the Cognitive Behavioral Tradition*. New York: Guilford Press.

Hayes, S. C., Masuda, A., Bissett, R., Luoma, J., & Guerrero, L. F. (2004). DBT, FAP, and ACT: How empirically oriented are the new behavior therapy technologies? *Behavior Therapy*, 35, 35-54.

Hayes, S. C., Pankey, J., Gifford, E. V., Batten, S. V., & Quinones, R. (2002). Acceptance and commitment therapy in experiential avoidance disorders. In T. Patterson (ed.), *Comprehensive Handbook of Psychotherapy: Cognitive-Behavioral Approaches* (vol. 2, pp. 319-351). New York: Wiley.

Hayes, S. C., & Smith, S. (2005). *Get Out of Your Mind and Into Your Life: The New Acceptance and Commitment Therapy.* Oakland, CA: New Harbinger Publications.

Hayes, S. C., & Strosahl, K. D. (2004). *A Practical Guide to Acceptance and Commitment Therapy.* New York: Springer Science and Business Media.

Hayes, S. C., Strosahl, K. D., Bunting, K., Twohig, M., & Wilson, K. G. (2004). What is acceptance and commitment therapy? In S. C. Hayes & K. D. Strosahl (eds.), *A Practical Guide to Acceptance and Commitment Therapy* (pp. 3-29). New York: Springer Science and Business Media.

Hayes, S. C., Strosahl, K. D., & Wilson, K. G. (1999). *Acceptance and Commitment Therapy: An Experiential Approach to Behavior Change.* New York: Guilford Press.

Hayes, S. C., & Wilson, K. G. (2003). Mindfulness: Method and process. *Clinical Psychology: Science and Practice,* 10(2), 161-165.

Hayes, S. C., Wilson, K. G., Gifford, E. V., Bissett, R., Piasecki, M., Batten, S. V., et al. (2004). A preliminary trial of twelve-step facilitation and acceptance and commitment therapy with polysubstance-abusing methadone-maintained opiate addicts. *Behavior Therapy,* 35(4), 667-688.

Hayes, S. C., Wilson, K. G., Gifford, E. V., Follette, V. M., & Strosahl, K. (1996). Experiential avoidance and behavioral disorders: A functional dimensional approach to diagnosis and treatment. *Journal of Consulting and Clinical Psychology,* 64(6), 1152-1168.

Hirst, I. S. (2003). Perspectives of mindfulness. *Journal of Psychiatry and Mental Health Nursing,* 10(3), 359-366.

Hollon, S. D., & Kendall, P. C. (1980). Cognitive self-statements in depression: Development of an automatic thoughts questionnaire. *Cognitive Therapy and Research,* 4(4), 383-395.

Hopko D. R., Lejuez C. W., Ruggiero K. J., & Eifert G. H. (2003). Contemporary behavioral activation treatments for depression: Procedures, principles, and progress. *Clinical Psychology Review,* 23(5), 699-717.

Kabat-Zinn, J. (1994). *Full Catastrophe Living: Using the Wisdom of Your Body and Mind to Face Stress, Pain and Illness.* New York: Dell Publishing.

Keane, T. M., & Wolfe, J. (1990). Comorbidity in post-traumatic stress disorder: An analysis of community and clinical studies. *Journal of Applied Social Psychology,* 20(21), 1776-1788.

Kessler, R. C., Sonnega, A., Bromet, E., Hughes, M., & Nelson, C. B. (1995). Posttraumatic stress disorder in the National Comorbidity Survey. *Archives of General Psychiatry,* 52(12), 1048-1060.

Kuo, C., Tang, H., Tsay, C., Lin, S., Hu, W., & Chen, C. (2003). Prevalence of psychiatric disorders among bereaved survivors of a disastrous earthquake in Taiwan. *Psychiatric Services*, 54(2), 249-251.

Levy, M. S. (1998). A helpful way to conceptualize and understand reenactments. *Journal of Psychotherapy Practice and Research*, 7(3), 227-235.

Linehan, M. M. (1993). *Cognitive-Behavioral Treatment of Borderline Personality Disorder*. New York: Guilford Press.

Litz, B. T., Orsillo, S. M., Kaloupek, D., & Weathers, F. (2000). Emotional processing in posttraumatic stress disorder. *Journal of Abnormal Psychology*, 109(1), 26-39.

Ma, S. H., & Teasdale, J. D. (2004). Mindfulness-based cognitive therapy for depression: Replication and exploration of differential relapse prevention effects. *Journal of Consulting and Clinical Psychology*, 72(1), 31-40.

Marlatt, G. A., & Gordon, J. R. (eds.). (1985). *Relapse Prevention*. New York: Guilford Press.

Marlatt, G. A., & Kristeller, J. L. (1999). Mindfulness and meditation. In W. R. Miller (ed.), *Integrating Spirituality in Treatment* (pp. 67-84). Washington, DC: American Psychological Association Books.

Mayall, A., & Gold, S. R. (1995). Definitional issues and mediating variables in the sexual revictimization of women sexually abused as children. *Journal of Interpersonal Violence*, 10, 26-42.

McBee, L. (2003). Mindfulness practice with the frail elderly and their caregivers: Changing the practitioner-patient relationship. *Topics in Geriatric Rehabilitation*, 19(4), 257-264.

McCracken, L. M. (1998). Learning to live with the pain: Acceptance of pain predicts adjustment in persons with chronic pain. *Pain*, 74, 21-27.

McCracken, L. M., & Eccleston, C. (2003). Coping or acceptance: What to do about chronic pain? *Pain*, 105(1-2), 197-204.

McCracken, L. M., Vowles, K. E., & Eccleston, C. (2004). Acceptance of chronic pain: Component analysis and a revised assessment method. *Pain*, 107(1-2), 159-166.

McNally, R. J., Bryant, R. A., & Ehlers, A. (2003). Does early psychological intervention promote recovery from posttraumatic stress? *Psychological Science in the Public Interest*, 4(2), 45-79.

Messman, T. L., & Long, P. J. (1996). Child sexual abuse and its relationship to revictimization in adult women: A review. *Clinical Psychology Review*, 16(5), 397-420.

Najavits, L. M. (2001). *Seeking Safety: A Treatment Manual for PTSD and Substance Abuse*. New York: Guilford Press.

Naugle, A. E., Bell, K. M., & Polusny, M. A. (2003). Clinical considerations for treating sexually revictimized women. *National Center for PTSD Clinical Quarterly*, 12(1), 12-16.

Orsillo, S. M., & Batten, S. V. (2005). Acceptance and commitment therapy in the treatment of posttraumatic stress disorder. *Behavior Modification*, 29(1), 95-129.

Orsillo S. M., & Roemer, L. (2005). *Acceptance and Mindfulness-Based Approaches to Anxiety: Conceptualization and Treatment.* New York: Springer.

Ouimette, P., & Brown, P. J. (2003). *Trauma and Substance Abuse: Causes, Consequences, and Treatment of Comorbid Disorders.* Washington DC: American Psychological Association.

Palm, K., Polusny, M. A., & Follette, V. M. (2004). Vicarious dramatization: Potential hazards and interventions for disaster and trauma workers. *Prehospital and Disaster Medicine*, 19(1), 73-78.

Pistorello, J. (2005). DBT and acceptance and commitment therapy. Workshop at the ACT Summer Institute. Philadelphia, July.

Polusny, M. A., Rosenthal, M. Z., Aban, I., & Follette, V. M. (2004). Experimental avoidance as a mediator of the effects of adolescent sexual victimization on negative adult outcomes. *Violence and Victims*, 19(1), 109-120.

Prigerson, H. G., Bierhals, A. J., Kasl, S. V., Reynolds III, C. F., Shear, M. K., Day, N., et al. (1997). Traumatic grief as a risk factor for mental and physical morbidity. *American Journal of Psychiatry*, 154, 616-625.

Prigerson, H. G., Bierhals, A. J., Kasl, S. V., Reynolds III, C. F., Shear, M. K., Newsom J. T., et al. (1996). Complicated grief as a distinct disorder from bereavement-related depression and anxiety: A replication study. *American Journal of Psychiatry*, 153(11), 1484-1486.

Resick, P. A., & Schnicke, M. K. (1992). Cognitive processing therapy for sexual assault victims. *Journal of Consulting and Clinical Psychology*, 60(5), 748-756.

Resick, P. A., & Schnicke, M. K. (1993). *Cognitive Processing Therapy for Rape Victims: A Treatment Manual.* Newbury Park, CA: Sage Publications.

Riggs, D. S., Cahill, S. P., & Foa, E. B. (2006). Prolonged exposure (PE) treatment of posttraumatic stress disorder. In V. M. Follette & J. I. Ruzek (eds.), *Cognitive-Behavioral Therapies for Trauma* (2nd ed.; pp. 65-95). New York: Guilford Press.

Roemer, L., Litz, B. T., Orsillo, S. M., & Wagner, A. W. (2001) A preliminary investigation of the role of strategic withholding of emotions in PTSD. *Journal of Traumatic Stress, 14, 2001, 149-156.*

Root, M. P. (1989). Treatment failures: The role of sexual victimization in women's addictive behavior. *American Journal of Orthopsychiatry*, 59(4), 542-549.

Rosenthal, M. Z., Rasmussen Hall, M. L., Palm, K., Batten, S. V., & Follette, V. M. (2005). Chronic avoidance helps explain the relationship between severity of childhood sexual abuse and psychological distress in adulthood. *Journal of Child Sexual Abuse*, 14, 25-41.

Ruzek, J. I., Polusny, M. A., & Abueg, F. R. (1998). Assessment and treatment of concurrent posttraumatic stress disorder and substance abuse. In V. M. Follette, J. I. Ruzek,

& F. R. Abueg (eds.), *Cognitive-Behavioral Therapies for Trauma* (pp. 226-255). New York: Guilford Press.

Sagula, D., & Rice, K. G. (2004). The effectiveness of mindfulness training on the grieving process and emotional well-being of chronic pain patients. *Journal of Clinical Psychology in Medical Settings*, 11(4), 333-342.

Schaaf, K. K., & McCanne, T. R. (1998). Relationship of childhood sexual, physical, and combined sexual and physical abuse to adult victimization and posttraumatic stress disorder. *Child Abuse and Neglect*, 22(11), 1119-1133.

Schnurr, P. P., Spiro III, A., Vielhauer, M. J., Findler, M., & Hamblen, J. L. (2002). Trauma in the lives of older men: Findings from the Normative Aging Study. *Journal of Clinical Geropsychology*, 8(3), 175-187.

Shear, M. K., & Smith-Caroff, K. (2002). Traumatic loss and the syndrome of complicated grief. *PTSD Research Quarterly*, 13, 1-8.

Shipherd, J. C., & Beck, J. G. (1999). The effects of suppressing trauma-related thoughts on women with rape-related posttraumatic stress disorder. *Behavior Research Therapy*, 37(2), 99-112.

Shipherd, J. C., Street, A. E., & Resick, P. A. (2006). Cognitive therapy for posttraumatic stress disorder. In V. M. Follette & J. I. Ruzek (eds.), *Cognitive-Behavioral Therapies for Trauma* (2nd ed.; pp. 96-116). New York: Guilford Press.

Silverman, G. K., Jacobs, S. C., Kasl, S. V., Shear, M. K., Maciejewski, P. K., Noaghiul, F. S., et al. (2000). Quality of life impairments associated with diagnostic criteria for traumatic grief. *Psychological Medicine*, 30(4), 857-862.

Smith, D. W., Frueh, B. C., Sawchuck, C. N., & Johnson, M. R. (1999). Relationship between symptom over-reporting and pre- and post-combat trauma history in veterans evaluated for PTSD. *Depression and Anxiety* 10(3), 119-124.

Speca, M., Carlson, L. E., Goodey, E., & Angen, M. (2000). A randomized, wait-list controlled clinical trial: The effect of a mindfulness meditation-based stress reduction program on mood and symptoms of stress in cancer outpatients. *Psychosomatic Medicine*, 62(5), 613-622.

Steil, R., & Ehlers, A. (2000). Dysfunctional meaning of posttraumatic intrusions in chronic PTSD. *Behaviour Research and Therapy*, 38(6), 537-558.

Stevenson, M. R., & Gajarsky, W. M. (1992). Unwanted childhood sexual experiences relate to later revictimization and male perpetration. *Journal of Psychology and Human Sexuality*, 4(4), 57-70.

Stewart, S., Peterson, J. B., & Pihl, R. O. (1995). Anxiety sensitivity and self-reported alcohol consumption in university women. *Journal of Anxiety Disorders*, 9, 283-292.

Strosahl, K. D., Hayes, S. C., Bergan, J., & Romano, P. (1998). Assessing the field effectiveness of acceptance and commitment therapy: An example of the manipulated training research method. *Behavior Therapy*, 29, 35-64.

Tacon, A. M., McComb, J., Caldera, Y., & Randolph, P. (2003). Mindfulness meditation, anxiety reduction, and heart disease: A pilot study. *Family and Community Health*, 26(1), 25-33.

Taylor, S., Koch, W. J., & McNally, R. J. (1992). How does anxiety sensitivity vary across the anxiety disorders? *Journal of Anxiety Disorders*, 6(33), 249-259.

Tull, M. T., Gratz, K. L., Salters, K., & Roemer, L. (2004). The role of experiential avoidance in posttraumatic stress symptoms and symptoms of depression, anxiety, and somatization. *Journal of Nervous and Mental Disease*, 192(11), 754-761.

Twohig, M. P., Hayes, S. C., & Masuda, A. (2006). Increasing willingness to experience obsessions: Acceptance and commitment therapy as a treatment for obsessive compulsive disorder. *Behavior Therapy*, 37, 3-13.

Ulmer, C., Walser, R. D., Westrup, D., Rogers, D., Gregg, J., & Loew, D. (2006). Acceptance and commitment therapy: Adaptation of a structured intervention for the treatment of PTSD. ACT World Congress, London, July.

van der Kolk, B. A. (1996). The complexity of adaptation to trauma: Self-regulation, stimulus discrimination, and characterological development. In B. A. van der Kolk, A. C. McFarlane, & L. Weisaeth (eds.), *Traumatic Stress: The Effects of Overwhelming Experience on Mind, Body, and Society* (pp. 182-213). New York: Guilford Press.

Walser, R. D., Gregg, J., Westrup, D., & Loew, D. (2005). PMI: Acceptance and commitment therapy: Treating PTSD. Workshop presented at the International Society for Traumatic Stress Studies, Toronto, November, 2005.

Walser, R. D., & Hayes, S. C. (1998). The effects of acceptance and suppression on thought and emotion. Workshop presented at the Association for Advancement of Behavior Therapy (AABT), Miami Beach, November 19-22.

Walser, R. D., & Hayes, S. C. (2006). Acceptance and commitment therapy in the treatment of posttraumatic stress disorder: Theoretical and applied issues. In V. M. Follette & J. I. Ruzek (eds.), *Cognitive-Behavioral Therapies for Trauma* (2nd ed.; pp. 146-172). New York: Guilford Press.

Walser, R. D., & Pistorello, J. (2005). ACT in group format. In S.C. Hayes & K. D. Strosahl (eds.), *A Practical Guide to Acceptance and Commitment Therapy* (pp. 347-372). New York: Springer Science and Business Media.

Walser, R. D., Ruzek, J. I., Naugle, A. E., Padesky, C., Ronell, D. M., & Ruggiero, K. (2004). Disaster and terrorism: Cognitive-behavioral interventions. *Prehospital and Disaster Medicine*, 19(1), 54-63.

Walser, R. D., & Westrup, D. (2006). Supervising trainees in acceptance and commitment therapy for the treatment of posttraumatic stress disorder. *International Journal of Behavioral and Consultation Therapy*, 2(1), 12-16.

Walser, R. D., Westrup, D., Gregg, J., Loew, D., & Rogers, D. (2004). Acceptance and commitment therapy: Innovative treatment for PTSD. Workshop presented at the International Society for Traumatic Stress Studies, New Orleans, November.

Walser, R. D., Westrup, D., Rogers, D., Gregg, J., & Loew, D. (2003). Acceptance and commitment therapy: Treatment for PTSD. Workshop presented at the International Society for Traumatic Stress Studies, Chicago, November.

Weathers, F. W., Litz, B. T., Herman, D. S., Huska, J. A., & Keane, T. M. (1993). The PTSD Checklist (PCL): Reliability, validity and diagnostic utility. Workshop presented at the meeting of the International Society for Traumatic Stress Studies, San Antonio, October.

Wegner, D. M. (1994). Ironic processes of mental control. *Psychological Review*, 101(1), 34-52.

Wegner, D. M., Erber, R., & Zanakos, S. (1993). Ironic processes in the mental control of mood and mood-related thoughts. *Journal of Personality and Social Psychology*, 65(6), 1093-1104.

Wegner, D. M., & Zanakos, S. (1994). Chronic thought suppression. *Journal of Personality*, 62(4), 615-640.

Weissbecker, I., Salmon, P., Studts, J. L., Floyd, A. R., Dedert, E. A., & Sephton, S. E. (2002). Mindfulness-based stress reduction and sense of coherence among women with fibromyalgia. *Journal of Clinical Psychology in Medical Settings*, 9(4), 297-307.

Williams, L. M. (2006). Acceptance and commitment therapy: An example of third-wave therapy as a treatment for Australian Vietnam War veterans with posttraumatic stress disorder. Unpublished dissertation, Charles Stuart University, Bathurst, New South Wales.

Wilson, K. G., & Groom, J. (2002). The Valued Living Questionnaire. Available from the first author at the Department of Psychology, University of Mississippi, University, MS.

Wilson, K. G., & Murrell, A. R. (2004). Values work in acceptance and commitment therapy: Setting a course for behavioral treatment. In S. C. Hayes, V. M. Follette, & M. Linehan (eds.), *Mindfulness and Acceptance: Expanding the Cognitive-Behavioral Tradition* (pp. 120-151). New York: Guilford Press.

Zettle, R. D., & Hayes, S. C. (1986). Dysfunctional control by client verbal behavior: The context of reason giving. *Analysis of Verbal Behavior*, 4, 30-38.

Robyn D. Walser, Ph.D., works as a consultant, workshop presenter and therapist in her private business, TLConsultation Services (walser_robyn@sbcglobal.net) and she is a psychologist at the National Center for PTSD, Veterans Affairs Palo Alto Health Care System. Dr. Walser has expertise in traumatic stress, substance abuse, and acceptance and commitment therapy (ACT). She has been doing ACT workshop trainings both nationally and internationally since 1998; training in multiple formats and for multiple client problems. Dr. Walser continues to investigate the use of mindfulness and ACT in trauma populations.

Darrah Westrup, Ph.D., is an experienced ACT clinician with a private practice in Menlo Park, CA. She has conducted numerous ACT trainings and workshops, and provides ACT supervision on an ongoing basis. Dr. Westrup has extensive training and experience in PTSD, and along with her practice, is Program Attending of the Women's Trauma Recovery Program at the National Center for PTSD, and Program Director of the Women's Mental Health Center at the VA Palo Alto Health Care System.

Index

A

acceptance: definition of, 19; experiential, 200-201, 223-224; harmful situations and, 221; mindfulness and, 26; radical, 61; self-, 186-190

Acceptance and Action Questionnaire-2 (AAQ-2), 223, 224, 228, 233

acceptance and commitment therapy (ACT): anxiety and, 218; assessment tools for, 221-227; CBT alternatives to, 17-18; central ideas of, 199; comorbidity and, 216-221; core skills for, 198-202; decision factors for using, 209-210; depression and, 216-217; evaluating effectiveness of, 228-230, 233-234; experiential acceptance and, 200-201; explaining to clients, 36; exposure therapy and, 207-208; harmful behaviors and, 218-219; informed consent and, 36-37; last session considerations, 191-192; medication use and, 217; methods for exploring, 196; mindfulness and, 16-17, 202; orientation for therapists, 34; overall goal of, 40; overview of components in, 199; psychotic symptoms and, 220-221; PTSD treatment using, 1-2, 18; questions and answers about, 198-199, 209-210; research studies on, 233-234; settings for treatment in, 208-209; somatization and, 219-220;

substance abuse and, 217-218; supervision groups, 197; telling the story of, 165-166; therapist qualities for, 202-204; training in, 197-198; trauma populations and, 212-216; treatment structure for, 35; vicarious traumatization and, 205; workshops, 196, 197

Acceptance and Commitment Therapy: An Experiential Approach to Behavior Change (Hayes, Strosahl, and Wilson), 2, 3

Acceptance and Commitment Therapy for Anxiety Disorders: A Practitioner's Treatment Guide to Using Mindfulness, Acceptance, and Values-Based Behavior Change Strategies (Eifert and Forsyth), 3

Acceptance and Mindfulness-Based Approaches to Anxiety (Orsillo and Roemer), 3

ACT. *See* acceptance and commitment therapy

action. *See* committed action

alcohol abuse. *See* substance abuse

American Psychiatric Association (APA), 9

anxiety: ACT and, 218; about the future, 24-25; mindfulness and, 27, 87-88; welcoming, 87-88

assertiveness training, 17

assessment, 221-230; of ACT effectiveness, 228-230; of avoidant thoughts and cognitive defusion, 224-225; of client satisfaction, 228-230; of committed action, 225-226, 227; of experiential avoidance and acceptance, 223-224; of mindfulness, 225; of trauma and PTSD, 221-223

Association for Contextual Behavioral Science, 3

Association for the Behavioral and Cognitive Therapies, 2

authenticity, 203-204

automatic thoughts, 224

Automatic Thoughts Questionnaire (ATQ), 224

avoidance symptoms, 9, 10, 224-225. *See also* experiential avoidance

avoidant thoughts, 224-225

awareness: experiential, 202; present moment, 20-21, 132. *See also* mindfulness

B

Baer, Ruth, 3, 26

Beautiful Mind, A (film), 220

Beecher, Henry Ward, 85

believability scale, 224

bereavement, complicated, 12, 215

be-still mindfulness, 86-87

body scan, 44-46

box-with-stuff-in-it metaphor, 124-126

breathing: attending to, 43-44, 66-67; light imagery with, 66-67

burnout, 26

C

cancer patients, 27

character of commitments, 182-186

chessboard metaphor, 116-118

child exercise, 186-190

childhood sexual abuse, 212, 213. *See also* sexual trauma

childhood trauma, 193, 212, 213

Chinese finger trap metaphor, 75

choice making, 144-145, 182, 185-186

chronic pain, 26, 223-224

Chronic Pain Acceptance Questionnaire (CPAQ), 223-224

citizenship values, 158

Clarifying Values Worksheet, 155-159

clarity, 25-26

clients: central ideas about ACT for, 199; committed action challenges, 192; control-as-the-problem challenges, 81; creative hopelessness challenges, 57-59; evaluating satisfaction of, 228-230; explaining ACT to, 36; mindfulness introduction, 27-31, 32; self-as-context challenges, 131-132; trying to convince, 60; valued living challenges, 152-154; willingness challenges, 107-108

clinging to conceptualized self, 179-181

Clinician Administered PTSD Scale (CAPS), 221

clinician self-care, 205-206

cognitive defusion, 28-29, 91-102; assessment of, 224-225; eyes-on exercise, 100-102; taking-your-mind-for-a-walk exercise, 94-100; two computers metaphor, 92-94

cognitive processing therapy (CPT), 18

cognitive therapy, 17, 210

combat trauma, 214

committed action, 161-194, 199; ACT storytelling and, 165-166; assessment of, 225-226; barriers related to, 170-181; character of commitments and, 182-186; client sticking points, 192; conceptualized self and, 179-181; forgiveness and, 170-174; homework assignments, 194; issues of right and wrong and, 174-178; mindfulness exercises, 162-165; monsters on the bus metaphor, 183-185; overview of, 161; prior session review, 165; regaining values, 166-170; responses of others to, 166-169; seeking an outcome to, 169-170; session format, 162; skiing metaphor, 169-170; stand and commit exercise, 190-191, 193; therapist sticking points, 192-193; willingness and, 181-182, 186

comorbidity: ACT and, 216-221; PTSD and, 11-12, 216-221

compass metaphor, 148-149

compassion, 202-203

compassion mindfulness, 141

complicated bereavement, 12, 215

conceptualized self, 179-181

concession, willingness vs., 104-107

confidence, 192

consciousness, continuity of, 111, 131

content: context distinguished from, 124-126; getting caught in, 59-60

context. *See* self-as-context

contextualists, 231-232

continuity of consciousness, 111, 131

control as the problem, 65-84, 199; Chinese finger trap metaphor, 75; client sticking points, 81; fighting-the-wave metaphor, 75; helping clients connect with, 69-71; homework assignments, 82-83; mindfulness exercises, 66-68; misapplied control and, 79-80;overview of, 65; paradox-in-action examples, 71-73; polygraph metaphor, 71-72; prior session review, 69; quicksand metaphor, 73-74; recognizing costs of control, 76; session format, 66; therapist sticking points, 81-82; tug-of-war exercise, 77-79

control strategies: discovering problem with, 65-84; excessive use of, 82; experiential avoidance and, 12-13; language and action and, 81; paradox of, 72-73; self-as-context and, 115

convincing clients, 60

corpus delicti metaphor, 105-107, 174

creative hopelessness, 41-64, 199; clarifying the issue of, 54-55; client sticking points, 57-59; creating in clients, 48-52; false solutions related to, 52-54; getting caught in content, 59-60; giving hope to clients, 56-57; homework assignments, 61-64; listing strategies tried, 48-50; mindfulness exercises, 43-46, 63-64; overview of, 41-42; prior session review, 46; questions for clients, 47; radical acceptance and, 61; recognizing costs of prior efforts, 55; session format, 42-43; staying with feeling stuck, 55-56; therapist sticking points, 59-61

Credibility/Expectancy Questionnaire, 230

D

daily diary, 228-230

defusion techniques, 28-29, 91-102; eyes-on exercise, 100-102; taking-your-mind-for-a-walk exercise, 94-100; two comput-

ers metaphor, 92-94. *See also* cognitive defusion

deliteralization, 29, 92

depression: ACT and, 216-217; mindfulness and, 26; PTSD and, 11, 216

Detroit Area Survey, 8

dialectical behavior therapy (DBT), 210

domestic violence, 212

drug abuse. *See* substance abuse

DSM-IV-TR (APA), 9

E

education values, 158

Eifert, George, 3

emotions: mindfulness of, 25; numbing of, 232. *See also* feelings

employment values, 158

Euripides, 139

exercises: child, 186-190; eyes-on, 100-102; forgiveness, 173-174; funeral service, 145-147; hands-on, 89-91; headstone, 149-150; labeling, 126-131; letting-go-of-identity, 136-137; observer, 119-124; right-wrong game, 176-178; stand and commit, 190-191, 193; taking-your-mind-for-a-walk, 94-100; tug-of-war, 77-79; what-do-you-stand-for, 145-147. *See also* mindfulness exercises

experiential acceptance, 200-201, 223-224

experiential avoidance, 8, 200-201; assessment of, 202, 223-224; comorbidity and, 11-12; control strategies and, 12-13; PTSD and, 10-12, 232-233; research studies on, 232-233

experiential knowing, 189

exposure therapy, 17, 18, 31, 207-208

eyes-on exercise, 100-102

F

family relations values, 157

feelings: defusing from, 115; mindfulness of, 25; stuck, 55-56; willingness confused with, 103-104

fibromyalgia, 27

fighting-the-wave metaphor, 75

finding-the-center mindfulness, 113-114

Follette, Victoria, 3

forgiveness: exercise about, 173-174; meaning of word, 171; trauma survivors and, 170-174; willingness confused with, 103-104; worm-on-a-hook metaphor, 173

Forsyth, John, 3

Frank, Anne, 235

freedom, burden of, 107-108

friendship values, 157

Fromm, Eric, 107

Full Catastrophe Living (Kabat-Zinn), 3

functional contextualism, 34, 231

funeral service exercise, 145-147

fusion: with an identity, 132; with mind, 14-16, 132

future, anxiety about, 24-25

G

game playing, 182-183

Get Out of Your Mind and Into Your Life (Hayes and Smith), 3, 197

goals: of ACT, 40; setting, 185; values vs., 185

grief, traumatic, 12, 215-216

H

hallucinations, 220

hands-on exercise, 89-91

harmful behaviors, 218-219

Hayes, Steven C., 1, 3, 232

headstone exercise, 149-150

heart disease, 27

historical events, 15

Høeg, Peter, 41

homework assignments: on committed action, 194; on control as the problem, 82-83; on creative hopelessness, 61-63; on mindfulness meditation, 63-64, 83; on self-as-context, 133-137; on valued living, 155-159; on willingness, 109-110

hyperarousal symptoms, 9, 10

hypnosis, 30

I

identity: exercise on letting go of, 136-137; holding too tightly to, 132; therapist issues of, 133

imagery exercises, 66-67, 82-83

imagined ideals, 15

informed consent, 36-37

International Society of Traumatic Stress Studies, 2

interpersonal trauma, 212-213

intimate relations values, 156-157

Iverson, Kate, 212

J

Joe-the-bum metaphor, 181-182

just listening exercise, 68

K

Kabat-Zinn, John, 3

Kentucky Inventory of Mindfulness Skills (KIMS), 225, 233

kiss-the-earth-with-your-feet exercise, 164-165

Kornfield, Jack, 7

L

labeling exercise, 126-131

language: of control, 81; fusion with, 14-16; trauma and, 13-16

letting-go-of-identity exercise, 136-137

Levertov, Denise, 231

Lewis, W. M., 33

Linehan, Marsha, 3

listening exercise, 68

loss, traumatic, 12, 215-216

lost values exercise, 159

M

marital satisfaction, 26

marriage values, 156-157

mattering, 152, 186

meaning: finding after PTSD, 152; identifying values and, 145-147

medications, 217

memories: acceptance of, 193; fear of activating, 193; traumatic, 21-24, 193

metaphors: box-with-stuff-in-it, 124-126; chessboard, 116-118; Chinese finger trap, 75; compass, 148-149; corpus delicti, 105-107; fighting-the-wave, 75; Joe-the-bum, 181-182; monsters on the bus, 183-185; person-in-a-hole, 55-56, 70; polygraph, 71-73; quicksand, 73-74; skiing, 169-170; swamp, 108; two computers, 92-94, 131; worm-on-a-hook, 173 mind: defusing from, 28-29, 91-102; fusion with, 14-16, 132; trauma and, 13-16

mindfulness, 20-32, 202; acceptance and, 26; ACT and, 16-17; assessment of, 225; characteristics of, 26; clarity and, 25-26; definitions of, 16, 20, 26; homework assignments on, 63-64, 83; introducing clients to, 27-31, 32; misconceptions about, 29-31; past memories and, 21-24; present moment awareness and, 20-21; projected future and, 24-25; research on benefits of, 26-27

Mindfulness and Acceptance: Expanding the Cognitive-Behavioral Tradition (Hayes, Follette, and Linehan), 3

Mindfulness Attention Awareness Scale (MAAS), 225

mindfulness exercises: attending to breathing, 43-44, 66-67; be-still mindfulness, 86-87; body scan, 44-46; compassion mindfulness, 141; finding-the-center, 113-114; just listening, 68; kiss-the-earth-with-your-feet, 164-165; light imagery, 66-67; overview of, 32; place of peace, 142; recognizing mind quality, 112-113; session structure and, 37; we-are-all-in-this-together, 162-164; welcome anxiety, 87-88. *See also* exercises

"Mindfulness Training as a Clinical Intervention: A Conceptual and Empirical Review" (Baer), 3

mindfulness-based stress reduction (MBSR), 27

misapplied control, 79-80

moment-by-moment awareness, 132

monsters on the bus metaphor, 183-185

N

Nash, John Forbes, Jr., 220

National Comorbidity Study, 8

natural disaster survivors, 214-215

O

observer exercise, 119-124

observer self, 111, 115, 119-124, 131

ongoing experience, 132

Orsillo, Susan M., 3

P

pain: assessment of, 223-224; mindfulness and, 26; suffering added to, 21-22

paradox-in-action examples, 71-73

past, memories of, 21-24

person-in-a-hole metaphor, 55-56, 70

physical well-being values, 159

place-of-peace exercise, 142

polygraph metaphor, 71-73

Post-Traumatic Cognitions Inventory (PTCI), 222

post-traumatic stress disorder (PTSD): ACT and, 1-2, 18; alternative therapies for, 17-18; anxiety disorders and, 218; assessment of, 221-223; comorbidity and, 11-12, 216-221; complicated bereavement and, 12; depression and, 11, 216; experiential avoidance and, 10-11, 232-233; finding meaning after, 152; overview of, 8-9; substance abuse and, 11-12; symptom clusters in, 9; therapist training in, 206-208; treatment structure for, 35; vicarious traumatization and, 205. *See also* trauma

Practical Guide to Acceptance and Commitment Therapy, A (Hayes and Strosahl), 3

present moment awareness, 20-21, 132

prisoners of war (POWs), 214

psychodynamic approach, 17

psychological burnout, 26

psychotic symptoms, 220-221

PTSD. *See* post-traumatic stress disorder

PTSD Check List (PCL), 221, 222, 233

punishment, 174

Q

questions: for clients on creative hopelessness, 47; for therapists on ACT, 198-199

quicksand metaphor, 73-74

R

radical acceptance, 61

rape. *See* sexual trauma

recognizing mind quality exercise, 112-113

recreation values, 158

reexperiencing symptoms, 9, 10

relational frame theory (RFT), 17, 34, 197, 232

Relational Frame Theory: A Post-Skinnerian Account of Human Language and Cognition (Hayes, Barnes-Holmes, and Roche), 17

relaxation exercises, 30

revictimization, 213-214

right and wrong: addressing issues of, 174-178; game related to, 176-178

right-wrong game, 176-178

Rilke, Rainer Maria, 211

Roemer, Lizabeth, 3

Rowling, J. K., 195

S

self: conceptualized, 179-181; observer, 111, 115, 119-124, 131; whole, 116

self-acceptance, 186-190

self-as-context, 29, 111-137, 199; advantages of, 115; box-with-stuff-in-it metaphor, 124-126; chessboard metaphor, 116-118; client sticking points, 131-132; exploration exercise, 134-136; homework assignments, 133-137; identity issues and, 132, 133, 136-137; intact-self concept, 131; labeling exercise, 126-131; letting-go-of-identity exercise, 136-137; mindfulness exercises, 112-114; objectives pertaining to, 131; observer exercise, 119-124; overview of, 111; power of, 115; present-focused work, 132; prior session review, 114; self-as-observer concept, 119-131; session format, 111-112; therapist sticking points, 132-133; tracking sheet, 135; trauma survivors and, 115-116; two computers metaphor, 131

self-blame, 171

self-care, 205-206

self-forgiveness, 171

session structure, 37-39

sexual trauma: ACT and, 212-213; exposure therapy and, 207; mindfulness exercises and, 46; revictimization and, 213; valued living and, 152

skiing metaphor, 169-170

Smith, Spencer, 3

social relations values, 157

solutions, false, 52-54

somatization, 219-220

spirituality values, 158

stand and commit exercise, 190-191, 193

strategies list, 48-50

stress: mindfulness and, 27; workplace, 234. *See also* post-traumatic stress disorder

stress inoculation therapy, 17

Strosahl, Kirk, 2, 3

Structured Clinical Interview for DSM-IV (SCID-II), 221

stuck feelings, 55-56

substance abuse: ACT and, 217-218; mindfulness and, 26; PTSD and, 11-12, 217

suffering: added to original pain, 21-24; self-as-context and, 115

suppression, 71, 232, 233

swamp metaphor, 108

symptoms of PTSD, 9

systematic desensitization, 17

T

taking-your-mind-for-a-walk exercise, 94-100

terrorism survivors, 214-215

therapists: authenticity of, 203-204; committed action challenges, 192-193; compassion of, 202-203; control-as-the-problem challenges, 81-82; core skills required for, 198-202; creative hopelessness challenges, 57-59; exploration of ACT by, 196; importance of self-care for, 205-206; orientation to ACT for, 34; PTSD training for, 206-208; qualities desired in, 202-204; question and answers on ACT for, 198-199; self-as-context challenges, 132-133; training in ACT for, 197-198; treatment setting issues, 208-209; valued living challenges, 154; vicarious traumatization of, 205; willingness challenges, 109, 192

third generation behavior therapies, 232

thoughts: automatic, 224; avoidant, 224-225; deliteralizing, 29, 92; mindfulness of, 25; observation of, 115; suppression of, 232; therapist problems with, 133

Tolle, Eckhart, 65

training values, 158

trauma: assessment of, 221-223; fear of activating, 193; forgiveness and, 170-174; interpersonal, 212-213; memories of, 21-24; natural disaster, 214-215; prevalence of exposure to, 8; revictimization, 213-214; self-as-context and, 115-116; terrorism, 214-215; values and, 151-152; verbal behavior and, 13-16; veteran and POW, 214; vicarious, 205. *See also* post-traumatic stress disorder

trauma populations, 212-216

Trauma Symptoms Checklist-40 (TSC-40), 222

traumatic grief, 12, 215-216

treatment: decision factors for, 209-210; evaluation of, 228-230; settings for, 208-209; structure of, 35

tug-of-war exercise, 77-79

two computers metaphor: self-as-context and, 131; willingness and, 92-94

U

unwillingness: client, 108, 182; therapist, 109, 192

V

Valluvar, Tiru, 19

valued living, 139-159, 199; choice making and, 144-145; clarifying values worksheet, 155-159; client sticking points, 152-154; compass metaphor, 148-149; explanation of, 148; finding meaning, 152; funeral service exercise, 145-147; goals vs. values and, 151; headstone exercise, 149-150; homework assignments, 155-159; identifying values for, 143-147, 150-151; lost values exercise, 159; mindfulness exercises, 140-143; missing the point of, 153-154, 166-170; overview of, 139-140; prior session review, 143; session format, 140; therapist sticking points, 154; trauma survivors and, 151-152; what-do-you-stand-for exercise, 145-147

Valued Living Questionnaire (VLQ), 225

Values and Goals Worksheet, 225-226, 227

verbal behavior: fusion with, 14-16; trauma and, 13-16. *See also* language

veterans, 214, 233

vicarious traumatization, 205

victim role, 104

visual hallucinations, 220

W

walking meditation, 164-165

war-zone trauma, 214

we-are-all-in-this-together exercise, 162-164

welcome anxiety exercise, 87-88

what-do-you-stand-for exercise, 145-147

White Bear Suppression Inventory (WBSI), 224, 228, 233

whiteboard list, 48-50

whole self, 116

Williams, Lynn, 233

willingness, 85-110, 199; barriers to, 102-107; being right vs., 108; client sticking points, 107-108; cognitive defusion and, 91-102; committed action and, 181-182, 186; concession confused with, 104-107; eyes-on-exercise, 100-102; feelings confused with, 103-104; hands-on exercise, 89-91; homework assignments, 109-110; introducing to clients, 89-91; Joe-the-bum metaphor, 181-182; mindfulness exercises, 86-88; overview of, 85; prior session review, 88-89; session format, 86; swamp metaphor, 108; taking-your-mind-for-a-walk exercise, 94-100; therapist sticking points, 109, 192; two computers metaphor, 92-94

Wilson, Kelly, 2, 3

workability, 185, 209, 232

workplace stress, 234

worksheets: Clarifying Values, 155-159; Values and Goals, 225-226, 227

worm-on-a-hook metaphor, 173

more **acceptance & commitment therapy** titles
from new**harbinger**publications